To 6B · from Brent.
Xmas-2001

D0847274

EVERYBODY PAYS

EVERYBODY

TWO MEN, ONE MURDER AND
THE PRICE OF TRUTH

G.P. Putnam's Sons   New York

PAYS

Maurice Possley
and
Rick Kogan

G. P. Putnam's Sons
Publishers Since 1838
a member of
Penguin Putnam Inc.
375 Hudson Street
New York, NY 10014

Library of Congress Cataloging-in-Publication Data

Possley, Maurice.
Everybody Pays : two men, one murder, and
the price of truth / by Maurice Possley and Rick Kogan.
p. cm.
ISBN 0-399-14810-8
1. Aleman, Harry Peralt, 1939- 2. Lowe, Bobby Dean, 1948-
3. Murder—Illinois—Chicago. 4. Trials (Murder)—Illinois—Chicago.
5. Witnesses—Illinois—Chicago. I. Kogan, Rick. II. Title.
HV6534.C4 P67   2001   2001019982
364.15'23'0977311—dc21

Printed in the United States of America

1 3 5 7 9 10 8 6 4 2

This book is printed on acid-free paper. ∞

BOOK DESIGN BY MEIGHAN CAVANAUGH

For Cathleen and Herman and Marilew

Acknowledgments

No book comes to life without the advice, aid, and support of many people, and we are grateful and indebted to, among too many to mention, judges, prosecutors, defense lawyers, members of law enforcement, Colleen Sims, Ted Jones, Sam Sianis, Harlan and Paul Draeger, Scott Cassidy, Vic Switsky, Scott Mendeloff, Vincent Bugliosi, Bouchaib Khribech, Harold Ramis, Arnie Rissman, David Black, Kevin McNally, Scott Turow, Nancy Watkins, the family of Billy Logan, David Mamet, Michael Monico, Sharon Barrett, Allan Brown, Bill Kurtis, the many reporters and writers who came before us and those who now chronicle Chicago, and colleagues and bosses at the *Chicago Tribune*. Our editor, Denise Silvestro, provided insightful and careful editing of the manuscript. Our agent, Caroline Carney, helped us keep the faith during difficult times. We owe a most profound debt to Bob and Fran Lowe and their family for opening their lives up in intimate detail and, most of all, for their courage.

Author's Note

All the dialogue in this book was carefully reconstructed from court transcripts and from conversations with at least one of the participants. Joe and Jane Reese are not real names, but were used to protect Bob and Fran Lowe. Harry Aleman declined to be interviewed.

1

When you are going out to murder a man, it's always a good idea to know where he is. But on the night of September 27, 1972, Harry Aleman and Louie Almeida were still new to the killing game and so their evening plans were shadowed by a mixture of uncertainty and hope that manifested itself in the quiet mumblings of Almeida as he made his way along Taylor Street on the Near West Side of Chicago.

"Where the hell was he? He better be there tonight, better be there tonight," Almeida said over and over as he walked. "He better be there tonight. That's all."

No one on the street appeared to notice Almeida's muttering even though the street was crowded, filled with ears eager for all sorts of gossip.

In the shadow of the city's skyscrapers that formed a wall two miles to the east, Taylor Street was the heart of what remained of one of Chicago's oldest Italian neighborhoods, a commercial strip of restaurants, bakeries, hot-beef sandwich joints, taverns, sausage shops, and lemonade stands, peppered with neatly kept two- and three-story brick and wood-frame houses. When the weather was warm—and it was on this night—the stoops and porches and sidewalks were crowded with people sharing the neighborhood news that has always knitted such communities together.

But there were strangers here, too. Much of the neighborhood around Taylor Street had been gobbled up and bulldozed to make way for the University of Illinois at Chicago campus, and now thousands of students and faculty members had begun to rent and buy and to shop and eat in the area.

Most of the longtime neighborhood residents accommodated these strangers, though they bridled at the new nickname, "Little Italy," which the college kids, the trend-seekers, and the media had begun affixing to a neighborhood that was always, to them, just Taylor Street. They thought of themselves, proudly, as survivors, and they grudgingly tolerated the new faces. They were, after all, good for business and housing prices.

Louie Almeida and Harry Aleman had been children of Taylor Street, yet their considerable energies were not given to matters of real-estate speculation and urban gentrification, but rather to home invasion, extortion, and other dark activities. And tonight, for the second time in a week, their focus was murder.

Louie mumbled his way across the two lanes of Taylor Street traffic and, taking a deep breath and closing his eyes as if in short prayer, opened the door of the Survivor's Social and Athletic Club. It was a small storefront, wedged inconspicuously between the Gentle Care dry cleaner, with its guarantee of 1 HR DRIVE IN CLEANING, and a clothing store called Ups and Downs, which offered in its window the promise of JEANS, T-SHIRTS, HATS AND PURSES.

The windows of the club were painted with a thick strip of yellow, the same color as the diamond centered on a recessed glass door and containing the address, 1140, and a message so terse it might have been seen as a warning—MEMBERS ONLY. Dimly lit and heavy with the smell of espresso, the club was one of a number of such private gathering places that dotted the city, financed by organized crime money and operating primarily as fronts for illegal gambling and other outfit activities.

Louie saw Harry right away, sitting alone at a table in the corner. The room was filled with other tables, chairs, and a few couches, none of them new. A television flickered in another corner, the volume turned low. The soft slap of cards drew Louie's eye to a halfhearted game of gin in the back.

The faces were familiar—there were no strangers here—and Louie nodded to a couple of the old men who were playing.

Harry was at the same table at which he had been sitting six nights before and he said the same thing: "Sit down."

Louie had waited at the table that night as Harry had gone to get his shotgun and .45 automatic. The pair had then driven, Louie behind the wheel, to kill Billy Logan. They had parked on a quiet street on the city's Far West Side. Harry had climbed into the back seat, and they waited. And waited.

They waited, the super-charged engine of the dark Plymouth sedan becoming an increasing annoyance as minutes stretched into more than an hour. They waited, watching the front door of the two-story white frame house of Logan's sister. They waited for their victim to walk out into the night on his way to his job as a dispatcher at the trucking yard.

"Where the fuck—?" Harry said finally. "I thought you said you—"

"I did, Harry. I did. I seen the guy," Louie said. "Every night, the last two weeks, same time, I swear it, same time every night."

"Then, where the—?" Harry snapped from the back seat. "Let's go."

"But—" Louie protested.

"Go," Harry said.

"You wanna get in front?" Louie asked.

"I have to say it again?" Harry barked. "Just drive."

There was anger in his voice—Louie knew that sound well, the words coming in crisp, explosive bursts. He put the car in drive and took off. He would, many years later, say that he feared for his life that night during the fifteen-minute ride back to Taylor Street.

"I knew Harry since we was kids," he would say. "There was always an anger in him. He could kill, didn't think nothin' of it. We all knew that. And I didn't much like the idea of Harry sitting in the back seat of a car I was driving, holding a loaded shotgun and a forty-five."

Louie first heard Billy Logan's name in August. He and Harry had been eating lunch at Guido's, a sandwich shop just down the street from the club. Harry was digging through his wallet.

"What are you looking for?" Louie asked.

"Nothing," Harry said. "Give me something to write on."

Louie took out his wallet and thumbed through it. He found the business card of a mechanic who worked at a nearby gas station and who for months had been acting as his fence, buying whatever stolen goods Louie could provide.

"Here," said Louie. "I don't need this. I know the number."

"I want you to lay on someone for me," Harry said, taking the card.

"Who?" Louie asked.

Harry's left hand worked the pen slowly. He shoved the card back.

"This is the address. He's staying with his sister," Harry said.

Louie picked up the card. He couldn't read well, but he did know the three words printed in ink on the reverse side: "Death to Billy."

"Who's Billy?" Louie asked.

"Billy Logan," Harry said. "He works in Cicero. Interstate Motors. A dispatcher. Find him. Follow him. Tell me where he goes and when he goes. When you know, come and tell me."

That's all Louie needed to know. He didn't ask Harry a lot of questions. Harry didn't like answering Louie's questions. Instead he would stare at Louie with those eyes. "Dead eyes. Black and empty," Louie would later say. "Shark's eyes."

For more than two weeks, Louie shadowed Logan. It had been easy. A man with a routine and two jobs is easy to tail. Louie didn't take notes. He kept it all in his head: Walks out of the house at eleven five nights a week, drives to the midnight shift at Interstate, leaves front gate of Interstate little after eight in morning, then goes to Elmwood Park to pick up his taxi, drives till noon, and then to his sister's place to sleep.

Louie had given Harry his report at the Survivor's Club.

"He leaves the house and goes straight to work," Louie said, emphasizing what he thought was the most important detail. "He leaves at eleven every night."

"That's good," Harry had said, raising a cup of coffee. Pursing his lips, he blew softly, and then sipped. His voice was low, matter of fact. "Let's go," he said. "You drive."

So, Louie had driven Harry out to the Far West Side where they sat in the Plymouth, waiting to kill Billy Logan. But Logan didn't show.

That was six nights ago.

On this night, the night of September 27, 1972, when Louie had made his nightly call to Harry, the instructions had been simple: "Meet me at the club at nine." Though Harry had not been explicit, Louie knew intuitively that Harry wanted to go after Logan again.

And so Louie's silent urgings had become vocal—"he better be there"— as he made his way along Taylor Street. And now here they were again.

"Sit down," Harry said, and, for what seemed like minutes, Harry just stared at Louie.

Finally, Harry said, "Let's go. You drive."

Neither spoke as they walked to an alley off Taylor and May streets, to a brick one-car garage. The overhead door rattled as Louie shoved it open. Inside was a chocolate brown Plymouth. It was one of several of Harry's "work cars," stolen cars equipped with stolen license plates or with plates purchased on the black market for an under-the-table fee. The car had other unusual characteristics: an engine souped up by a nearby auto shop; a heavy-duty suspension in the rear because Harry was contemplating a gold heist; and five hundred pounds of extra weight to prevent fishtailing when a foot might have to slam down on the accelerator.

Louie backed the car out and drove to the mouth of the alley.

"Turn left and pull in to that gas station on the corner," Harry said.

Louie stopped and waited, nervously drumming his fingers on the steering wheel, while Harry opened the trunk of another car and retrieved his shotgun and the .45-caliber pistol. He climbed back into the passenger seat.

"What are we gonna do?" Louie asked, even though he knew.

"Hit Logan," Harry said.

As he eased the car onto the Eisenhower Expressway for the short ride west, Louie pressed down on the gas and silently repeated his mantra of the night: *He better be there tonight, better fucking be there.*

2

Bob Lowe was hungry. It seemed that he was almost always hungry and now the gnawing in his stomach was made more urgent by the bag of White Castle hamburgers he spotted on the otherwise empty passenger seat of the black Chevy Malibu convertible.

"Fill it up, please," said the female driver, a perky blonde, middle-aged, Bob guessed, in a white blouse and green skirt.

He unscrewed the gas cap and rammed the nozzle in, then walked to the front and lifted the hood. As the gas pump clicked lazily, he checked the oil, then unscrewed the radiator cap and topped it off with water from a can sitting next to the garbage container on the pump island. He slammed down the hood and walked to the rear to finish pumping the gas.

He approached the driver's window, wiping grease from his stubby fingers on the red rag that perpetually dangled from the back pocket of his blue jeans.

"The oil's fine, but I'd keep an eye on it," he said.

He offered a polite grin to the woman. He thought she was a little old to be driving such a sporty car and wondered if it belonged to someone else. "It might need a quart in a week or two. Stop by and I'll put it in for ya."

"Thanks," the woman replied, reaching for her purse. "What do I owe you?"

"Five bucks even for the gas. The water's free," Bob said, grinning and shaking his collar-length brown hair to flick it away from his face. Gingerly, to avoid soiling the woman's hand, he plucked a $5 bill from her fingers and tucked it into a wad he retrieved from the right front pocket of his blue shirt. He stepped back as the car rolled off, watching it pull onto Division Street and turn north onto Laramie Avenue, then he walked between the gas pumps and into the station office.

The phone rang and Bob grabbed the receiver, his response automatic: "Joe's Super One-hundred."

It was his father. "Bob," he said. "I'm finished with dinner and I'm running by the other station to pick up today's cash. Then I'll be over and you can catch dinner yourself."

"OK, Pop. Hurry it up, though. I'm a starving dog today," Bob said.

He was always starving because he was always moving. Bob worked two jobs. In the mornings he drove a truck for a milk company. In the afternoons and most evenings, he pumped gas, changed oil, inflated tires, and did minor mechanical work at one of the two gas stations his father owned on the Far West Side.

It was not a schedule that allowed for rest. Up every day at five, he was out the door of his house only thirty minutes later. He often didn't return until after 10 P.M. But tonight he was going home early, if his father would ever get here. He was through working deep into the night.

Tonight he would be home before 9 P.M. He would see his wife, Fran, and the kids. Tina was only three weeks away from her fourth birthday. Joey was four months old. And there were the other "babies," the Doberman pinschers, German shepherds and Labrador retrievers that Bob kept in pens out next to the garage. He had them for a reason: The neighborhood was changing.

There had been several burglaries in recent months. Some neighbors now had pistols for protection and others talked of getting watchdogs. Bob sensed a business opportunity, and though Fran was never enthusiastic about her husband breeding and selling watchdogs—the barking drove her crazy—she had learned to tolerate it even though, in the first three months of their back-yard business, they'd yet to sell a dog.

It was almost nine when Bob headed south on Central Avenue, slowed as he turned west on Walton Street, and stopped at the curb in front of 5903, the corner house, a two-story wood-frame building surrounded by a chain-link fence.

Several piles of tree branches lined the curb on the south side of the street, the work of city tree-trimmers. He had seen them earlier that week, working their way westward on Walton. *Now that would be a good job,* he had thought, *working outdoors, getting city money.* He paused on the sidewalk for a moment. The late-September air, tinged with the odor of wood chips and shavings, offered him a modest reminder of the Tennessee valley forest where he had been raised.

As he walked through the gangway between houses, he was greeted by a chorus of barks and yips from the dog run out back.

"Hold your horses, boys and girls," he said, pulling a sack of dried dog food from a storage bin. He filled several bowls with food and water, pushing eager snouts away. "Wait a second, will ya?"

The rear stairs creaked as he clomped up to the back door on the top floor. He paused to kick at a soft board. *Got to fix that,* he thought.

The smell of roasted meat hit him the moment he pushed through the door, and he felt and heard his stomach growl. He hadn't eaten since noon.

"That you, Bob?" Fran asked from the bathroom.

"Yeah, and I'm hungry. What's to eat, babe?" he said.

Bob stood over the kitchen sink, washing his hands. His hands always looked dirtier under the harsh kitchen light. He rinsed off the lather and wiped his hands on a dish towel, hoping Fran wouldn't notice the dark stains left behind.

"Pork chops in the oven," she replied. "I'm changing Joey's diaper."

His dark-haired little girl burst into the room, shouting, "Daddy!"

Bob smiled.

"Well, how's my Tina-girl tonight?" he asked.

He forked two chops onto his plate and popped the oven door shut. Lifting a lid on a pot on the stove, he grimaced.

"I hate mashed potatoes," he muttered.

"I'm fine, Daddy," Tina said, hanging on the back of a kitchen chair. "Will you read me a story tonight? When I go to bed?"

"Sure will, baby doll. Daddy's gonna eat now," he said.

"Tina, come here and help your brother get his pajamas on," Fran called.

"OK, momma. Coming," she said, bolting from the room.

A cold, wet nose nudged Bob's arm. Ginger, a frisky three-year-old German shepherd, sat next to his chair. Ginger was the family dog, the only dog allowed to live indoors.

"What do you want?" Bob asked. "Some of this? Nope. This is my dinner; you had yours." The dog cocked its head. "Anyway, you may not be long for this house, Ginger, my girl. We'll see."

Bob ate in silence, listening to the muffled voices of Fran and Tina. He rinsed his dish and was putting it in the sink as Fran came back with Joey on her hip.

"Get enough to eat?" she asked, inspecting the stove. "You didn't touch the potatoes."

"Still don't like 'em," Bob replied. "Never have. Never will. You make 'em though, don't you?"

"I like them. So does Tina," she said.

"Keep trying," he said. "Now, bring that little one over here."

"They need to go to bed, Bob," Fran said. "Give your daddy a kiss, Tina."

Fran leaned over so Bob could run his hand over Joey's head.

"My boy," he murmured. "Good night, my baby boy."

Tina tugged on his sleeve.

"Read to me, Daddy. Read to me," she said.

They walked to the bedroom together. The two-bedroom apartment was a welcome change from the cramped quarters of the one-bedroom flat they had left just a few months earlier. When his parents, Joe and Mary, bought the two-family house at West Walton Street, Fran and Bob and the kids had joined them, moving into the second floor. They were now saving for new furniture. This was the first place they'd lived where they planned to stay. The investment in new furniture would, they believed, make it a home.

As Tina crawled under the covers, Bob grabbed a book from among the half dozen or so that peeked from underneath the bed. He picked up *A Child's Garden of Verses* by Robert Louis Stevenson, a gift from Bob's mother.

"That's a good one, Daddy," Tina said, pulling her pink, satin-trimmed blanket up to her neck.

Bob opened the book and began to read:

I wish I lived in a caravan, with a horse to drive, like a peddler man!
Where he comes from nobody knows,
or where he goes to, but on he goes!

"No, not that one," said Tina. "The shadow one, the shadow, please."

"OK, honey," he said, flipping the pages and finding the poem titled "My Shadow." He read, slowly and in a voice barely above a whisper:

I have a little shadow that goes in and out with me,
And what can be the use of him is more than I can see.
He is very, very like me from the heels up to the head;
And I see him jump before me, when I jump into my bed.

He continued to read, not taking his eyes off the page. At the poem's end, only three verses later, he looked up. Tina was asleep, her breathing slow and measured. This was the sort of moment he had come to savor. In the quiet of this moment, there was only "My Shadow" and the peace he felt watching the rise and fall of his daughter's chest, the delicate curve of her cheek, the curl of her brown hair. It made him feel good. *This,* he thought, *makes the working worth it. This is worth the hours, and the hunger.* Quietly, he bent down to kiss Tina's forehead.

She's sleeping," he said to Fran, who was sitting in the living room, flipping through the September issue of *Reader's Digest* magazine.

"Sit down for a minute," she said.

"I gotta go out, take Ginger for a walk," he said.

"I walked her earlier," said Fran.

"That's OK. I want to see if I can catch Billy on his way to work," said Bob. "He said something the other day about buying one of the dogs. Says he needs a watchdog for something. He seems a little nervous."

"You're going to sell Ginger?" asked Fran, surprised by her feelings.

"She'll make a great watchdog," Bob said. "Besides, I didn't think you liked any of the dogs."

"Just sell her, then," said Fran, who had indeed grown fond of Ginger. "Not like we don't have other dogs."

"And if Billy buys her, she'll just be down the street," Bob said.

"Billy always goes to work this late?" asked Fran.

"Same time every night, like a watch," said Bob.

"You guys work too much," said Fran. "Hurry back."

3

Just after two in the afternoon on the day he would die, Billy Logan trudged up the steps that led to the second and top floor of his sister's white frame house at 5916 West Walton Street. He pushed open the door and walked down the hall and into the bathroom where he turned on the shower and let the water run hot.

"Where were you?" asked his sister, Betty Romo. "You drive the cab today?"

"Nah," Billy said, pulling off his shirt. "Went horseback riding instead."

"After you shower, come to the kitchen," Betty said. "I've made you something to eat."

"Will do," said Billy. He was a solidly built man who stood a little over 6 feet and weighed more than two hundred twenty-five pounds. He was thirty-six years old but most people, meeting him for the first time, would have put him at least five years younger. If they'd asked him, though, he would have told them he felt like an old man.

The last several months had not been easy. He had just been through a lengthy and messy divorce and was still involved in a contentious battle with his ex-wife over when and how often he could see their two children. Billy and Phyllis Chiapetta had married in 1964, both for the second time. Billy had legally adopted Joseph, her son from her first marriage, and late in 1964, she and Billy welcomed Billy Logan, Jr., into the family.

The family had lived in a modest ranch house nestled on the edge of Melrose Park, a bedroom community abutting Chicago's western border. They were not far from the home of Phyllis's second cousin, Harry Aleman, his wife, Ruth, and their four kids. Many of Melrose Park's newest arrivals hailed from Taylor Street, some brought there after being displaced by construction of the University of Illinois at Chicago campus and the encroachment of blacks brought about by the building of public housing projects. For many, the move to the suburbs provided proof of success and a patina of respectability. Still, for virtually all, Taylor Street would always be home.

Though Billy and Harry had known each other since childhood, growing up within blocks of one another on Taylor Street, they were vastly different types and Billy was ever disdainful, in a quiet fashion, of Harry's flashy style. But Phyllis and Harry were close, "as close as cousins could ever be," Phyllis would later say.

After his relationship with Phyllis disintegrated, Billy moved into the two-flat where his two sisters lived. Joanna Dietrich and her son, William, lived on the first floor, while Billy lived in a spare room in Betty's second-floor apartment. Beyond blood, Billy and Betty shared a strange bond: His first wife and Betty's husband had decided being in-laws was not as good as being lovers. They divorced and were married. While Billy had remarried, Betty had not.

Betty was eager to have Billy live with her. "I'm here for you," she told him. "I know what you're going through, too." The move turned out to be a greater comfort than Billy had imagined, especially with Joanna and her son around. It felt like home. But although Billy was eager to get on with his life and was happy to no longer be in a bitter and unpleasant marriage, he felt a constant ache for his children.

"I want to see the kids," Billy had said to some friends one Sunday afternoon in a bar near his sister's house. They had heard it all before, heard how Phyllis had cheated him out of the proceeds when she sold their Melrose Park home; how she wouldn't let him see the kids; how much he loved the kids.

He left his friends and drove to his wife's new house, where she was living with her new husband, Mario. Billy rapped on the door and Phyllis answered, though she refused to open the screen door.

"I want to see the kids," Billy said. It was a demand, not a request. He pulled on the door.

Phyllis could smell the booze. "No," was all she said.

Billy persisted. "Open this door, you bitch," he shouted.

Billy heard a man's voice from inside the house: "That's it."

The door was flung open. A man appeared, almost filling the frame. "Get the fuck out of here," he said.

"What the—?" said Billy.

Even in his fogged up state, he recognized Butch Petrocelli, a man he had known since they were kids. He was easy to recognize, with his thick lips and heavy eyebrows framed by a shock of black hair, a weight lifter's chest and massive arms. Butch stepped onto the front stoop, eye to eye with Billy.

"What are you doing here?" Billy said.

He knew that Butch and Phyllis were friends and had often worried that there was more to their relationship than that. He was not wrong. After the divorce from Billy, Phyllis and Butch began an affair. At one point he proposed marriage, but she had turned him down, later saying it was "because I had a great deal of respect for his dark side. He had a very violent nature and temper." Still, they had remained close after Phyllis remarried and on the day that Billy came by, Butch was at the house paying a condolence call; Phyllis's mother had died a few weeks before.

Butch and Billy began to argue, so loudly that it attracted the attention of seven-year-old Billy Logan Jr., who was playing in a tent in the back yard. "I saw them screaming at each other at the top of the stairs," he would later say. "They walked by the tent. I could hear them swearing at each other. I had never heard anybody really talk like that."

The little boy sneaked out of the tent and, as the two men made their way to an alley behind the house, peeked at them from behind the garage.

His loyalties were torn. He loved his father, but now saw him only on

Saturdays when Billy took him and Joseph horseback riding. "Butch," he would later say, "took me fishing. He took me hunting. He taught me how to shoot a gun, a shotgun. He took me out to play ball. He gave me my first dog."

The men tussled and pushed. Punches were thrown. Billy's hat was knocked to the ground. "Other than the time my grandmother had a heart attack in front of me, that was the most scared I had ever been in my life," said Billy Jr.

The fight ended with loud threats and only minor bruises, but a week later Billy was back, waking up the family in the middle of the night, banging on the door. That time Phyllis called the police, who hauled him away and warned him not to come back. This had no effect. All summer long, Billy continued to contact his kids, in person and by telephone.

Phyllis threatened to call Harry.

"Harry?" answered Billy. "Fuck that guinea."

Bill. It's ten o'clock."

He shifted in the bed. His eyelids fluttered.

"You up?" Betty asked.

Billy's eyes tried to focus.

"Yeah," he said.

Minutes later, he ambled into the kitchen, pulling a black cardigan sweater over a white T-shirt that was tucked into his jeans. He put a brown paper sack on the counter.

"What's that?" Betty asked.

"My medicine and some shaving lotion—for work," he said.

"What about that dog?" she said.

"I talked to Bob Lowe the other day," he said. "He says he's got one to sell. I'll talk to him the next time I see him."

Billy had brought up the idea of getting a watchdog a couple of weeks before. He had been hearing things. Hearing that Harry was angry about his treatment of Phyllis, hearing that Butch was mad, too. Billy hadn't told his sister about his fight with Butch. He didn't want to worry her. And what did he have to worry about? It was months ago, and who were Harry and Butch besides small-time Taylor Street punks?

The telephone rang and Betty picked it up. Billy sat for a few minutes at the kitchen table and then, realizing his sister was going to be chatting for some time, got up and grabbed his paper bag.

His sister didn't notice as he stood up and headed for the door.

"See you in the morning, baby," Billy called over his shoulder as he walked out the door, down the stairs and into the still-warm darkness of the September night.

4

Louie Almeida drove north on Racine Avenue and west on the Eisenhower Expressway, past the miles of crumbling apartment buildings, dusty lots, and dangerous streets that formed the heart of the city's West Side ghetto. He didn't say a word on the trip. Neither did Harry Aleman. Louie kept his eyes on the road. Harry occasionally glanced at his forty-five and the shotgun in the back, as a parent might cast an eye at an infant in a car seat.

The shotgun, a Browning twelve-gauge, was Harry's favorite weapon. It was his instrument and he treated it with same tenderness with which a musician might treat his violin. He had sent it to California to have it Parkerized, a process in which a gun is taken apart down to the smallest screw, meticulously cleaned, and the metal parts dipped in a special solution that protects against rust, then reassembled. The barrel was only eighteen inches long and the stock had been cut down so that it could be concealed easily under a coat.

On this night Harry was wearing a dark shirt and slacks topped by a dark windbreaker. Louie was dressed similarly.

The car eased onto the Central Avenue exit ramp and headed north. After a few blocks, Louie turned off the main drag and into the quiet streets of Austin. He circled the block where Billy Logan lived. The pair spotted Billy's black Pontiac parked at the curb. Louie eased the car to the curb on the same side of the street, several car lengths behind Billy's. He put the car in neutral and leaned back in the seat. The clock on the dashboard read 9:35 P.M.

Harry climbed over the seat and took up a position in the rear, next to the passenger-side window. He rolled the window down. He loaded three shells into the shotgun and laid it across his lap. Deer slugs were his ammunition of choice for human beings. He disdained the smaller loads—shotgun shells filled with bb-sized pellets. Those were for target practice at the skeet range on Lake Michigan where the pellets would spread out in a wide pattern to knock down clay targets launched out over the water. Tonight his target would be closer and, optimally, standing still. Deer slugs would do more damage.

His .45 was filled with hollow-point bullets. "Cop killers," Harry had explained to Louie many months before, during one of their frequent visits to a suburban shooting range. "They flatten out inside the body. They do the job."

Now, as they settled back to wait, Harry said, "If you see any police, shoot them."

"What do you mean, shoot 'em?" Louie asked, fingering the pistol jammed under his waistband.

"You know what I mean," Harry said.

After that, they waited in silence.

Ginger eagerly clawed the bottom of the door and, as it opened, dashed down the front steps. Bob followed.

Louie didn't pay much attention to the man and the dog when they first emerged, but he did see them.

Reaching the sidewalk, Bob paused as his ear caught the sound of an idling car engine. He spotted the source, a dark car parked at the curb at the corner of Mayfield and Walton. He paid no more attention to it.

"Ginger. Come," he called, starting to walk west.

Quickly, Ginger was three houses ahead and angling for the street. Bob looked up and saw Billy walking across the lawn toward his car. He waved, but Billy didn't see him. Bob stepped off the curb and into the street.

"Ginger," he yelled again.

And then it all began, a series of sights and sounds that would stay with Bob forever. It commenced with the bright flash of headlights behind him. The harsh roar of a revving engine. The dark car moved swiftly past him and jerked to a halt. A gun barrel slid out of the car window.

A voice shouted, "Hey, Billy! Hey, Billy! Come here!"

Billy stopped and put his paper sack on the front fender of his car. Billy took a step off the curb. Then Billy backed up.

A blast tore through the night—thunder and a flash.

Billy flew backward and was lifted off the ground, his legs and arms flailing. He landed on his feet and, for a moment, stayed erect. Then wobbling, his knees buckled. A crimson stain grew on his left shoulder.

"Oh, God!" Billy screamed. "Oh, God!"

The shotgun roared again, lifting Billy up and back and onto the lawn. Blood spurted from a hole in his chest.

Bob was frozen. His legs would not move. He was a statue at the rear bumper of the Plymouth. The back door of the car opened and Harry stepped into the street, his left hand hanging by his side, clutching the .45.

On the grass, Billy rolled to his side and tried to scrabble away.

Suddenly, Ginger appeared, leaping toward the car. Bob lunged for the dog, but was too late. When he looked up, he found himself staring into Harry's face. Bob's pale blue eyes locked into the coal-blackness of Harry's. Neither man moved. Neither spoke.

Ginger's sharp bark pierced the air, shattering the strangely intimate moment. Bob turned and ran across the street. As he dove over the pile of freshly cut branches, hugging the ground and burying his face in the grass, he heard the flat crack of a pistol.

He did not hear Harry say to Louie, "Let's go. He's gone."

What he heard was a car door slam and an engine roar. He did not hear

Billy, gasping for breath, his car keys still clutched in his right hand. What he heard were the screams of the living as Billy's life ebbed away, flowing onto the newly clipped grass of the front lawn.

Betty was still on the phone when she heard the first blast. When she heard the second and third shots, she dropped the phone and raced down the stairs, nearly colliding with Joanna, who was flinging open the front porch door. Her dress was wet with blood.

She was shaking and screaming: "Billy, Billy! He's hurt real bad! There's blood all over! I got to call the ambulance."

Half-stumbling down the steps, Betty ran across the yard.

"Billy!" she screamed. "Biiiiilllly!"

She knelt, grabbing his arm. Billy slowly turned his face to look at her. His hand rose and the car keys dropped, landing by Betty's knee.

"Hold on!" Betty pleaded. "Billy, hold on! An ambulance is coming! Hold on!" She could still feel his pulse. She begged him to live.

5

To the uninformed or those who gather their knowledge from television, the processing of a real crime scene can seem chaotic, rushed, and disorganized. It is anything but to the cops who make their living at such chores. It begins even before that familiar yellow tape bearing the words POLICE LINE—DO NOT CROSS is stretched across sidewalks, around parked cars, and tied off on bushes or low tree limbs.

It begins when the first cops arrive on the scene, tires squealing, sirens blaring, and lights flashing. As the officers hastily begin to sort the wounded from the dying and the witnesses from the gawkers, they are scanning the scene for the particulars of the crime: a dropped knife or pistol, a trail of blood drops, the pattern of broken glass. Their eyes are watchful as they begin to protect areas where evidence could be hiding.

Shortly, the forensic cops arrive—the "techs," or evidence technicians, whose job it is to dust for fingerprints, to bag up expended cartridges, and to hunt for clues that might help solve the case or provide a physical link to the perpetrator.

Across from Billy Logan's house, Bob Lowe stood smoking a Marlboro on the sidewalk as some cops stretched the yellow tape from the street to

Billy's car and well past the blood-soaked lawn, while others picked through the grass near the curb.

The strobe of a tech's camera flashed as he recorded the blood, the trees, the streetlight glowing overhead, and Billy's brown paper sack resting on his black Pontiac. Another tech stretched a tape measure from the Pontiac to the largest of the bloodstains.

They looked for evidence, but there were no bullets to be found; the pathologist who examined Billy at the autopsy would recover the pellets. There were no fingerprints to process. There was no evidence to be placed in plastic bags. There was nothing but Billy's blood.

As the cops went quietly about their tasks, both sides of the street filled with people and lights and noise and talk.

"Hell of a thing," said Joe Lowe. "What happened?"

"Car pulled up," Bob said. "Guy stuck a shotgun out the window and shot Billy. Guy got out of the back seat. I think he shot once at me. But I jumped over them branches."

"You see him?" Joe asked, his eyes narrowing slightly.

"Yeah, I seen him," Bob said. "We were eye to eye, right there on the street. I was right behind the damn car, Dad."

From across the street, a uniformed police officer approached.

"You see what happened?" he asked.

Bob took a step forward.

"You see anything about this?" the officer asked.

Joe stepped up behind his son. "Don't say nothing," he whispered.

"You see what happened?" the officer repeated. "See the car?"

"It was dark-colored," said Bob.

"You see the license plate?"

"Only part of it. It was Illinois," said Bob.

"Model?"

Joe gripped the back of his son's arm.

"Not sure," Bob said. "Could've been a Mercury."

"You see the shooting?"

Joe's grip tightened as the question was repeated.

"You see the shooting?"

Bob took a long drag on his Marlboro and exhaled hard.

"Yeah," he said.

The officer motioned and said, "Come with me. You need to give a statement to my partner. I'll drive you to the hospital."

Bob rode in a squad car the five blocks to West Suburban Hospital. Joe followed in his car, driving alone. At the hospital, he found Bob sitting in a waiting area outside the emergency room.

"You talk to them yet?" asked Joe.

"Nope," said Bob.

Joe looked squarely into his son's eyes.

"Listen to me, Bob," he said. "You don't want to get involved in this. This ain't just any killin'.'"

Bob stubbed a Marlboro into the canister ashtray next to his chair.

"This is a hit, dammit. An assassination, son," Joe said. "This is mob business. That's the way they take care of things."

"Billy was in the mob?" Bob asked.

"Hell, I don't know and I don't care," Joe replied. "This is none of your business, Bob. It's just trouble. For you. For your family."

"How's that?" Bob asked.

"Figure it out, son," said Joe. "You want to be a witness?"

Bob pulled the pack of Marlboros from his shirt pocket, shook one halfway out, and raised the pack to pull the cigarette out with his lips. He struck a match and held it to the end, aware of commotion in the background. Through a door and behind a curtain, a doctor was making the official pronouncement of what everyone else already believed: Billy was dead. He had died on the lawn of his sister's house; the last thing he had heard was Betty's plea to live and the distant siren of the ambulance.

Patiently, Joe watched his son.

"I saw what I saw," Bob said, finally.

"Don't do it, Bob," said Joe.

"I'd expect Billy woulda done the same for me," Bob said.

Joe sighed and sat back in his chair. He knew his son well enough to know that further conversation was pointless. Bob had always bridled when told what to do. He'd been that way since he was a kid, not rebellious in any frivolous way, just strong-willed, independent. In this case, Joe, for all his worry, felt a grudging admiration and even pride at Bob's decision. He had always taught his kids to be honest.

Alfred Joseph Lowe's life was shattered at age six when his Baptist preacher father was accidentally electrocuted and his family was plunged into the hardscrabble poverty that was not uncommon to the towns of the Houston Valley in the northeast corner of Tennessee. It is an area of extraordinary physical beauty, situated in the forested foothills of the Appalachian Mountains. It was also a place where poverty hung as heavy as the fog that sometimes turns the hollows into eerie wonderlands.

In the 1950s, Joe, as he was called, was attempting to raise a family in the town of Greeneville. It was a struggle. He tried his best, but with his salary from working at the local water plant barely enough to feed and clothe his growing family, he reluctantly decided to move to Chicago.

Joe wanted to try his hand at running a gas station—he had always been good with cars—and figured there would be no shortage of cars in a city as large as Chicago. So, in the fall of 1958, he kissed his wife, Mary, a nurse's aide, good-bye and headed north. Two of their children were out of the house—Cordell was in the Navy and Frances was married—but three remained at home with Mary—Delbert, Bob, and Joetta. In Joe's wake were the promises that he would send money and bring them to Chicago when he got settled. They knew he would. He was a man of his word.

Bobby Dean Lowe, born on September 14, 1948, was a rambunctious ten-year-old at the time and found himself with new responsibilities. In addition to his regular chores—hauling drinking and bath water from the spring in the back of the family's tin-roofed house—Bob earned money suckering tobacco fields in the valley before school, rising at dawn to pull and chop weeds. After school, he headed back to the fields until it was too dark to strip the small shoots from the tobacco plant stalks.

It took two years for Joe to send for Mary. He was working nights at a gas station on the West Side and living in an apartment in Uptown, an area of the city that had become an entry point for many working-class whites from the South, who shared the area's streets with Native Americans. Mary left with Joetta to join him. Delbert, two years older than Bob, had already moved up to be with his father.

Bob, exercising the independent streak that would punctuate his life, balked at moving away from the valley he loved, and moved in with his sister and her husband. However, by 1962, Frances, her husband, and their new baby were on their way to Chicago. They found a one-bedroom apartment in a building near Wrigley Field, the home of the Chicago Cubs. Bob, then fourteen, and Delbert, then sixteen, moved into a $20-a-week one-room apartment one floor below their sister.

In Chicago, Bob spent an undistinguished and forgettable couple of years at Lake View High School, working afternoons flipping burgers at a Henry's, a hamburger joint, and often spending mornings ditching classes in the company of like-minded teens.

On one such morning he was sitting with some friends in a local hangout called Nellie's when, to his horror, he saw his father stride by, clearly in a foul mood. Usually he slept during the day after working the night shift. Bob left Nellie's and raced back to school. In the principal's office, Joe Lowe said nothing. After school, Bob was summoned to his parents' apartment.

"What's up, dad?" he said with false cheer.

"I work nights, you know that," said Joe. "I don't have time to be woke up by the people at your school and told to come in because you're not there. You understand?"

"But I was—" Bob started to say.

"Don't you lie to me, Bob," Joe said, his voice rising with anger.

Bob realized it would be pointless to make up a story as his father unlooped his belt for what would be a harsh and stinging punishment.

Bob would never lie to his father again.

They sat in the hospital, waiting for the police officers to return.

"Are you gonna talk to them?" Joe asked.

"I saw what I saw," Bob said.

"Bob Lowe?"

A police officer stood in the doorway. Behind him, Bob could see a nurse parting curtains from a treatment area.

"There a Bob Lowe out here or not?" said the cop.

Bob stood and walked toward the officer, who led him down a hall to a room bare but for a small table in the middle and three chairs. Bob sat on one side of the table, two cops on the other. One asked the questions, the other took notes with a Bic pen on a pad of yellow paper. Dispassionately, Bob began to speak.

"I went outside to walk my dog, Ginger," he began. "I noticed a car at the curb."

"Why did you notice it?"

"The engine was running," he said. "Idling."

It went on for ten minutes, after which Bob and his father left the hospital together. They did not speak during the ride home. On the sidewalk outside their house, they stood together before going inside.

"Smells good out here," said Joe.

"Does," said Bob. "Think it's the cut trees."

"And fall's in the air," said Joe.

The street was still filled with people, neighbors gathered in small groups up and down the sidewalks. It was well after midnight, but many children were about, dressed in pajamas and pointing at the lawn where Billy Logan had died. The police were gone, leaving behind only the yellow tape, a garish reminder of death.

"You told them everything, didn't you?" asked Joe.

"I answered what they asked," said Bob.

"I hope you know what you're doing."

"I saw what I saw," Bob said.

6

Louie Almeida parked the brown Plymouth in the garage on May Street. "You want me to clean off the car tonight?" he asked. Blood splatters, he was thinking.

"No," said Harry Aleman. "I'll do it tomorrow."

Together they walked to the Survivor's Club. Harry stepped inside and Louie continued west to Aberdeen Street. He ate an Italian beef sandwich at the late-night stand on the corner and then went home to sleep.

Later, when Harry left the club, he walked to the gas station where his car was parked and drove to his home. In his suburban life, Harry was seen as a doting father. Nobody ever asked what he did for a living. His neighbors liked and admired him. On Taylor Street, he was respected and feared. Some saw him as a rising mob star. Many more, though, saw him differently. When he walked the streets, along Taylor and Bishop and Racine and Aberdeen and Loomis, Harry Aleman was a man whose dark eyes would fix on the teenagers who stood on the corner, cigarettes in hand, and he would usually stop to lecture in a kind but firm manner. "Don't smoke. Throw those away," he would say. "I don't smoke and I don't drink. Take care of yourselves and you'll stick around for a long time." He would allow a hint of a smile, perhaps a friendly cuff on the back of the head, and walk on.

For some, Harry was a father figure and counselor. With a month left to go before graduating, a family friend's son quit high school and refused to return. Harry paid a visit to the house and, after a private conversation, the boy returned and graduated. Harry sponsored a neighborhood hockey team and regularly dropped in to watch games and the occasional practice. Years later, one of those players would recall the night he dropped his gloves and fought an opponent who had clobbered him against the boards. Harry approached him after the game. "I didn't come to watch you fight," he said. "I come to watch you play."

On occasion, Harry would stop into the park district field house and watch the wiry, dark-haired teenagers trade punches in the boxing ring, as he once had. He would lean against the wall and just watch, his eyes seemingly missing nothing. One afternoon, he noticed one particularly feisty youth wearing canvas tennis shoes in the ring.

"What's with the kid with the gym shoes?" Harry asked one of the park staffers, a man he had known since they were kids themselves.

"He doesn't have the money for boxing shoes," the staffer said. "He's from a big family and they don't have a lot of dough, the kid says."

Harry dug into his pocket, pulled out a roll of cash and peeled off three $20 bills. "He's got guts," Harry said. "Buy the kid some shoes."

Harry Peralt Aleman was born January 19, 1939, and was raised, along with his two younger brothers, Fred and Anthony, on Bishop Street, a quiet avenue of two- and three-flat brick buildings separated only by the narrow gangways leading from the sidewalk in front to the alley behind. Their parents were an unusual union. Louis Aleman was a native of Durango, Mexico, a hoodlum who supplemented his income from a small-time drug trade with an occasional stickup, and a man with a violent temper. Mary Virginia Baratta was Italian and Taylor Street had long been her home.

Like many residents of the neighborhood, the family lived in an apartment, in a building owned by Harry's maternal grandmother. It was always full of uncles, aunts, and cousins, a center of generally joyful gatherings. But behind this pleasant domestic picture were beatings, unpredictable and furious. They started early, soon after Harry was old enough to walk, prompted by almost anything: spilled food, crying, a misplaced toy. As the brothers grew older, the spankings and seemingly unprovoked cracks with an open palm escalated into beatings with closed fists.

When Harry was seven, the violence ceased for four years while his father was in prison for robbery. Upon his release, the family learned he had not been rehabilitated during his absence. The beatings resumed. On occasion, his father used a horsewhip, but the worst came when he handcuffed Harry to a radiator and went at his son until he was too tired to go on. When his mother intervened, she got hit, too.

Harry, like most male children who have been victims of this type of violent rage, would carry his father's behavior into the street. At first he expressed it in the controlled violence of the football field, playing halfback on the Crane Tech High School football team. He also boxed, learning the art at the Duncan YMCA on the Near North Side, where his hard left hand earned him the nickname "The Hook." Despite his slight build, he was good. After winning one boxing competition at a neighborhood tournament, he faced the choice between a trophy and $7.50.

The choice was easy. Harry took the money. He likely spent it on clothes, for Harry was always a snappy dresser. His was a fastidious look in an era of chinos and blue jeans. He wore dark slacks with a razor-sharp crease, knit shirts, and sport coats. While many of his friends were emulating the styles of Marlon Brando or James Dean, his style attracted a nickname from another era, "The Sheik," for a Rudolph Valentino movie role decades earlier.

Harry was drawn to life's finer things and was passionate about art. After graduating from high school in 1956, he enrolled in the Chicago Academy of Fine Arts. While at school, he worked part-time in the market district, lifting crates of fruit and vegetables. He graduated two years later with a commercial art diploma. While some would later suggest that Harry had studied art so he would know the right pieces to steal, his passion for art and painting would be lifelong, and were perhaps even a desperate attempt to cultivate something soft within himself.

He arrived home from killing Billy Logan to find his wife, Ruth, asleep. So were the four kids. They were her kids from her first marriage, but Harry was more a father to them than Frank Mustari, their biological father, had ever been.

Mustari was not very good at anything. A nickel-and-dime hoodlum, he had a lengthy criminal record, including arrests for hijacking truckloads of pinball machines, whiskey, and jukeboxes. In 1956, when he was twenty-nine years old, he was arrested in what police said was a racket to extort protection money from prostitutes operating in downtown Chicago.

The following year, he foolishly attempted to graduate to hit man by agreeing to kill an ex-convict who owned a tavern called the Rio Vista in the Chicago suburb of Lyons. In the company of two other would-be assassins, Mustari shadowed Willard Bates for weeks. It was three-forty-five in the morning on July 1 when Bates walked to his car with Duchess, his eight-year-old Doberman. The dog started to growl and Bates reached for his pistol. As he opened the door of his car, he saw Mustari aiming a gun at him from the back seat. Bates fired his .38 caliber pistol and Mustari fired back. The bullet from Mustari's gun nicked Bates's finger, but Mustari was shot fatally in the head.

Bates later speculated to police that the assassination attempt might have resulted from his testimony in a 1951 hijacking case or from problems he was having with a business associate. Whatever his trouble, it was serious. Four months after foiling Mustari and his pals, Bates was riddled by rifle, carbine, and shotgun slugs in an ambush in front of his home. One of those brought in for questioning in the slaying, a minor hood named James Rini, flippantly told police, "I don't think it was a murder; I think it was a suicide."

So Ruth Felper Mustari was a widow when she first met Harry. She was working as a cocktail waitress in a club on Rush Street. It was not a profession or a place for those with delicate sensibilities. The area was one of hustle and heartbreak, a neon-splashed section of the city that catered to conventioneers and locals and offered, in its night clubs, gin mills, restaurants, and strip clubs, as vast and varied an array of seedy diversions as existed in any city. Sailors on leave, businessmen away from home, and locals seeking cheap thrills filled the nightspots and sidewalks. Uninhibited and usually well-lubricated, this nightly gathering posed considerable challenges for those in the service industry. But Ruth was good at what she did. And she was a knockout. Compact and curvaceous, she was possessed of a biting tongue and quick wit. Her taste in men, however, was questionable.

One man she dated was a twenty-nine-year-old ex-convict named Richard Fanning. On December 10, 1960, he was found beaten and stabbed to death in his car parked near his South Side home. He was last seen alive three days earlier by a real-estate salesman named George Jurkish who testified at a January 1961 coroner's inquest that the slain man had been dating a waitress named Ruth, with whom he was "having trouble," and that she "had it in for him." Ruth was subpoenaed to attend the inquest, but she refused to testify on the grounds that her testimony might be self-incriminating.

Her relationship with Harry was a happy one from the beginning. Seven years older than Harry, she had a self-assured spark that he found irresistible. He realized the girl he was engaged to—a proper Italian and Roman Catholic—was a child by comparison. Ruth was taken with Harry's dashing good looks and what she would ever refer to as his sensitive side. They were married in a civil ceremony at City Hall on April 4, 1964.

Ruth would later recall how, in those early years, Harry's domestic side was dominant as she made the transition from cocktail waitress to full-time stay-at-home mother. She learned to cook under Harry's tender guidance, particularly the intricacies of melding garlic, tomato paste, oregano, and basil into the rich red sauce that was a staple of their lives.

The sudden transformation from life as a bachelor to a man with a wife and four children was seamless. Harry embraced Ruth's children as his own father had not embraced him. Each day, Harry would help make the children's lunches and see them off to school. "He treated those kids like they were his own," Ruth would later recall. "He came home every night and we sat around the table for dinner and he asked them about their school and what they were doing."

It seems that no one, though, dared ask what Harry was doing with the rest of his life.

7

Fran Lowe was pacing in the kitchen when Bob returned from giving his statement to the police at the hospital. She all but leapt on him when he walked in the door.

Bob held her briefly, sat down, and said, "Billy's dead."

"I know. Everybody knows. It's terrible," she said. "Are you OK?"

"I think so," he said. "You should have seen it."

He didn't mean that. He was glad she hadn't seen Billy die.

"Do they know who did it?" she asked.

"No," said Bob. "I'm the only one who seen the car."

"Did you see who shot him?" asked Fran.

"Yeah."

"And you told the police?" asked Fran.

"I told them what I seen," he said.

"So much dying to see in a year," said Fran, shuddering. "So much killing."

"I know," he said, suddenly feeling tired, extremely tired. "I know."

Better than nothing," Bob said to himself as he grabbed a handful of popcorn and lifted it to his mouth. It was three o'clock on an uncharacteristically cold morning in mid-April 1972, five months before Billy Logan was killed. Snowflakes swirled outside the windows of the gas station office. Bob could see cars moving slowly on the streets, when there were cars to see.

He grabbed the carton of chocolate milk and washed the popcorn down and turned his attention back to the *Playboy* magazine on his lap.

He heard the click of the door and, lowering the carton, looked up to see two black men standing in front of him. Bob flinched and the popcorn that had been balancing on his leg fell and scattered on the black-and-white tile floor. The men both carried revolvers.

"Open the safe, motherfucker. Now," said one man. He was the taller of the two, his voice firm, controlled.

"There ain't no safe," Bob said, his eyes on the pistols.

The shorter man spoke. "Give us the money." His voice was squeaky.

"Don't have it," Bob said. He had locked the day's receipts in a back room. "All I got's this—"

He reached for his shirt pocket.

"Easy, motherfucker. Move that hand real slow," the tall man said.

Bob froze. "I got bills in my pocket," he said, slowly drawing $38 from his left shirt pocket with his left hand. With his right, he levered $2.38 from the metal coin changer on his right hip. "This is it."

"Damn," the shorter man snapped, grabbing the money. Beyond them, out in the snow, Bob spotted a third man standing near the gas pumps.

"Where's the rest?" the tall man asked. "I ain't gonna tell you twice."

"Like I told you, that's it," Bob said, his voice rising.

The smack of the pistol on the side of his cheek reverberated through his skull and sent Bob spinning from the chair. He rolled over to face them, but the short man pounced on him and put a knee on his chest.

The cold metal smacked him again. Bob tasted his own blood.

"Fuck it, let's git," the tall man said, edging toward the door.

The short man grabbed the front of Bob's shirt, pulled his head from the floor, and whacked his face again. As the robbers backed out the door, Bob rolled to his side and reached under a shelf next to his chair. His hand groped under a towel until he felt the .38-caliber pistol—a gun he had purchased a year earlier from a friend.

As he pulled it to his chest, he could hear voices outside through the open door. It was the voice of the tall man. "Go on. I'm telling you, he seen our faces. You go back and shoot that honky motherfucker."

Bob heard feet shuffle across the floor. He felt a shoe slide under his chest and then reactive rage took over. He rolled and came up firing. The bullet found the chest of the short man and he fell back, against the door, shattering the glass.

Bob leaped to his feet and stepped over the short man's bleeding body. He raised the gun and snapped off five more shots at the figure clambering over the fence that separated the station from an empty lot to the east. The last shot found its mark and the tall man slumped to the ground. Bob was on him in a flash. He held his now-empty gun to the man's head and wrested the gun from his hand. He stared into the man's eyes, raised the robber's gun and shot him in the stomach.

"I hope you die, you son of a bitch," Bob said.

He dropped the guns and, with blood dripping from his nose, cocked his right fist and delivered a punch squarely to the man's mouth. The man didn't move and as Bob rose, he saw a tooth embedded in one of his knuckles. Only then did he feel his body begin to shake violently. The rest of that early morning and what followed is now largely a blur: Bob was charged with failing to register his pistol; he pled guilty and was put on probation; the third robber had fled to the rear porch of a nearby building, where a resident, aroused by the gunfire, had subdued him with the aid of a butcher knife; Bob testified in court that summer; the third man and tall man both were sent to prison; the short man was dead when he hit the ground.

Two detectives showed up at Joe's 100 about a week after the murder of Billy Logan. Bob was sitting in the office. The detectives asked him to come to the police station.

"We want you to look at some pictures," they said.

They were homicide investigators, men who followed up on leads in the days after a killing. They had already talked with Billy's sisters and his nephew. They had also talked with Billy's ex-wife, Phyllis, who told them she thought the murder was a "tragic accident."

Now they were here for Bob. Both were dressed in the typical 1970s Chicago detective garb—cheap brown or navy blue sport coats, white shirts, and dark slacks, with ties from the sale rack at Sears.

Bob ducked his head into the back room. "Dad, some detectives want me to look at pictures," he said.

"How long's it gonna take?" Joe asked.

"An hour, maybe. I don't know," Bob said.

"OK," Joe said. "Just be back by four o'clock. I've got to run by the other station for a while."

The detective headquarters for the West Side of Chicago, like the five other detective bureaus scattered across the city, was a square and squat red brick building surrounded by a concrete parking lot. Bob followed the two detectives up a flight of worn stairs and pushed through a swinging door. Along one wall were small cubicles that served as offices for the commanders of several detective divisions. Typewriters clacked as detectives, many in shirtsleeves with their ties loosened, pecked away at reports.

"Sit here," one of the detectives said, pointing to an empty table.

Bob waited silently while the two men pulled open the doors to a metal cabinet and hauled four fat photo albums to the table. Hand-printed across each was a label corresponding to a detective division: HOMICIDE/RAPE, BURGLARY, ROBBERY, AUTO THEFT. The volumes contained police booking photographs of men arrested for the various crimes, the detectives explained.

"Take your time and go through them," said the one with the blue jacket.

"See if the guy you saw get out of the car the night Logan was murdered is in there," said the other.

The detectives left Bob alone as he opened the AUTO THEFT book. It was interesting at first, examining the expressions on the faces. Some were blank, others angry, and a few, apparently used to the routine, even smiled. There were white men, black men, brown men staring at him from the pages. No names, only booking numbers.

Bob put the book aside: nothing. The same for HOMICIDE/RAPE and BURGLARY. He picked up the final book. His initial interest had waned as the task turned tedious and tiring—a waste of time. But he opened the book and began to flip the pages, no longer studying each face, but scanning, looking for a glimmer of recognition. He did not expect to find one.

But there it was, midway through the gallery: the narrow face, the coal-black eyes, the dead stare. The hair was different, longer. But there was no doubt. Bob motioned to the two detectives, who were lounging at a table a few feet away. One was smoking. The one with his feet propped on a chair read the newspaper.

"Officers," Bob said. "Got him."

The two men exchanged a quick look, then casually sauntered to stand behind Bob.

"That's the guy," he said, pressing a stubby index finger to the photograph.

"You're sure?" asked the detective in the blue jacket.

"Yeah, I'm sure," Bob said, pointing again at the black eyes. "This is the guy who got out of the car when Billy got shot."

"Okay then. Thank you, Mr. Lowe," blue jacket's partner said. "We'll take it from here. My partner will give you a lift back to work."

Bob left without learning the identity of the man he had picked out. He didn't even bother to ask. "We'll take care of it," he had been assured on the drive back to the gas station. "We'll find the guy."

And that, he thought, *would be that.*

8

When he died on the front lawn of his sister's house, Billy Logan became a member of an exclusive, if unfortunate, club. He was Chicago's 1,015th mob killing.

It is, of course, impossible to know exactly how many people have been shot, stabbed, garroted, blown up, beaten, or tortured to death during the bloody history of organized crime in Chicago. Even the Chicago Crime Commission, a citizen's watchdog organization formed in 1919 by members of the business community in outraged response to the bribery and corruption even then plaguing the criminal justice system, can't be precise. The leading arbiter on such matters, the Crime Commission began tabulating mob murders the year it was formed, and it freely admits that its figures have always been conservative. Unlike other terrorist organizations, the mob has never felt the urge to take credit for its handiwork.

Ironically, the Crime Commission was formed in the same summer that Chicago saw the arrival of a young and vicious man who would define and help romanticize the image of a gangster. Even now, more than fifty years after his death and more than seventy years after leaving Chicago, the mere mention of the city's name abroad often triggers a familiar response: using two hands to mimick the posture of a man sweeping a submachine gun from side to side while mouthing a steady rat-a-tat-a-tat and the chilling name "Al Capone."

There has always been crime in Chicago, but in the 1880s it became organized, thanks to the pioneering efforts of Michael Cassius McDonald, a prominent gambler, who created a system where all betting establishments and brothels paid him a tribute to continue operating without police interference. His methods were refined by the turn of the century by 1st Ward Alderman "Bathhouse" John Coughlin, with the help of tavern owner Michael "Hinky Dink" Kenna. They created the framework for organized crime in Chicago by establishing a legal defense fund for gamblers and prostitutes, drawing on tributes and monthly fees collected for police protection.

The system worked so well for the powerful duo—often referred to as the "Lords of the Levee" for the thriving red-light district in their ward— that they enlisted the help of saloon owner "Big Jim" Colosimo. As the 1st Ward's precinct captain and its tribute gatekeeper, Colosimo collected enormous sums from the saloons and brothels in the ward. It was said that of every $2 a prostitute made, $1.20 went to Colosimo.

A former street-sweeper, shoe-shine boy and newspaper hawker, Colosimo was Chicago's first real gangster and he appeared to relish the role, turning out in a finely tailored wardrobe that glistened with a small fortune in diamonds. He ruled Chicago's underworld without many challenges until about 1910, when the Italian Mafia—the vestiges of the notorious extortionists known as the Black Hand, abetted by some imported muscle from New York—attempted to extract its own tribute from Colosimo.

Not about to share the turf, he sent for his nephew in New York City. Johnny Torrio was a member of New York's infamous Five Points Gang and had the New York connections necessary to help eliminate his uncle's tormentors. Sometimes this was done with words. Sometimes words were not enough, and quickly the twenty-eight-year-old Torrio established himself as a terror.

But he, too, needed extra muscle and in 1919, he sent to New York for his tough young cousin named Al Capone. By then, Capone had acquired a wife and a jagged scar running from his left ear to his mouth that gave rise to the nickname "Scarface," which no one dared to utter in his presence. He got it in a fight but, showing the imaginative flair that made him a favorite of quote-starved reporters, he claimed that it was the result of shrapnel in World War I.

The next year, in the face of Colosimo's refusal to get into bootlegging after the Volsted Act banned the sale of legal liquor, Torrio ordered Capone to kill their mentor. And Colosimo was dead, compelling the Crime Commission to begin its list of mob killings. Virtually all of them would be the result of competitive business practices; the battle to consolidate and control criminal enterprises was waged not with pens on contracts, but with bullets and bombs.

Torrio escaped the list, barely. After ordering the 1924 assassination of North Side gangster Dion O'Banion, who was taken out in the flower shop he owned on State Street directly across from Holy Name Cathedral, Torrio was seriously wounded by a shotgun blast and four bullets. In the hospital, surrounded by thirty bodyguards around the clock, he fought successfully for his life and got the message. This had been the second attempted hit; the first had cost Torrio his chauffeur and his dog. By the time he emerged from intensive care, he had seen the light. With an estimated $30,000,000, he took a trip to the Mediterranean and then settled into a quiet life in Brooklyn. Before leaving Chicago, he said to his closest associate, "It's all yours, Al. I retire."

And Capone grabbed it with bloodthirsty gusto. He and his associates figured in many of the 697 gangland killings recorded from 1919 to 1932. The annual toll of gangland murders had been running about two dozen a year beginning in 1919, but, as the struggle for control of Chicago's illicit businesses heated up, the flow of blood became a torrent. Dead bodies began popping up like spring crocuses: fifty-four in 1924, sixty-six in 1925, seventy-five in 1926, fifty-eight in 1927 and seventy-two in 1928.

The bloodbath climaxed in 1929 at about 10:30 A.M. on St. Valentine's Day when four men burst into the S.M.C. Cartage Co. garage at 2122 North Clark Street, which Capone rival George "Bugs" Moran was using for various illegal doings, most notably bootlegging.

Two of the men who entered the building were dressed as police officers.

They ordered the seven men inside the garage—six Moran associates and Reinhardt Schwimmer, an optometrist who got his kicks hanging out with mobsters—to line up against a whitewashed brick wall. Immediately the intruders opened fire, spraying the wall and the seven men with more than 100 bullets.

For six of the victims, the time of death was noted on police reports as 10:40 A.M. Despite fourteen slugs in his body, Frank Gusenberg, a top Moran aide, lived for nearly three more hours. Dying, but blindly adhering to that code of honor among hoodlums, Gusenberg refused to tell his pal, Sergeant Thomas J. Loftus of the old 36th District, who had done the shooting. But everyone knew.

"Only Capone kills guys like that," said Moran.

None of those who followed in Capone's footsteps would ever attain his mythic stature. Some were smarter, some even more vicious, and others more adept at playing the press to their advantage. But none had the combination of Capone's evil skills and media savvy that so firmly embedded his character into the fabric of American culture.

After Capone was convicted of tax evasion and sentenced to seven years in prison, most of it at the new maximum-security prison at Alcatraz, his enterprise fell under the control of two men, Frank Nitti and Paul Ricca.

Nitti, nicknamed "The Enforcer," had started his career fencing stolen goods out of his barbershop and later proved clever at smuggling booze from Canada into Chicago. Ricca, nicknamed "The Waiter" for his profession in his humble early years in America, was an elegant man, clean and neat with a thick Italian accent. He was far more powerful than his colleague, who was the focus of greater press attention at the time (and later in mythologized Hollywood treatments). Ricca often countermanded Nitti orders with a quick, "We'll do it this way and let's say no more about it." When he ordered a hit, it was with a simple, "Make'a him go away."

Though the Nitti/Ricca alliance was an effective one, expanding the mob's reach into the policy and numbers rackets in the city's black neighborhoods, as well as positions of power in various trade unions, the most influential post-Capone mob leader would prove to be Antonino Leonardo Accardo. The Chicago-born son of an Italian immigrant shoemaker, he dropped out of school at age fourteen and, after working jobs as a delivery boy for a florist and a grocery clerk, found a home behind the wheel of a truck carrying Capone's bootleg booze.

Though Accardo officially changed his name to Anthony Joseph Accardo, he was better known by the menacing nickname "Joe Batters," testimony to his skills as an enforcer. His driving prowess and physical toughness catapulted him into a position as Capone's chauffeur as well as membership in the Circus Cafe gang, whose members are believed to have participated in the St. Valentine's Day massacre.

With Nitti and Ricca in charge, Accardo became more visible, even acting as front man for the two mobsters and picking up another nickname, "Big Tuna," in part for the frequent fishing trips he took.

Nitti committed suicide in 1943 after a few too many run-ins with the law caused some of his colleagues to question not only his intelligence but also his loyalties. And Ricca became little more than an adviser, consumed with legal and deportation battles after serving a four-month prison sentence in 1947 for extortion.

With Accardo in command, the rackets expanded outside Chicago as the population began to invade the surrounding counties of Lake, Will, and DuPage.

A short-tempered man who stood little more than five feet tall, Accardo continued operating the mob in a businesslike fashion, ceding day-to-day operating control to capable underlings. He was greatly admired by his mob colleagues, one of whom told a newspaper columnist, "Accardo has more brains before breakfast than Al Capone ever had all day." He brooked no protests and misbehavior was punished swiftly and with finality. But the violence of the 1920s had gradually toned down once liquor was legalized. Gangland killings tapered off, with no more than ten deaths a year in the 1930s, 1940s and 1950s.

Some mob-watchers officially retired Accardo in 1958, during an appearance at a televised hearing of a U.S. Senate investigating committee. Although he invoked his 5th Amendment right against self-incrimination one hundred thirty times, he did say he was "retired" and receiving Social Security. He declined to say what he had retired from and, had truth been known at the time, he was actually many years away from his rocking chair and slippers.

The Chicago mob entered the 1960s as an efficient and increasingly ambitious operation, with Accardo playing mentor to Sam "Momo" Giancana. Initially considered a low-profile type, and living in a modest bungalow in Oak Park, Giancana was no shrinking violet. He loved the limelight, courted the press, and seemed to bask in the celebrity that followed his love affair with singer Phyllis McGuire. Through his association with her celebrity pals, including Frank Sinatra, he met another man not immune to the delights of Hollywood, a handsome senator named John Fitzgerald Kennedy. Both men, the gangster and the president, also shared a relationship with a pretty starlet named Judith Exner.

Giancana was a brazen man who would, according to a former FBI agent, "have someone hit at the flick of an eye." He was said to have put out a contract on Desi Arnaz, angry because of the way the mob was portrayed in *The Untouchables* television show, which Arnaz produced; and to have put out murder contracts on FBI agents. It has been widely suggested that he was involved in unsuccessful assassination plots against Fidel Castro and that he may have had a hand in the assassination of JFK.

It was with some relief on the part of elder mob bosses, then, that Giancana was sent to prison in 1965 for failing to testify in front of a grand jury investigating organized crime. Released in 1966, Giancana remained a powerful local mob figure, but he no longer played top man.

A number of others filled that spot, characters such as Sam "Teets" Battaglia and Felix "Milwaukee Phil" Alderisio, but they were mere front men. The mob was being run by Accardo and two principal aides: Gussie Alex, an experienced and intelligent mobster not of Italian descent, and Joseph "Doves" Aiuppa, another holdover from the Capone days who, though lacking many administrative skills, was, in the words of a later mob turncoat, "The Pope (who) sits in a chair and decides who gets what in Chicago."

Together, they cultivated the next generation, men such as Joseph Ferriola who, like Accardo, was a product of the West Side and worked his way up the crime syndicate ladder by being an enforcer for Giancana.

Ferriola had a reputation for business acumen, but he also was a fearless, take-no-prisoners terrorist. He cut his teeth as a juice loan operator, lending cash to gamblers for obscenely high interest rates and managing the mob's vending machine business. He earned a justifiable reputation as a man who always got what he and his bosses were owed. He was, in the words of an FBI agent, a "monster with brains."

He also was Harry Aleman's uncle.

9

"City desk, Royko," said the twenty-eight-year-old reporter.

"This is security, downstairs," said the guard on the other end of the line. "Maybe you wanna get somebody down here. Cops are here. Two guys tried to bust into the vending machines."

Mike Royko looked around the offices of the *Chicago Daily News*. It was after midnight and the room was empty. He gathered up a pen and notebook and took the elevator to the basement, his instincts telling him his efforts wouldn't amount to anything. Such petty crimes, even one on site, rarely made the papers.

The *Daily News* shared a seven-story building at the edge of the Chicago River at Wabash Avenue with the *Chicago Sun-Times*. The guard had spotted two men attempting to break into the row of vending machines and called the police. Officers were placing the two young men under arrest by the time Royko arrived. He talked to the security guard and the cops. He noted that the men had netted only $82 for their unsuccessful efforts. He recognized one of the men, an apprentice pressman who had been working in the building for a few months. The other he had never seen, but he jotted down his name: Harry Aleman.

The story of the botched robbery never did make the paper and a few months later, a judge would place both men on probation for their crime. But Royko, later a Pulitzer Prize–winning columnist and astute mob observer, ever kept his eye on Harry's career.

Decades after his first encounter with Harry, Royko would write:

New York mobsters have so little dignity that they collaborate on books about themselves. They hold press conferences. . . . But members of Chicago's Outfit have always demonstrated Midwestern virtues, such as restraint, modesty, and a desire for privacy and anonymity. As little more than tots, they were taught that in the presence of cameras, a proper gentleman always wears his gray fedora over his face.

But Harry was not a restrained or modest man. Though he desired anonymity, his increasingly violent streak made that impossible. One of his most explosive scenes took place on an early 1960s night when he was visiting a bar on North State Street in the Rush Street nightclub district. There was an argument with a woman. Words were exchanged, becoming harsher and louder. Suddenly, with little warning, Harry shoved the woman through a plateglass window and then fled with his brother, Freddie, and two friends. In a noble if foolhardy gesture, Howard Pierson, the twenty-three-year-old son of a Chicago police robbery commander, gave chase. The foursome was stopped several blocks away by police and, as officers questioned them, Pierson caught up. Without a word, Harry delivered his left hook, breaking Pierson's jaw. Harry was put on probation for two years.

There were other minor scraps with the law during the early 1960s, reflected in an arrest sheet that was not unlike those of hundreds of other young toughs of the time: arrests for bar fights, for riding in a car that turned out to be stolen, for lying on a loan application. Without the benefit of hindsight, these might have appeared to be simple acts of juvenile delinquency rather than the building blocks of a successful career in organized crime.

By the late 1960s, Harry had organized a gang of thugs of varying degrees of intelligence and viciousness. With his uncle a rising power in the mob and Harry facing the new responsibility of matrimony and of raising four children, he had the clout and the reasons to start his own business.

His principal associate was Butch Petrocelli, a childhood friend, and their first jobs involved collecting money from those who refused to pay for protection or refused to do their bidding. They employed such tried-and-true methods as threats, strong-arming, damaging various body parts, and, when necessary, bombings. Petrocelli built some of the bombs in the back room of the Survivor's Club, packing black powder with a high concentration of nitroglycerine into a ten-inch section of two-inch-wide pipe and attaching a three-minute fuse. They bombed a currency exchange after the owner balked at providing "clean" license plates for their work cars. They bombed the garage of a prison guard who was not treating their pals well behind bars. The list of bombings was long and eclectic: a restaurant, a beauty salon, an optometrist's office, and any number of taverns.

In January 1969, state agents were called in after a painting contractor said mobsters threatened to kill him. The painter had lost $6,000 to syndicate bookmakers and borrowed the money to pay—a "juice loan," in mobster parlance. But, as often happens, the painter fell behind in his $600-a-week payments and, as happens just as often, some very nasty men paid the painter a visit.

The painter thought he was meeting two men about getting hired for a painting job. But when he showed up, the two men dragged him into a nearby camper. They started with threats: "We'll dynamite your home," the two men said. "We'll kill your wife, and then we'll kill you." Then they pistol-whipped him until, whimpering, he agreed to pay $3,000 within two days. However, lacking such resources, he called the authorities. Two agents, posing as friends of the contractor, set up a meeting with the loan collectors to pay the debt. The meeting was arranged to take place at the mouth of the Chicago River in the office of a lock-tender. There, at the meeting, the lock-tender had been arrested. Harry and Butch were spotted in a car nearby, and when the contractor identified them as the men who had beaten him, both were arrested. And both were released on bond.

Two days later, Butch was arrested again. It seemed that when the agents opened the lock-tender's trunk after the arrest by the river, they found clothing that was part of a $100,000 shipment of women's apparel that had been recently hijacked. A search warrant had been executed at Butch's home, where the rest of the clothing was recovered.

A grand jury was convened, but no indictment was returned. Harry and Butch seemed to be living a charmed life. It was a life that would turn particularly violent just two years later.

Sam "Sambo" Cesario had been Harry's uncle by marriage until he divorced Harry's aunt Viola in the late 1960s. A heavyset man with a broad nose, heavy eyelids, and a thick neck made more so by a double chin, Cesario was for decades a well-known and feared member of the outfit. Once arrested in the 1950s along with two of Al Capone's brothers for questioning in murder and bombing investigations, he was what the cops called a "middle-echelon hoodlum," whose main activity was illegal gambling, specializing in horse-race betting and card games.

What was not so well known about Sambo was his secret marriage to a woman named Nan Partipilo in June 1971. The reason for the hush-hush nature of the union was that Nan was the girlfriend of Felix Alderisio, the high-ranking and much-feared mob boss from Milwaukee.

Given the number of people who might have wanted to ingratiate themselves with Alderisio, it is not surprising that word of the marriage reached him, even though he was in prison. He was understandably displeased.

On the night of October 19, 1971, Sambo and Nan were sitting on the lawn in front of their unassuming two-flat on Polk Street, just north of Taylor Street, when two men wearing cloth masks approached.

One of them told Sambo to remain seated but the other knocked him off his chair with a rifle and began to savagely beat him with the butt. The other man pumped four pistol shots into Sambo as he lay on the ground. As Nan screamed, the two men fled through a gangway.

The event was of no comfort to Alderisio, who had died in prison about three weeks before the slaying. There would never be an arrest for the murder, but law enforcement officials will say that one of the assassins was Butch Petrocelli. The other, they say, was Harry Aleman and it was his first killing.

Early risers shivered their way to the Survivor's Club on the morning of April 8, 1972. The temperature was in the 20s and three inches of snow covered the ground. A cup of espresso steamed in front of Harry as he stared at the front page of the *Chicago Tribune*. The last night's storm was front-page news. But a number in another story caught Harry's eye: $500,000. That's how much United Airlines had paid a hijacker using the name "A. T. Johnson" before he parachuted from the plane as it flew over Provo, Utah.

The other stories in the paper were of little interest for a man such as Harry: The North Vietnamese Army continued its offensive push toward Saigon; George Meany, president of the AFL-CIO, appeared at the National Press Club to denounce the economic policies of President Nixon; an Illinois Democratic State Representative named Harold Washington got 40 days in jail for failing to file state income tax returns. Those were not the stories that intrigued Harry that cold spring morning. The article that drew his full attention was on page six.

Mob Chief Gallo Killed; Fear New York Gang War

NEW YORK-April 7-Mobster leader Joseph (Crazy Joe) Gallo was shot to death as he celebrated his 43rd birthday with his wife of three weeks early today in a restaurant in the Little Italy section of Lower Manhattan.

Police expressed fear his murder would touch off another Gangland war.

Gallo had gone to the restaurant after attending a nightclub. Just before dawn, a lone gunman entered by a back door, walked up to the Gallo table and fired three times. Gallo was hit in the back and in the buttocks. The third shot slightly wounded his bodyguard, Peter (Pete the Greek) Diapioulis.

Gallo staggered from the restaurant and fell dead on the street.

The story went on for many more paragraphs, but its impact was immediate and profound. For the rest of that day and for days afterward, Harry could talk about nothing else but the hit on Gallo. In the car with Louie Almeida, at his table at the Survivor's Club, over lunch at Guido's, everywhere but at home. "Now, that was a hit," he would say, "in a restaurant, in the open, in front of plenty of witnesses." Louie heard it again and again, so often that he felt like telling Harry to "shut up about Gallo."

But he didn't. He knew better

Wake up," said Harry.

Louie Almeida, still half-asleep, blinked, then sat up in bed.

"Meet me at the club. Noon," Harry said.

"Sure, Harry," Louie replied, now fully awake.

"Be on time," Harry added, and then hung up.

It was early September 1972 and by then Harry and his associates, building upon his successes at extortion, had invested in police radios to monitor police calls and accumulated a stable of stolen cars—"work cars"—that were crucial to the expansion of their activities beyond extortion and bombings, to include home invasions, robberies, and an industrial cleaning business that also brokered stolen semitrailer loads of merchandise. Harry would plot strategy and dispense orders: Don't take rope to tie up victims, use shoestrings because they are easier to conceal and carry; wear hats and masks; get in and out quickly.

It was important that no one be harmed. In fact, after raiding the home of one elderly couple and leaving them both tied up and gagged, Harry ordered Louie to pull over on the way back to the Survivor's Club so he could call the police from a phone booth. He was concerned that the couple would not be immediately found.

Butch and Harry were already at their regular table when Louie strolled into the dimness of the club a few minutes before noon. Two other men were there, Tommy Versetto and Lennie Foresta. Lennie he knew as a wannabe hood with a liking for home invasions and holdups, and who had been recruited to work for Harry's gang of thieves. Versetto, Almeida soon learned, was a buddy of Petrocelli who had a good tip for a score. Harry cast a neutral gaze at Louie, motioned him to sit down and continued speaking, "Tommy here says there's forty grand in the basement. In cash."

"How do we know that?" Butch asked.

"This guy's old man owns concession stands at Chicago Stadium," Harry said. "Every fuckin' time there's a show, his kid takes the money home. It doesn't go to the bank 'til the next day. The split will be even—five ways."

Harry turned to Louie and Lennie and said, "I want you two to handle this."

"When?" Louie asked.

"Right now."

"Now?"

"Tommy says nobody's home during the day except the kid's wife," Harry said.

"I don't have a gun," Louie said.

"You don't need one," Harry replied. "It's a housewife, for fuck's sake."

Harry shoved a set of car keys across the table toward Lennie. "There's a work car in the lot out back." He jerked his head toward the rear door of the Survivor's Club. "Take the Fairlane."

Lennie drove only three blocks before he pulled over and ducked into a telephone booth. Louie watched as Lennie dialed, then quickly hung up. "She's home, all right," Lennie said as he slid behind the wheel and pulled away.

"Man, I got no gun," Louie said. "It just don't feel right, us having nothing. What if something happens?"

Lennie kept his eyes on the street as he dropped his right hand and pulled back his jacket to reveal a .32-caliber Browning semiautomatic pistol. Then he grinned.

The ride took less than 30 minutes, as Lennie maneuvered the car through the side streets of Oak Lawn, a southwest Chicago suburb.

"I'm gonna stop and call her again," he said. "I'm gonna tell her that I have a package—no, how about an antique?—that her old man bought for her."

"We ain't go no package," Louie said.

"Look in the back seat, dummy," Lennie said. "There's a shopping bag with some shit in it. She won't know the fuckin' difference."

Louie began to relax and Lennie continued to talk, pulling on a pair of dark gloves. "I'll pull up a coupla houses down, go up with the bag. You wait in the car. I can bullshit her better than you. Wait five minutes and then come in."

A woman and a young girl, both bound with shoelaces, were lying face down on the kitchen floor when Louie entered. Lennie was heading down to the basement. An infant sat quietly in a high chair. The faucet was running in the sink and a cloud of steam mushroomed from the stove where a pot of water boiled.

"Where's the fucking money?" Lennie shouted over his shoulder.

"There's no money down there," the woman said, her voice trembling. She was terrified. "The only money is upstairs, in the bedroom. Take it, and leave us alone."

Louie heard a crash from the basement. Several thuds. Lennie swore. A dog began whining from below. Louie surveyed the room, glanced out the back window, and then stepped in the living room to peek at the street. All was quiet. He walked back into the kitchen, turned off the flame under the boiling water and calmly ripped the telephone off the wall.

"Please, sir," the woman implored Louie, "can you take the baby out of the high chair? I want my baby next to me."

Lennie tromped up the stairs. "Leave the kid right there," he commanded. "You want the kid to crawl over and fall down to the goddamn basement? The kid is fine right there." Louie watched him walk into the living room and then heard him stomping around upstairs.

They were out of the house and walking back into the Survivor's Club in less than thirty minutes. Harry, Tommy, and Butch appeared not to have moved. Lennie got right to the point. "There wasn't no forty grand in the fucking basement," he said. "I swear. The broad said they didn't have it and I couldn't find it."

"What'd you get?" asked Harry as he watched Lennie toss a wad of bills on the table. He followed with a handful of jewelry: necklaces, rings, and earrings.

Butch counted out $1,800 in bills and handed it to Harry, who peeled off $500 and passed it to Lennie. He handed another $500 to Louie.

"I'll handle the rest," he said.

No one said a word. Harry was not pleased.

Their next caper, a few days later, was a bit more successful, but it too did not meet expectations. At the home of a wealthy Indianapolis physician, Lennie flashed a Cook County sheriff's badge, said he was with the CIA, and then pushed his way past a maid. He ransacked the house while Louie tied up the woman and stood guard. They left with $25,000 in cash, diamonds, and furs—far short of the tipster's claim that the doctor kept a stash of several hundred thousand dollars in a bedroom safe. Louie and Lennie drove straight back to Harry's home in Melrose Park.

"This is a disappointment," Harry said, surveying the take. He handed Lennie and Louie $500 each. "I'm gonna have to piece these diamonds out to make any fuckin' money."

There is no way of knowing if evil is born or made, or how a bad and quick temper can be transformed into a taste for killing. Does a man wake up one morning, wipe the sleep from his eyes, and say, "I think this would be a good day to become a hit man"?

Could it have started one day, when, hearing his uncle complaining about some problem, Harry offered to help? Did he say, "Uncle, I'll take care of it"? Or did his uncle Joe Ferriola tell him to kill?

What turned this man, who by many accounts was a loving husband and doting father—one who others would later refer to as "a respectful person who could not hurt another human being"—into a man that law enforcement officials would one day describe as the most prolific killer in the history of organized crime in Chicago?

The life of a hit man as portrayed in films such as *Prizzi's Honor* and scores of television shows that focus on and glamorize organized crime is far from reality. Robert Walsh, once the FBI's top organized crime expert in Chicago, said, "Someone being paid big money . . . for a hit is a myth. If a mob boss tells an underling to kill someone, they do it."

It was, on some level, just business—death as a way of life in the skewed moral universe of crime. Mike Royko put it best in a column written more than twenty-five years after his first encounter with Harry:

> *The trouble with most people writing about . . . organized crime [is that] the authors aren't content with appreciating these men for the rare quality that brought them great financial success: their willingness to maim, maul and kill.*
>
> *[These writers] credit them with executive and economic skills beyond those of a Harvard MBA . . . Oh, they were involved in payoffs, kickbacks, rigged union votes . . . and other deals that sounded sophisticated . . . But there's nothing to that. Any sharp CPA or lawyer can structure a deal if all the parties are willing.*
>
> *It's persuading everybody to be willing that's the secret of the mugs' success. And the secret can be described in these little words: "I'll kill you."*

Law enforcement officials would later say that they believed Joe Ferriola tapped Harry Aleman for the job of chief enforcer sometime in late 1972 or early 1973. But while they speculated how and when that occurred, what became abundantly clear was that bodies began piling up around Chicago beginning shortly before Christmas in 1973. Among the first and highest-profile victims was Richard Cain, one of the most charismatic and complex characters in the annals of Chicago crime.

Born in Chicago, Cain began his career as an investigator with a detective agency in Dallas before returning to his hometown and attending classes at a polygraph school run by a Chicago Police Department captain. The captain helped get Cain on the force, where he spent a flashy five years. A smooth talker, he was able to ingratiate himself with superior officers as well as some local columnists who chronicled his career. The good press ended, for a time, in 1960 when Cain resigned from the force after it was discovered that he and a partner were spying on Mayor Richard J. Daley's commissioner of investigations. Law enforcement officials would later say they believed Cain was trying to keep one step ahead of Daley's investigators.

Cain spent the next two years in Mexico, claiming to be doing work for the CIA, before returning to Chicago, where he organized a group of private detectives as volunteers for the Republican gubernatorial campaign of Richard B. Ogilvie. After Ogilvie's victory, Cain was named his chief investigator.

But his career as a crime fighter ended for good when he was convicted and sentenced to four years in prison for conspiracy and concealment of evidence as well as perjury in connection with staging a phony recovery of drugs from a warehouse robbery. Paroled from prison in 1971, he began working as driver, bodyguard, courier and financial adviser for Sam Giancana, the syndicate chief, who by then was in self-exile in Cuernavaca, Mexico. Cain became well known in the press and on the street as "Momo's man," and investigators speculated that all along Cain had been, in fact, the mob's most successful mole and one of the most corrupt police officers in the history of the country.

On December 20, 1973, Cain walked into Rose's Sandwich Shop at 1117 West Grand Avenue for what he believed was a meeting with upper-echelon mobsters. Witnesses would later tell police that Cain spent some time talking with four men and that shortly after they left, two masked gunmen arrived, carrying a shotgun, a pistol, and a two-way radio. They ordered the forty-nine-year-old Cain, three other customers, and a waitress against a wall. The shotgun blast that killed Cain struck him in the lower jaw, so disfiguring his face that he was not officially identified for several hours. The gunmen were last seen driving west on Grand.

The next day's papers played the story big: "Ex-cop Cain shot to death," read the *Tribune's* front page, along with "Slain gangland style by 2 masked hoods." Investigators believed that Cain's demise came as the result of his stepping on some tender toes while "seeking investment opportunities for Giancana." Or, as another headline put it, "Cain played mob game and lost big."

Less headline-grabbing but equally vicious, the killings continued.

On February 24, 1974, Socrates "Sam" Rantis, forty-nine, a counterfeiter, was found in the trunk of his wife's car at O'Hare International Airport with his throat slashed and with puncture wounds in his chest.

On April 21, 1974, William Simone, twenty-nine, another counterfeiter, was found in the back seat of his car in the 2400 block of South Kedvale Avenue, with his hands and feet bound and a gunshot wound in his head.

On July 13, 1974, Orion Williams, thirty-eight, a suspected mob informant, was found shotgunned to death in the trunk of his girlfriend's car on East 33rd Street in the shadow of Comiskey Park, where the White Sox played.

On September 28, 1974, Robert Harder, thirty-nine, a jewel thief and burglar who had become an informant, was found shot in the face in a bean field near Dwight, Illinois.

On January 16, 1975, Carlo Divivo, forty-six, a mob enforcer, was cut down by two masked men who opened fire with a shotgun and a pistol as he walked out of his home at 3631 North Nora Avenue.

On May 12, 1975, Ronald Magliano, forty-three, an underworld fence, was shot once behind the left ear and his Southwest Side home was set ablaze.

On June 19, 1975, Christopher Cardi, forty-three, a former cop turned loan shark, was waiting in line with his wife and children at Jim's Beef Stand in Melrose Park. Two masked men pushed through from the door, calmly walked up, and pumped eight bullets into his back, then one in the face.

And the killings continued.

On August 28, 1975, Frank Goulakos, forty-seven, a federal informant, was shot six times by a masked man as he walked to his car after finishing a shift as a chef at a Northwest Side restaurant.

On August 30, 1975, Nick "Keggie" Galanos, forty-eight, a bookie, was shot nine times in the head in the basement of his home in the 6800 block of West Wabansia Avenue.

With each murder, with each whispered, "I heard it was Aleman," Harry's reputation for violence and death reached every corner of the underworld.

10

Vincent Rizza got the first call in September 1975. A former Chicago traffic cop, he had quit the force, decided to make bookmaking his calling, and set up a sports betting operation in an apartment on the South Side. Business was brisk until, shortly after a police raid shut down his operation for a few days, he got a phone call from Harry and a terse message: *We need to meet. You owe us some money.*

The timing of the call prompted speculation that Harry got some of his intelligence from newspaper stories (the three major dailies that existed at the time invariably ran short items about police raids) as well as from the informants, snitches, and wannabe hoods who weaseled out of tight situations or sought to ingratiate themselves with tips and snippets of gossip.

A meeting was arranged in a Southwest Side restaurant and Rizza slid into a booth across from Harry and Jimmy Inendino, one of Harry's Taylor Street crew. Harry said nothing, fixing Rizza with that ominous stare—a grim look marked by depthless dark eyes. In negotiations such as these, Harry preferred working with a partner who did the talking at first. Harry listened, determining by some mysterious intuitive sense whether their companion was a snitch or was wearing a wire to record the conversation.

After several long, uncomfortable moments and finally convinced that Rizza was clean, Harry began to speak, softly explaining that he was operating on instructions of Ferriola, who wanted to organize the bookmakers. In Chicago, where organized crime has controlled all forms of illegal gambling—except for perhaps office NCAA pools—operating as an independent bookmaker has always been a risky proposition. And the stakes went up considerably after Ferriola put out the word that anyone operating without mob sanction had to deal to stay in business. A good deal was considered to be a fifty-fifty split on the bookmaker's profits, as well as an additional payment known as street tax. In return, bookmakers got a package of benefits not unlike those a small company might receive after a takeover by a large corporation: debt-collection services, in the form of mob enforcers adept at convincing clients to pay what they owed; resources, in the form of a large bankroll to cover sudden and high losses; and a simple kind of health insurance, in the form of allowing the bookmaker to stay alive.

For small-timers such as Rizza, resistance to the mob's offer was usually pointless and frequently fatal.

"Harry told me I owed him forty-some thousand dollars," Rizza would later recall. That was not all. Rizza, from that day forward, would have to hand over 50 percent of his profits to Harry and pay a street tax of $1,000 a month. Rizza asked for time to get the cash—and got it.

He went to see a family friend, Angelo LaPietra, a mob lieutenant who oversaw organized crime operations in Chicago's Chinatown neighborhood. Rizza offered all he had—a paper sack containing a few thousand dollars.

"It is a very serious situation you have gotten yourself into," was all LaPietra said, but, family being family, he took the bag and promised to meet with Harry and smooth matters out. Harry, Rizza would happily learn, agreed to accept the smaller than requested payment. And so Rizza was in the fold. Not long afterward, Harry came to visit him again, this time asking Rizza to deliver a message to Anthony Reitinger, a bookmaker operating in an apartment near his home on the North Side, serving clients in the Uptown and Rogers Park neighborhoods. The message was, as usual, simple: "Come to the table and be part of the organization." Reitinger, Harry said, was believed to be booking as much as $100,000 a month.

Rizza tapped into his clientele, figuring correctly that one of them might place bets with Reitinger. He got a phone number and called, explaining that Harry wanted to speak with him.

"Go fuck yourself," Reitinger said. "I will not pay any fucking street tax to anybody."

"Meet with Harry," Rizza insisted.

"No," Reitinger replied and hung up.

That afternoon, Rizza saw Harry.

"What's with Reitinger?" Harry asked.

"Tony told me to fuck myself," Rizza declared. "He doesn't want to have anything to do with you is how he put it."

Harry was silent for a long minute before he spoke.

"I will kill that motherfucker," he said.

"Let me try him again," Rizza said. "Give me—him—another chance."

Silence.

"Fine," Harry said. "We will meet with him anywhere he wants. Tell him all we want to do is talk."

Over the following days, Rizza repeatedly reached out to Reitinger through one of his workers and one of his customers, imploring them to convince Reitinger to meet, but Reitinger would not budge. Once more, Rizza called him directly.

"I'm not interested," Reitinger said. "I just don't want to pay that motherfucker a dime."

It all seemed not to have mattered by the time Rizza reported his latest conversations with Reitinger.

"It's a dead deal," Rizza offered. "He's not coming in."

"Forget it," Harry said. "He's a fucking dead man."

"I still might be able to bring him in if I have some more time," Rizza said.

"Don't worry about it," Harry snapped. "He's dead."

Days passed. Rizza met Harry for dinner at a restaurant in Melrose Park, minutes from Harry's home. Matter-of-factly, Rizza recounted how he had gotten a call from Reitinger, that he had finally come around, and that he wanted to do some business with Harry after all.

"It's too late for that motherfucker," Harry said.

"What are you going to do?" Rizza asked.

"Whack him," Harry replied.

Rizza said nothing. Harry asked, "You want to go along?"

Slowly, Rizza shook his head. "No, everybody on the street knows I've been asking for him," he said. "Why don't you give Tony a little more time? I think he is gonna come up with the money."

"I don't want his fucking money anymore," Harry said.

"Well, can't you wait 'til this cools down a little?" Rizza pleaded. "If he gets killed, the finger is going to point at me."

Harry ignored him.

"Halloween might be a good night," he said. "Nobody is gonna pay attention to guys wearin' masks."

On Halloween night, Reitinger strolled down the aisle of Mama Luna's restaurant on the city's West Side to the front window where he paused to survey Fullerton Avenue. He was nervous. Before leaving the house, he told his twelve-year-old daughter, "If anything happens to me, get in touch with Grandma."

He slid into his booth and began studying the menu. He ordered spaghetti and meatballs, then touched the arm of the waitress.

"Has anyone called here looking for a customer?" he asked.

"No, sir," she said.

"If a call like that comes in, it's probably for me," he said.

Diners would later tell police that they saw Reitinger rise from his seat and stand at the window, gazing at the street for ten minutes until his food arrived. He sat back down in the booth and began spooling his spaghetti. As he ate, a red Mercury Montego quietly drew to the curb outside and stopped. The driver and a passenger emerged.

Inside, the waitress was on her way to the kitchen when the two men walked in the door. The first man was wearing a three-quarter-length leather jacket, a black hat, black pants, and a flesh-toned hockey goalie mask covering his face. The second man wore a field jacket and a red ski mask.

Reitinger saw them at once and began to rise, but the man wearing the goalie mask walked directly toward him and withdrew a pump-action shotgun from underneath his coat. Before Reitinger could speak, the man shot him once in the head.

As patrons screamed and some dived for cover, the first gunman yanked the table and Reitinger, blood spurting, fell forward on top of it. The gunman jacked another round into the chamber of the shotgun and shot Reitinger just below the neck. The roars were thunderous in the confined area of the restaurant. He jacked another round into the chamber, fired once more into Reitinger's lower back, then stepped back next to the window and menaced the room.

The other gunman stepped forward. He was armed with a rifle. He placed his finger over the trigger and pulled several times, firing rounds into the body that was now lying on the floor.

It was redundant: Reitinger had been dead by the time his face pitched onto the table. Without a word, the two men turned, waved their weapons at the horrified diners and departed as calmly as they had arrived.

Inside, no one moved until the Montego screeched away.

At home, sitting on his couch, Rizza was watching the television news when the phone rang.

"I told you we would kill that guy," a voice said.

"Harry?" Rizza asked at almost the same time he realized it was.

"Watch the news."

"I am watching the news."

"Watch the news—we killed that motherfucker," Harry said.

With a click, the line went dead. As Rizza dropped the receiver onto the cradle, he saw it on TV: klieg lights illuminating the street outside Mama Luna's, the black body bag stretchered into a waiting police van, grim-faced uniformed cops standing alongside the yellow tape, and detectives in plainclothes standing in the restaurant doorway.

A TV reporter was saying something but to Rizza the words sounded like gibberish. His mind was on fire with worry. *How many guys have I told that Reitinger was about to be killed? Did I mention Harry's name? Won't those very same cops come looking for me?*

He arranged a meeting with Harry the next day.

"You put me on the spot," Rizza said, emboldened by his own fears. "At least two guys know I was trying to get Tony to come on board. I told them he would be hit. You should've waited, goddammit. Now what's gonna happen to me?"

Harry laughed.

"You know what, Vince?" Harry said. "You'll sink or swim just like everybody else." He laughed again.

Harry, police would later say, had finally killed "New York style"—in the open, in front of plenty of witnesses. Reitinger, the police would later reckon, was number thirteen in Harry's hit parade.

Even on a sunny day, the Cook County Criminal Courts Building is grim, dark, and foreboding. Seven stories of limestone and concrete near the corner of 26th Street and California Avenue on Chicago's South Side, it is a structure that says, "Important matters take place here."

On weekday mornings, as the sun breaches the parking garage across the street, the tempo in front of the courthouse builds to a crescendo as the morning court call approaches. As if in attempt to delay the inevitable, men and women, some with children tugging at their hands, linger on the steps and the sidewalk, slapping hands and smoking cigarettes, flicking the dying butts into the gutter. Across the street, a small van—"the roach coach," the regulars call it—dispenses coffee, sweet rolls, and juice to lawyers, judges, witnesses, jurors, and defendants. Standing in line to get their roach-coach fix, these players in the theater of criminal justice are all equals. Across the avenue, past the revolving doors, roles become more defined.

By 1976, Assistant State's Attorney Nick Iavarone had been part of the cast of characters for three years, long enough that as he pushed through the revolving doors and walked across the art deco vestibule to the elevators, the particulars of the daily criminal court drama barely registered. It was the smell that hit first—a mixed perfume of fried bacon from the first floor stand-up cafeteria, shoe polish from the stand in the corner, stubbed-out cigarettes, bad cologne, and morning-after sweat from a night of booze. A cacophony of sounds—jangling keys, shuffling feet, rumbling evidence carts loaded with files and guns and drugs and the bloody detritus of crimes—echoed through the marbled halls.

Babies wail. Deputies boom: "No smoking in the halls. No hats in the courthouse. You, take your hat off. No smoking in the halls." Defendants buttonhole men wearing suits, beseeching them for advice and representation. And cutting through the crowd are the hallway hustlers, a particular breed of defense lawyers. These are men who carry no files, who trade their talents for the surety of a defendant's bond money—up front. They do not invest their income in well-appointed offices with a staff of paralegals and investigators. Their offices are their cars. For $5 or $10 slipped to a court clerk, they rifle the files of that day's cases to find defendants with the biggest bonds and then troll the halls to sign them up. Manila folders under their arms, these men stand sentry outside courtrooms, calling out to clients they have never met. It is part of the morning dance, the parade of justice in Cook County.

Clerks broke the morning silence in the courtrooms, arriving to assemble docket sheets and files; the crimes stamped in bold block letters: MURDER, ARSON, ASSAULT, and RAPE. The spectator pews gradually filled with victims' families sitting across from the families of the accused.

With the appearance of judges, justice was administered for those who were free on bail—burned-out dope users and angry-eyed robbers and burglars—as well as the murderers, rapists, and ghetto gangsters escorted from the jail behind the courthouse.

His left hand gripping a bulging brown leather briefcase, Iavarone took an elevator to the State's Attorney's Office on the second floor. On his mind was the first meeting of the day, a meeting he would run, a meeting that was the subject of an article in that morning's *Chicago Tribune*.

> *A State's Attorney's task force Monday will begin an intensive investigation of 12 gangland-style slayings in the Chicago area during the past three years. . . .*

> *The task force will be made up of six investigators from*
> *the Chicago Police Department, the Illinois Bureau of*
> *Investigation, and the state's attorney's office, according to*
> *assistant State's Atty. Nicholas Iavarone, who will head*
> *the unit.*
>
> *"By organizing the unit, we can coordinate all the files*
> *on suspected gangland slayings in one place without hav-*
> *ing different police departments in the city and county*
> *working on them," said Iavarone, head of the organized*
> *crime unit. "We believe that two to four syndicate killers*
> *are responsible for the murders."*

The reporter hadn't asked Iavarone why the task force was being assembled now. If he had, Iavarone might have told him the truth—the number
of unsolved mob hits in Chicago and its surrounding suburbs embarrassed
law enforcement. In the past ten years, the Chicago Crime Commission had
logged no more that seven organized crime killings in any single year, a total
of only thirty-two.

But 1974 marked a surge in mob violence with ten murders, followed
by nine in 1975. And while there had only been six in the first nine months
of 1976, mob informants were hinting that more death was to come. In particularly biting fashion, *Tribune* columnist Bob Weidrich had hammered law
enforcement about the bloody toll of hoodlums. His latest blast had been
particularly cynical and went so far as to suggest that Bernard Carey, the
State's Attorney and Iavarone's boss, should look no further than "a social
and athletic club on Taylor Street."

A second generation Italian-American, Iavarone was reared on Chicago's
South Side and had, from the time he was a child, planned a career as a
teacher. His plans were detoured when he was drafted by the Army in 1966
and dispatched to Vietnam as a member of the 17th Air Cavalry. After two
years of fighting what ultimately seemed to him an unwinnable war, Iavarone
returned to Chicago a changed man. "There were too many things wrong,
as I saw it," he would later say. "I wanted to do something about it."

He began working for Zenith Radio Corporation as a computer pro-grammer while attending Chicago-Kent College of Law at night. His final year, he became a law clerk in the Cook County State's Attorney's office and a year later, in 1974, he was sworn in as an assistant state's attorney.

Bespectacled, with a wiry build, dark eyes, and straight brown hair, the thirty-three-year-old Iavarone had a reputation for being able to handle tough and politically sensitive cases; he had successfully prosecuted a state insurance investigator who had falsified answers on the test of one of Mayor Richard J. Daley's sons, and obtained convictions in a parking concession shakedown racket at the Chicago Stadium, home of the city's professional basketball and hockey teams.

A Roman Catholic with a strong sense of right and wrong and a belief that "too many wrongs had yet to be righted," Iavarone was frustrated as he read Weidrich's latest column. It not only sarcastically suggested that in-vestigators stop in at the Survivor's Social and Athletic Club, but also men-tioned that one of the more prolific killers was thirty-seven years old and left-handed. Iavarone realized what many others in law enforcement be-lieved as well but could not prove—that the column was referring to Harry Aleman.

Weidrich could not be easily dismissed. A veteran of more than twenty years as a reporter, columnist and mob-watcher, Weidrich had a vast network of sources within law enforcement and, perhaps more significant, a loose col-lection of sources from within organized crime.

"A crying need for the talents of executioners arose in recent years when scores of independent bookmakers moved to cash in," Weidrich wrote. "The gangland ruling council didn't like seeing one of their last solid revenue sources disturbed by opportunists. So they . . . hired professional killers. And the end result of their reign of terror is to be found in the grave."

Iavarone realized that tackling the mob in Chicago would be difficult. Beyond the usual conditions, such as a code of silence and the fact that wit-nesses often turned up dead prior to trial, Iavarone knew that more than a few Chicago police officers and judges were under the mob's control.

In many respects, Iavarone believed, the police department's organized crime unit was similar to the mob itself—a tightly controlled, insulated group, whose responsibilities largely amounted to attempting to tail mob-sters around the city in order to assemble dossiers of intelligence that, for the most part, gathered dust instead of arrests. Far too much of the "intelligence," Iavarone suspected, flowed from the cops to the hoods. "The basic differ-ence between the cops in the intelligence unit and the guys in the mob was that the cops were Irish and wore badges," Iavarone would later recall. "They all carried guns."

At Iavarone's urging, the task force would be small—two Chicago police homicide detectives and two agents from the Illinois Bureau of Investigation. Starting small, Iavarone thought, would allow for fewer leaks of information and closer supervision.

Although Iavarone had told the papers that the task force was just be-ginning, the work actually began weeks earlier when Richard Law and Ronald Mudry were assigned to Iavarone's unit. Both were veteran Chicago homi-cide detectives known for dogged pursuit and careful attention to detail. They had begun by criss-crossing the city and suburbs to collect investigative files relating to several unsolved murders—most of them, Iavarone believed, the work of Aleman. Now, as he arrived at his office, Iavarone found Mudry and Law waiting just outside the door. He ushered them inside, where stacks of files, resembling paper tombstones, awaited.

"I've gone through these in a cursory fashion," Iavarone began. "One seems like it might have possibilities."

"Which one?" Law asked.

"Billy Logan, shotgunned to death over on Walton Street, near Austin Boulevard in 1972. Car pulls up, Logan is walking to his car, and boom, boom, he's down, car pulls off," Iavarone said. He tugged at a stack of manila folders to his right and opened a file. "The police reports list a witness, a guy named Bobby Lowe. Doesn't say what he saw. Or if he saw anything. That's the last piece of paper in the file. Just ends there. It's not much, but it's a lead. Let's try to find this guy, talk to him, show him some pictures. This is a shot-gun case. Show him Aleman and Petrocelli and put a couple of Aleman's other pals in there, too. Who knows?"

Iavarone knew it was a long shot, but that's the way it always is in cold case investigations. Read the police reports, locate and re-interview wit-

nesses, canvass the neighborhood again. Study the autopsy. Recreate the
crime scene and look for unanswered questions—leads that were ignored,
witnesses who weren't questioned. It was a painstaking process, and often a
fruitless one, as witnesses moved away and became difficult to find. Memories faded. Evidence was misplaced or lost. Understandably, the impetus to
solve a crime begins dropping within weeks after its occurrence and, expo-
nentially, solving it becomes more difficult. Iavarone did not kid himself: This
task force was prompted by media criticism, which is not the purest moti-
vating factor. Expectations of success were low—no one was aware of a hitman ever being nailed for one of his murders.

Still, when he handed Law and Mudry the Logan murder file he felt a
sudden whiff of optimism. He looked at the calendar on the wall. That was
it. The date was September 27, four years to the day from the killing. After
Law and Mudry left the room, Iavarone allowed himself to smile and lean
back in his chair. When trying to catch a killer, even the smallest symbols
can provide a flash of hope.

Tracking down Bob was easy, even though four years had passed. Unlike
most Austin residents, the Lowe family had resisted the "white flight" that
had so quickly changed the neighborhood. They still lived in the corner
building on Walton Street. There was no answer at Bob's home, but the
officers found his father, Joe, downstairs. After some soft persuasion, he had
directed them to Augustana Hospital. Fran, he said, had undergone surgery
and Bob was there.

They found Bob sitting next to Fran's bed, surrounded by Tina, two days
from her eighth birthday; Joey, an infant the night Logan was killed, now
four; Tammy, not quite three; and, Bobby, fifteen months old.

Mudry and Law flipped out their detective shields and asked Bob to step
into the hall. "We just need a minute of your time," Law said.

"What's this about?" Bob asked, folding his arms on his chest.

"We have some photographs we want you to look at," Law replied. "It's
about the Billy Logan matter."

"I thought that was taken care of a long time ago," Bob said.

"Let's go down the hall," Law said. "This won't take long. We just need you to help us out."

They walked to a waiting room and sat down. Law shoved aside a scattering of magazines on a small table in the center of the room and carefully positioned a half-dozen photographs in a neat line.

"See anyone you recognize from the night Logan was killed?" Law asked.

Bob eyed the photographs, then pressed an index finger down. "This is the guy I saw get out of the car. He's the one that shot Billy."

"You're sure?" Law asked.

Bob leaned back in his chair. "Why are you doing this now?" he asked. "I did this four years ago. I thought this was all taken care of. What's this about?"

Not sophisticated in the ways of law and justice, Bob had assumed that police had acted upon his identification in the days after Billy was killed. It was not his habit to scan the newspapers daily and he was just naïve enough to believe that when a police detective said a matter would be taken care of, it would be handled.

"What do you mean, you did this four years ago?" Law asked.

"Two detectives picked me up, took me to the station, and gave me big books," Bob replied. "I went through these books, picture books—guys who were criminals, I guess. What took you guys so long?"

"Who were the detectives?"

"I don't remember their names."

"And you looked through books?" Law asked.

"Yeah, four or five of 'em."

Law and Mudry were stunned.

"And what did they tell you, the detectives?" Law asked.

"They said they would take care of it," Bob replied. "I figured it was taken care of. Then when I didn't hear nothin' for a long time, I just figured they didn't need me anymore. What's the deal now?"

Law scooped up the photographs. "We'll get back to you. We have your number. Just keep this to yourself, though."

"Who would I tell?" Bob said, grinning.

He said what?" Iavarone asked.

"Yeah," Law repeated, "he said he looked at mug-shot books right after the shooting and picked out Harry's picture."

"That was *four* years ago!" Iavarone said. "What else? Did he pick out Harry's picture for you guys?"

"Right away. Went right to it," Law said. "And then he says, 'What took you so long? I did this four years ago.' I couldn't believe it, either. He says two detectives picked him up, took to the station, and showed him the books and he found Harry. They told him not to worry about it, they would take care of it."

Instantly, Iavarone realized that someone had buried the report of Bob's identification. And looking down the road, if and when Iavarone was able to bring Harry to trial for murder, a defense attorney would surely attempt to exploit the botched—intentionally torpedoed was more like it—investigation of the murder back in 1972. A coverup such as this would not play well to a jury of citizens and would muddy the prosecution. This skepticism could be enough to poison jurors to the point where they would not convict, even with the most solid evidence.

Before he could try to get to the bottom of it, Iavarone wanted to meet Bob, and the next day Law and Mudry brought him in. Iavarone showed him the photographs again and Bob immediately selected Harry.

"Did Law and Mudry suggest this was the right guy?" Iavarone asked.

Bob shook his head. "They just laid 'em out and asked if I recognized any of 'em from the night Billy got shot."

Iavarone again felt a surge of intense anger at the cops who had either dropped the original investigation or somehow scuttled it. At the same time, he experienced the adrenaline rush that prosecutors know so well when they start to see the pieces of a case begin to fall into place. Standing in front of him was that rarest of creatures: an eyewitness to a mob hit.

"Do you know who this is?" he asked, tapping Harry's photo.

"No," Bob said. "Just the guy who shot Billy."

Iavarone inhaled, then let it go slowly.

"I want to explain something to you," he said. "This is Harry Aleman. We believe he is a hitman for organized crime. We believe he has killed more than a dozen men in the past few years."

Bob merely nodded, but inside recalled the words of his father on the night of the shooting. "This is a hit—an assassination—mob business," Joe Lowe had said. "This is none of your business. It's just trouble. For you. For your family."

Iavarone studied Bob. His face was inscrutable. This was a delicate moment. Iavarone would not lie to Bob, yet he did not want to frighten him to the point where he might make himself difficult to find or loath to testify; a reluctant witness on the stand also does not look good to a jury. He wanted Bob to commit to him now, even though Bob couldn't possibly realize the meaning of this commitment. Iavarone knew that Bob's life would be transformed forever. Harry would not accept a prosecution without fighting back in the only way he knew—with violence. And that would mean Bob would have to get out of harm's way. He would have to go into hiding. He would have to disappear.

Iavarone didn't have to mention that now. He was a prosecutor and his job was convicting criminals for their misdeeds. In the end, his duty was not to Bob.

"So this is a bad, very bad individual," Iavarone continued. "He is a very dangerous man. Now, I don't know what happened with this other thing four years ago when you picked out his picture—I'll deal with that, it's none of your concern right now. But I intend to prosecute Harry Aleman for this murder and I can't do it without your testimony."

Bob nodded again.

"It's your choice. But I will say this: If you refuse, I can force you to testify. I could have you arrested for refusing to cooperate and put you in the grand jury," Iavarone said, "but I don't want to do that. I want you to testify. I need you to testify. If you are willing, fine. I want you do to this on your own. But I have to tell you, this is a very, very dangerous man and he has a lot of very, very dangerous friends. You would be putting yourself and your family in a very risky situation. So I'm leaving it up to you. It is your choice."

Without hesitation, Bob agreed.

"You're sure?" Iavarone said.

"I saw what I saw," Bob said, echoing the commitment he had made four years before.

With the approval and support of his boss, Joseph Urso, Iavarone had the muscle to haul in cops and accuse them of burying a murder investigation and within a week, he sat face to face with the two detectives who had interviewed Bob and showed him the mug-shot books in 1972. The tenor of the meeting accelerated from quiet intensity to shouts, denials, and threats. The detectives refused to acknowledge ever meeting with Bob until finally Iavarone began talking about subpoenas, arrests and indictments. And the detectives caved in, to a point.

"You can put me on the stand, you can put me in the fucking grand jury," one said, "but I will never—*never*—say this on the record, out loud, in court or outside of this room. Yeah, we picked the guy up, he picked out the picture. We wrote the report and filed it. Next day, we are called in. Our boss has the report on the desk. Says, 'Don't you worry about this anymore. I'll take care of it from here.' "

"And?" Iavarone prodded.

"I never saw the goddamned thing again," the detective said.

"Where is it?" Iavarone asked.

"I don't know," the detective said. "And I don't fucking care."

"We'll see about that," Iavarone snapped. The detectives stared at him. They said nothing. Iavarone could barely contain his rage. Through clenched teeth, he dismissed the officers.

Questioning whether the police department could be trusted to investigate its own, he pondered bringing in the FBI. It was a tough call. Once the FBI started poking around, word would surely leak that he was the one who had called them and the political heat would be intense. Instead, he gave the department a chance and took the matter there. In the end, Iavarone would later learn, the matter was dropped.

His most immediate concern, though, was the Logan case. He had no physical evidence tying Harry to the crime. Rarely would the State's Attorney's Office prosecute a "one eyeball" case and never in a high-profile case as, Iavarone knew, a prosecution of Harry would be. He needed more. He needed a break.

12

D on't speed." Those were the only instructions Louie Almeida gave his partner Joe Neary as he wheeled the new Buick out of Chicago and onto Interstate 80 early on St. Patrick's Day morning in 1975. "Just don't speed."

They were headed for Pittsburgh to kill a man, and if they accomplished it successfully, there would be nine more hits to handle. At $10,000 for each dead man, this was a deal worth the risk of traveling several hundred miles in a stolen car with a trunk full of guns. But Louie didn't want any hitches or mistakes.

He was already taking a chance with Neary, a virgin hit man with the long, undistinguished rap sheet of an unsteady criminal. But Louie didn't have a lot of options in selecting criminal cohorts. He had recently cut himself off from Harry Aleman and the rest of his Taylor Street crew. The break had come gradually and uncomfortably. Louie believed he was lucky to have been able to walk away alive.

The first hint of trouble had come in a casual conversation in front of Harry's Melrose Park home when Harry brought up the name of Anthony Raymond, a suburban police officer who had disappeared under mysterious and troubling circumstances. The press had reported that Raymond had van-ished after pulling over a car on the Eisenhower Expressway for some sort of traffic violation.

Louie had heard on the television news about Raymond's disappearance, but it meant nothing to him until the evening he had stopped by Harry's home to see if he was needed for any errands. Out of nowhere and for no apparent reason, Harry brought up the subject of Raymond's disappearance.

"You know that Hillside cop?" Harry asked. "The one that's missing?"

"Sure, Harry, I remember," Louie said. "I heard about it on the TV."

"I just got off the phone," Harry said. "He stopped a couple of my guys and they took him. They told me they took that fucker up to Wisconsin and killed him."

Louie drew back. "Why are you telling me this? I don't want to get in-volved in that. I don't want to know this."

In the instant that the words left his lips, Louie realized he had made a terrible mistake. Why couldn't he just keep his fat mouth shut? He had just told Harry he wanted no part of this. He might as well have slapped Harry in the face. Harry demanded loyalty and Louie's response implied otherwise.

Harry's eyes narrowed. Lips pursed, jaw muscles flexing, he stared at Louie. Abruptly and without a word, he turned and walked back into his house, slamming the front door.

"I thought he was going to have me hit," Louie would later recall. So, in the following days, Louie laid low. As the weeks passed and his worst fears were not realized, Louie resurfaced and was back sitting at Harry's table at the Survivor's Club. But their relationship was never the same.

Harry began playing with Louie's head, dropping seemingly offhand comments about the importance of loyalty and being on time and how easy it was to kill people. Increasingly, Louie was ill at ease in Harry's company, no more so than one night when he accompanied Harry and Jimmy Inendino to scout a future score. Louie was in his customary position behind the wheel. Inendino was beside him in the passenger seat. Harry, as always, was alone in the back seat. "Harry put a gun to my head," Louie would say later. "I looked back and he put the gun down. He and Jimmy started arguing and then it seemed Harry sort of forgot about it. I never really trusted him after that."

It fell apart for good in the spring of 1974. Louie had driven Harry and Jimmy to the North Side of Chicago to hit Robert Harder, a convicted armed robber who had led police to the location of Raymond's body after a yearlong nationwide search. The twenty-five-year-old cop's body had been found strangled and buried in a shallow grave in a northern Wisconsin resort community. Now, there was a very real concern that Harder might lead the cops to the Survivor's Club. For that, Harder had to die.

The trio stopped en route and parked in an alley. Jimmy was sitting in the passenger seat. Louie was behind the wheel. Harry was alone in back. Suddenly Harry opened his door. In the rearview mirror, Louie saw Harry walk to another car parked in the alley and open the trunk. He watched as the trunk slammed down and Harry walked back to the rear of the car, a shotgun in his left hand, dangling at his side.

"Look straight ahead," Harry commanded as he reached the driver's side. The moment froze Louie's blood. But nothing happened. The night stays with Louie still. "I really believed he was going to try to hit me. After that, I left and went my own way."

For reasons Louie never knew or attempted to learn, Harry had let him walk away. Louie stopped picking up the phone and he stopped coming around. Harry, as far as he heard, didn't miss him and wasn't going to whack him, either. Perhaps Harry believed that he could find Louie and get rid of him if and when that became necessary. Perhaps Harry believed that a man such as Louie, with a background of thievery and stickups and a sixth-grade education, could never harm him.

Louie didn't care—his break from Harry led to the ten-hit contract and his trip to Pittsburgh to find and kill John Badovinac, the leader of the Croatian Fraternal Union, a group known to support Yugoslav President Josip Broz Tito.

This was not a typical mob caper. Neary had been approached by Croatian-Americans living in Chicago who belonged to a rebel Croatian group, which was seeking Croatian independence from communist Yugoslavia. The Croats had a list of prominent Croatian-Americans across the country who had refused to join them. For their refusal, they had been sentenced to death and Neary, who had reached out to Louie for help, was to be the executioner. Louie didn't know international politics. He didn't care what Badovinac and the other nine men had done or refused to do. The price was right and that was all that mattered;—his share of $100,000 was a big score for a man whose life of crime had been launched by knocking off gas stations on Chicago's South Side.

The Buick coursed eastward past the corn and soybean fields along the northern border of Indiana, tires humming as the interstate dropped down just past the Angola exit and stretched into Ohio. In the noonday sun, Louie drifted off to sleep, his windbreaker bunched against the window as a pillow. Abruptly, his body shifted as the car suddenly began to slow down and he awoke. "What's going on?" he asked, sitting up straight. "What's wrong?"

Neary glanced at him, then looked into the rearview mirror. "State cop," he said. "Speed trap, I think."

"Goddammit!" Louie yelled. "I told you not to speed. What the hell did I tell you? Don't *speed*. Shit. Pull over, goddammit. Where are we anyway?"

"Almost to Toledo," a chastened Neary replied as he eased the car onto the shoulder and slowed to a stop. Louie was steaming. "Get out of the fucking car," he said. "Show him your license and take the ticket. Don't fuck with the guy. We're just two guys on the road."

Neary cut the engine and climbed out of the car. Louie pulled down the sunshield and flipped up the cover to the mirror, angling it to see an Ohio State police squad car, red lights flashing, sitting on the shoulder several car lengths behind.

"Dammit, dammit, dammit," Louie muttered as he watched Neary fish out his wallet and meet the trooper halfway between the two vehicles. As the trooper examined Neary's license, Louie nervously drummed a single index finger on the armrest. Neary and the cop walked back to the squad car where the cop got back in.

"Shit!" Louie yelped. He knew what was happening. He saw the cop reach down and come up with a handheld police radio and realized the trooper was calling in the Buick's license plate. It would only be a minute before the trooper would learn that the Buick was a rental car that had never been returned. *That's a minor beef,* Louie thought. *We can beat that.* But what about the three handguns, one equipped with a silencer, that rested in the trunk? Almost without thinking, Louie slid behind the wheel and grabbed the keys, still dangling from the ignition. The engine roared as he stomped on the gas pedal and, tires screeching and loose gravel flying, the Buick sped west on Interstate 80.

Much later that day, as Louie and Neary sat in separate cells in the municipal jail in Swanton, Ohio, he would wonder how close he had come to getting far enough ahead to stop, open the trunk and ditch the weapons without being seen. Apparently, not very. The state trooper had leaped from his car, cuffed Neary and slammed him into the back, then took off in pursuit. Louie had given up less than ten miles later.

Even then, the cop thought at most he had a speeding and eluding police case. But when the trunk was opened, out jumped the murder plot. Police found the three guns—a .38-caliber Colt revolver, an Italian .380 Beretta and a nine-millimeter German-made semiautomatic with a silencer. They also found two ski masks and several news clippings with photographs of the sixty-seven-year-old Badovinac, whose name was underlined in red. An X had been drawn across his face in one photograph.

That was enough for state police to summon the Federal Bureau of Investigation as well as agents of the Bureau of Alcohol, Tobacco and Firearms. They began the interrogation of Louie and Neary by threatening thirty-year prison sentences for hauling illegal weapons across state lines.

"Can I make a deal?" Louie asked. He was scared.

Asked what he had to offer, the agents were amazed at how easily Louie began to spill out the particulars of the Croatian murder plot. So compelling was his monologue, that the authorities immediately offered a sentence of ten years. But, feeling they might have a very eager songbird, they attached a string: Louie would have to detail all of his crimes.

"Leave anything out," he was told, "and the deal's dead."

Fueled by desperation, Louie started talking. He began with his first teenage stickups. The agents listened as he recounted going on bombing runs with Butch Petrocelli. Eventually, his chronology reached the name Harry

Aleman. They perked up increasingly as Louie mentioned the mob, gave details of Harry's occasional use of a .22-caliber Ruger that was equipped with a silencer and how he always changed the barrel, the ejector pin, and the firing pin after each use.

"What does he use the gun for?" he was asked.

"He kills people," Louie said.

The agents sat up in their seats but even before they could ask another question, Louie said, "I can tell you about a murder in 1972."

"How do you know about it?" one agent asked.

"I drove," Louie replied.

News of the arrest of Louie and Neary reached Chicago three weeks later but, as it was limited to disclosures about the assassination plot in Pittsburgh, there was no apparent link between Louie and any other organized crime figures in Chicago. Indeed, *Tribune* columnist Bob Weidrich speculated that Louie and Neary were pawns in a "Machiavellian plot" by either pro- or anti-communists "to spark reprisals by pro-Tito forces and somehow humiliate the Tito spy apparatus known to operate here."

Louie pleaded guilty and was sentenced to his agreed-upon ten years on April 18, 1975, almost exactly one month after his arrest. He was immediately shipped off to the federal prison on McNeil Island, off the coast of Washington. He was put in segregation "for his own protection," prison officials told him.

After just a few days, Louie cracked again—this time he dissembled mentally, and, in a halfhearted attempt at suicide, tried to slash his wrists, succeeding in causing only superficial scratches. Later, he would claim he had faked suicide to spring himself from the loneliness of segregation. Taken to the prison infirmary, Louie was examined there by Dr. R. T. Sargent, chief of psychiatric services, who filed a report to the warden: "He is in good reality contact, readily answers questions, and is realistically disgusted with his present situation. He feels that he should be out (of segregation) and wants to transfer somewhere near his family in Chicago. He is not psychotic, is not suicidal . . . he has some situational anxiety and some realistic anger at the situation in which he finds himself." Dr. Sargent recommended Louie's return to segregation.

But the following day, another examination found Louie was worse off. "Examination of this man," wrote Dr. Harold Johnston, another psychiatrist, "reveals a superficiality, which covers a great deal of anxiety, and perhaps even some depression. However, far more significant than any of these symptoms is his thought content, which contains paranoid ideation in profusion, attached to almost any circumstance and any relationship with another person. This man has been stressed to the point of developing a schizophrenic reaction. He will not take medication and it is obvious that he will not take it because he is suspicious of what it is or what it will do. . . . In his present paranoid state, he would be his own worst enemy and might blow into a full-blown schizophrenic reaction simply at the thought of being in a population where there would be so many threatening elements around him."

Dr. Johnston recommended that Louie be transferred to a medical facility for federal prisoners. But Louie wasn't going anywhere, right away. He stayed in the prison hospital for months. Then came an important phone call and Louie, like it or not, was headed back to Chicago.

|13|

More curious than nervous, and a little relieved to be within seconds of answers to his many questions, Bob Lowe escorted Nick Iavarone and Dave Williams up the stairs and into the apartment where Fran and his parents waited. The aroma of that night's dinner clung faintly in the air. The family had eaten together, spending most of the table conversation unsuccessfully speculating on what their visitors would want.

"Let's just wait and see," Bob had said repeatedly.

Iavarone and Williams took seats on the vinyl-covered chairs Bob had dragged into the living room earlier. Bob sat on the couch next to Fran and his mother, Mary, stood beside him, her hand resting on his shoulder. Across the room, leaning back in the recliner, his father, Joe, sat quietly, hands folded in his lap as if awaiting the kickoff of a televised football game. The four children were in bed.

After a few minutes of cordial small talk, Iavarone began to speak seriously, as he stared directly at Bob. His words came with the pacing of a man making a speech, for he had already rehearsed what he was going to say. "We are preparing an indictment for murder against Harry Aleman," he said. "What this means is that Harry will be arrested and go before a judge."

Bob nodded. He knew that Iavarone had asked for this meeting in order to discuss the progress of the case, and he appreciated that. He was, in fact, flattered by the attention. Still, he had not expected to have another visitor. The presence of Williams—introduced only as "Officer Williams"—seemed, at the moment, unnecessary. The man's significance escaped him.

He knew that he would be a witness against Harry. He had sealed that engagement a few days before when he was taken by detectives Law and Mudry to the Harrison Area detective station for a lineup. Harry was there, as was a lawyer he had summoned when a team of investigators came to his house earlier that day. Harry had come peacefully, but the presence of several armed men had been most upsetting to Ruth and the children.

"Why are you taking my daddy?" one of the boys had asked fearfully.

"Because he's a killer," one of the agents had snapped, causing Ruth to explode in anger and scream invective at the backs of the men as they escorted Harry down the sidewalk.

As soon as Bob arrived at the station, Law had rustled up five other men similar in size, stature, and coloring to Harry and herded them, along with Harry, into a nine- by twelve-foot room. Bob was ushered into an adjoining room where he was told to stand behind a one-way mirror. A knock on the door by Mudry signaled that Bob was in place and Law sent the six men through their paces. Individually, each man stepped forward two paces, looked straight ahead, turned left, then right, and then stepped back in line.

Without hesitation, Bob picked subject No. 2: "That's the one, number two," he said, selecting Harry. It was all over in a matter of minutes. Bob was driven home and instructed to wait for further contact, which was now coming in the form of Iavarone briefing the Lowe family in their living room. "And we are going to issue an arrest warrant for Harry before we publicly announce the indictment," Iavarone said.

"Why's that?" Bob asked.

"There is always the chance that he might try to disappear once the word gets out," Iavarone replied. "We know where he lives. We can just scoop him up."

"Then what happens?" asked Bob.

Iavarone turned his head to scan the room. Joe sat in the reclining chair, saying nothing. "Harry will be arraigned before a judge and bond will be requested by his lawyers," Iavarone said. "We will ask that bond be denied. After that, we would expect to get to trial sometime in the next several months."

"Am I the only witness?" Bob asked.

"No," Iavarone said. "We have other witnesses. One of them was the driver in the car on the night Logan was killed."

"Really?" Bob's eyes widened. "What did he say?"

"I really can't go into it," Iavarone said. "But you're not going to be alone in this." There followed a long pause. Iavarone planned it. He wanted that bit of good news to sink in and he noticed what he thought was the desired effect: Fran and Bob exchanging small smiles and nods, Bob's mother rubbing his shoulder, and Joe unclasping his hands.

And then Iavarone said, "But that's not the main reason we're here tonight."

The bodies of the Lowe family seemed to tense all at once, as if in direct response to Iavarone's now very sober tone. "You are going to need protection," he said, his words carefully chosen, his delivery measured. "You are a witness and you may be in some danger from Harry and his people."

"What do you mean, protection?" Bob asked.

"Agents," came the answer from the other man in the room. "Agents twenty-four hours, around the clock," he said.

Dave Williams was an agent for the Illinois Bureau of Investigation, a twenty-seven-year-old who had impressed his superiors with a no-nonsense attitude, sharp mind, and straight-arrow character. Though he had never before been charged with the protection of witnesses, his bosses were confident that he was the man to oversee the delicate and dangerous matter of handling the witnesses in the prosecution of Harry.

"I'm not going to pull any punches here," Williams said. "We think Harry is responsible for more than a dozen murders, maybe even closer to twenty. This is our chance—I've got to tell you, *you* are our chance—to put this guy away,—hopefully for good. Now, Harry knows that as well as anyone and, as far as we're concerned, if he could take you out of the picture, he would stand a better chance of beating this thing."

The room, for more than a minute, fell into uneasy silence.

"I don't know about this. I don't know if I want anyone following me around," said Bob. He could feel his heart racing.

"We want you to move," Williams said. "We want to relocate you and your family. It's for your own safety."

"That's bullshit!" Joe shouted. All eyes turned to the old man, his face red with anger. "I told you, Bob. I told you not to get involved in this."

"Let him talk," Bob said. "I just want to hear what he's got to say."

"Don't you—you're not thinking about doing this, are you?" Joe retorted. "Don't you let them—"

"Dad," said Bob, the words brusque, the tone authoritative, "let him talk."

Williams continued. "OK, then, what we would do is we would move you and your family. Again, it's for your own safety."

"I think I can take care of myself and mine," Bob said.

"It's for the safety of your family—your wife and your kids," Williams said. Iavarone was getting fidgety. He had warned Williams not to get in a dialogue with Bob over the particulars of the protection, but to merely state what would transpire as if it were *a fait accompli*. He was not pleased about the road this conversation was traveling.

"I don't think I want to do that," Bob said.

"Well, I've got to tell you, the fact is you don't have a whole lot of choice in this," Williams said. "We can take you into protective custody—"

"Arrest him, you mean?" Joe shouted, rising from his chair. "You can't threaten him like that. You can't threaten my boy."

Bob shot an angry look at his father, but said nothing.

"Not arrest him," Williams said. "Please, Mr. Lowe, just hear us out. Bob, we need your testimony and we want you to go along with this voluntarily. That's what we really want." He paused. "But I gotta tell you, it doesn't have to be that way."

What do you think, babe?" Bob asked.

They were in the bedroom; the agents and his parents were still sharing tense, uncomfortable space in the living room.

"I don't know, Bob," Fran said. "This is not what I was thinking would happen. I don't know. Do we really have to go?"

"You heard them," Bob said. "We got no choice, it sounds like."

In truth, Bob was excited. He had started to feel this way only minutes earlier in the living room as Williams began to explain how agents would come in a few days to pack up the family's belongings and move them out to a temporary location in the suburbs. "You go in, you testify, we convict Harry, and that's it," Williams said.

Now, he clutched Fran's hand hard. "Dad always taught me that if you see someone drop their wallet on the street, you pick it up and give it back to them," he said. "You understand? I got to do this. And the only way I'll do it is together. Will you please go with me?"

He gave Fran time to think. After their years together, he was confident that she would listen to him. Fran was only ten when Bob met her—bumped into her literally—while running to catch a pass in a schoolyard football game. They became friends, and flirted and then dated as teenagers. On July 30, 1967, when she was sixteen, eager to get away from her parents, and he a nineteen-year-old high school graduate, the youngsters rode the elevated train to the Cook County Clerk's Office and were married. He usually was able to persuade her to agree with him, even though the stakes had never been this high.

For many minutes in the bedroom, Fran said nothing. Bob studied his wife's face. It was a gentle face, he thought for the first time in a long time, even as its brow was furrowed with worry. The minutes passed and Bob could barely conceal a strangely giddy feeling brought about by the attention of respected and educated men; the spotlight of a trial that would surely be written up in the newspapers and be the subject of television broadcasts—the chance to put a notorious hit man in prison. It was invigorating and it was easy to imagine the outcome: The trial would be over in several months, Harry would go off to jail forever, and Bob's life would return to normal. Given that scenario, Bob reasoned, what the men in the living room were proposing seemed almost like a golden opportunity.

Fran took a deep breath and let it out. "I'll do it," she said. "If that's what you think we should do, I'll do it." She squeezed his hand. He bent her head down and kissed the top of it and together they walked back into the living room, which immediately fell silent. Bob did not say a word until he and Fran, still hand in hand, were sitting on the couch.

"I want to keep my job," Bob said. "I don't want to quit my job."

Williams paused before speaking, calmly collecting himself in the face of what he and Iavarone knew was great news: Bob was hooked and now all they had to do was reel him in. "That's fine, that's fine. Agents will drive you back and forth," Williams said.

"OK," Bob said. "We'll do it."

Iavarone and Williams spent the next few minutes detailing what would take place over the next several days, trying not to show their enthusiasm. Bob and Fran listened attentively. Mary went to check on the kids. Joe went out onto the porch. He was there when Iavarone and Williams came out and he said, "I don't agree with this. Not one damn bit. And I will tell you this right now. If anything happens to any of them, it's going to be personal. And this Harry will be dead, if I have to kill him myself."

A small army of agents descended on Bob's house almost immediately, packing boxes of clothing and stripping photographs from the walls. Light snow was falling when the nameless agents arrived shortly after dawn. They entered the house and hurriedly, without the formality of introductions or niceties, began to pack up the family's belongings. There were a dozen or so of them and at the same time, an equal number were elsewhere, scouring the city and suburbs in an attempt to arrest Harry. It was a frustrating hunt. Harry was not to be found, making Iavarone angrily conclude that Harry had been tipped off that an indictment was pending and had left town.

"Please be careful," Fran implored the agents. She was becoming increasingly agitated at the rising level of commotion in the second-floor apartment and she sat at the kitchen table smoking a cigarette, nervously tapping the smoldering end on a glass ashtray, watching the parade of agents go in and out the back door, down the stairs to the alley where five white vans waited.

She was getting angry with Bob, too, developing a *How did he talk me into this?* attitude. From outside came the sound of a crash and Fran scurried to the back door where she heard a loud "Jesus Christ!" come from a male voice on the landing below. She ran down the steps and almost collided with an agent who was coming up, swearing and shaking his right hand in pain. "Are you all ri—" Fran started to ask. She stopped and her mouth fell open. There, strewn over the bottom five steps, was the shattered detritus of her china. It was the only set of china she had ever owned, a gift from Bob's parents for their last anniversary. The dishes, cups, platters and bowls were in smithereens.

"Dammit! Dammit!" she shrieked. "My china! You've destroyed my china! What the hell were you doing?"

A series of rapid thuds signaled Bob's arrival behind her. "Oh, babe," he said. "The china." Fran turned, her eyes brimming with tears.

"How in the hell are they going to protect us?" she demanded. "They can't even take care of a box of china?" She bent down and began picking through the shards for the few pieces that had somehow survived.

The announcement came on Monday, December 13, 1976. A grand jury had returned a single-count murder indictment against Harry Aleman for the murder of Billy Logan. The indictment had been returned days before but had been kept under seal, as is often the case when there is a risk of flight. Police sent to Harry's home in Melrose Park did not find him or any evidence that he had been there in days. Iavarone knew that someone on the inside had to have leaked word of the grand jury vote. But he was not as angry as one might imagine. How could he be surprised that the mob had a mole inside his office? The police department was rife with mob sympathizers, if not outright members of organized crime, so why not in the State's Attorney's Office? He was worried, however, about his prize witness, Bob Lowe. Would his whereabouts be leaked, too?

Iavarone persuaded the FBI to obtain a federal fugitive warrant, charging Harry with crossing state lines to avoid prosecution. Police in Nevada and California were alerted, because Harry's uncle, Joe Ferriola, owned property there.

There was no press conference called that day to herald the indictment. State's Attorney Bernard Carey, a man with a savvy grasp of public relations and a taste for seeing his name in print, preferred to wait until Harry was in hand. The news media played the indictment without fanfare. The story was prominently placed in all three major papers, but without blaring headlines. All the stories noted that Harry was a suspect in as many as nineteen other unsolved gangland killings.

The papers also carried a photograph taken of Harry only weeks before, after the lineup at the Harrison Area detective station. It was the first time his picture had ever appeared in print and it was a grabber. Hooded lids shaded his black eyes as he stared straight out of the page, the corners of his mouth down-turned, his chin lifted just slightly, shoulders thrust back, the cords on his neck visibly standing out. Even in a police mug shot, he radiated the sort of arrogant appeal more common to movie stars than mobsters, and more than a few women thumbing through the papers stopped at his picture and found him handsome, even sexy.

In a few days, Harry voluntarily surrendered, striding up the steps of the Criminal Courts building with his lawyer, Thomas Maloney, a veteran criminal defense attorney with a reputation as a battler and rumored to be under consideration for a judgeship. Following at a discreet distance was Harry's wife, Ruth. The trio attracted little attention as they swept through the lobby and rode the elevator to the courtroom of Judge James Bailey for arraignment. This had all been prearranged by Maloney through Iavarone, who, as much as he might have wanted to see Harry suffer the indignity of being handcuffed and escorted to court by the police, wanted him to just appear even more. In front of the judge, Maloney formally entered a plea of not guilty. At the same time, he filed a motion for Substitution of Judge.

The SOJ motion, as it was called, was allowed under local court rules and permitted a defendant to automatically excuse two judges from hearing a case. Maloney listed Bailey and Frank Wilson, both veteran jurists with reputations, in the parlance of courthouse regulars, as hanging judges, men whose decisions typically favored the prosecution and who were likely to impose harsh sentences. Bailey, particularly, dispatched men to Death Row with far more frequency than any other judge in the building. The motion was granted as a matter of routine and the case was sent back to the assignment desk, there to be sent to another judge. Bailey then ordered Harry taken into custody and held without bail.

The kids were old enough to read the papers, but none paid attention to the stories about their father. Still, the indictment of Harry surely cast a gloom over the household. Iavarone believed that Ruth likely knew that Harry was involved in illegal activities. At the same time, she took great care to shelter her family from the particulars of his professional life. The four children adored their stepfather and he adored them. "I raised them," he would later say. "I consider them my own. I couldn't be any closer if they were my own blood."

At home, he was the loving and protective father, who forbade telephone calls during dinner, deeming it a private time for conversation exclusively for family, and often kept the kids at the table until 8 or 9 P.M. on some nights. He wanted to know everything about their lives, their friends, and their teachers. He seemed to glory in the time they spent together and he loved to take them on outings, on camping trips, to the zoo, and to Kiddieland, the amusement park less than a mile from the family home. On weekend nights, he tenderly washed his daughters' hair in the kitchen sink, patiently combing out snarls and tangles.

Perhaps driven by the memories of a childhood marked by beatings, or in response to the dark, often savage details of his work and the seamy characters with whom he associated, Harry created a home environment filled with tranquility, love, and the manifestations of prosperity. He showered the kids with gifts on their birthdays. At Christmas, when the house was filled with the smells of baked cookies and marinara sauce, the abundance was almost overwhelming.

As the older girls began dating, he hovered over them, carefully inspecting prospective boyfriends, even going so far as to lurk outside school to see just who his daughters were leaving with and to ensure they were exactly where they had promised they would be.

Harry was strict, but he could not—would not—do what his father had done. Once, in a moment of exasperation over the behavior of one of his teenaged sons, Harry had asked Louie Almeida to discipline the boy for drink-

ing and staying out past curfew. Louie, in a curious bit of surrogate parent-
ing, came to the boy with a rope in his hand and suggested that if the boy
didn't straighten up and listen to his father, he would be tied up and tossed
in the trunk of a car. Then Louie gave the boy a couple of light taps on the
head with the rope and walked away.

Having their father in jail was traumatic, even terrifying. The house was
painfully empty without him. A few days after he had surrendered and his
case had been reassigned to Judge Fred Suria, Harry's attorney argued for a
reduction in bond. Suria, known around the courthouse as "Fair Fred," set
it at $350,000. Harry would only be released after someone posted 10 per-
cent of it—$35,000.

As the blue-uniformed sheriff's deputies approached to escort him back
to the cell behind the courtroom, Harry turned halfway around. He spotted
Ruth, sitting in the front spectator pew, gave a slight nod, and then walked
quickly toward the lockup. Her lips pressed tightly together, Ruth, blonde
hair in short curls, nodded grimly in return. She left the courtroom and the
building and when she returned, less than two hours later, she was carrying
an attaché case in her right hand. She walked up to the sheriff's office bond
window.

"I'm here to post bond for my husband," she said. There was pride and
defiance in her voice. "My husband, Harry Aleman."

The clerk shuffled through some papers and as he pulled from them those
related to Harry, Ruth slid the court order across the counter, propped the
case next to the cashier's window, and swung it open to reveal rows of crisp
$100 bills, neatly bound.

"How much is *that?*" the cashier stuttered.

"The amount of the bond," Ruth declared. She waited patiently as the
money was counted, then she closed the case and waited for her receipt. Moments later, she and Harry left the building, ducked into a waiting car and
sped west, toward home.

Silver-haired and ramrod straight, Bernard Carey stood before the press
and touted the strength of the prosecution case. Without identifying Bob,

Carey said "an ordinary citizen" had stepped forward and would provide damning evidence. He branded Aleman "Harry the Hit Man," one of the first public references to Harry's apparent trade. And though he would not predict a victory, Carey privately confided to aides and friends that he had never seen a stronger murder case against a member of organized crime.

Soon after, informants began passing information to police and prosecutors that the mob had a standing $100,000 contract for the murder of Bob or Louie or both. FBI agents paid a visit to Iavarone and put a tape recorder on his desk and punched the button. "We picked this up the other day and thought you might get a kick out of it," one agent said.

Iavarone heard the voice of Joseph "Doves" Aiuppa, one of the highest-ranking mobsters in Chicago.

"Iavarone? Iavarone?" Aiuppa's voice dripped with sarcasm. "I remember when he was a kid and then that motherfucker turned bad."

Iavarone laughed that day, but not a few days later when his wife called in a panic. She was driving home on the Edens Expressway when a white van cut her off and slowed down to less than thirty-five miles per hour. She was unable to pass due to heavy traffic and after a mile, the van picked up speed and vanished into the traffic in front of her.

A few minutes later, as she left the expressway, the same van was waiting on the shoulder of the exit ramp and pulled in front of her again, forcing her to slam the brakes. With her voice trembling on the phone, she said, "It sped off again but then it was parked across the street from the house, parked right there when I pulled into the garage. Nick?"

"It's OK," said Iavarone, trying to sound calm for his wife's sake, though he was furious. "Did you get the plate number?" he demanded.

"No," she said.

"Go look," he said. "See if it's still there."

She put down the phone and Iavarone strained to hear a sound, any sound, for the next few anxious seconds. Finally, his wife picked up the phone and said, "Too late. It's gone."

Iavarone spent the next twenty minutes assuring his wife that everything would be OK, that she had nothing to worry about. And he was going to make sure of that with the call he then placed to the police department's Central Intelligence Unit, giving them the details of the episode and a description of the van. He didn't hear anything for three days and his wife's commute had been without further incident. Then, a detective he knew only slightly sauntered to his desk and said, "That van? That van that hassled your wife? Well, you don't have to worry about that van no more."

"Yeah, why's that?" said Iavarone.

"It's all taken care of," the detective said. "The other night a few guys from CIU spot the van. It was parked over on the West Side. So, they run the plate and, guess what, it comes up to some mope who works for the Turk." Iavarone knew the name. James "Turk" Torello was a west suburban mob boss who ran some gambling and extortion operations.

"And?" he asked.

"They blow the fucking windows out of the van," said the detective, pausing so long for effect that Iavarone finally asked, "And then?"

"That's it, the best part," said the detective, grinning. "Then these guys go over, drop by the Turk's house. They bang on the door and who comes out to answer the door but the fucking Turk. He says, 'Whaddaya guys want?' They don't say anything. Then one of them takes a shotgun, jams the fucking thing right in the guy's nose and says, 'Next time you're dead.' "

The detective laughed out loud. "So I don't think you gotta worry about it anymore. Tell your wife."

Dave Williams was at his desk in Iavarone's office when the phone rang. He picked it up, and heard a vaguely familiar voice ask, "Dave Williams?"

"Yes, this is Williams."

"Go to the pay phone, corner of 26th and California," said the caller.

"Who is this?" Williams asked.

"Just go there." The telephone clicked off.

Williams hung up.

"Who was that?" Iavarone asked.

"Didn't say, but I think it was Butch Petrocelli," Williams said.

"What did he want?"

Williams rose from his chair. "I'll be right back."

The door on the booth on the corner was barely closed when the phone began to ring. Williams lifted the receiver, but said nothing.

"Have you checked on your mother lately, agent Williams?" It was the same voice, but the tone was not matter-of-fact as it had been minutes before but rather was mocking. "Well, have you?"

Williams hung up the phone and though he almost laughed at what he considered a feeble attempt to cow him, he did call his mother just to say hello. He, of all those involved in the case, had anticipated this sort of thing. Indeed this was not the first time Butch had confronted him by phone.

That call had come after Harry was brought in for the lineup. Williams had been the agent who had so abruptly dismissed the plaintive question from Harry's children—"Why are you arresting my daddy?"—with a curt "because he's a killer."

Williams recognized Butch's voice immediately when the phone rang that time.

"Go to the middle pay phone on the fourth floor," Butch said and hung up.

A minute or two later, Williams and a fellow agent were standing on the fourth floor when the phone rang.

"Ruthie is very upset with what you said to her kids," Butch said.

"Well," Williams retorted. "Is it true? Is he a killer or not, Butch?"

"You didn't have to say that," Butch said.

"Was I wrong?" Williams asked back. "Was I lying?"

"I want to talk to you tonight," Butch said. "In Tom Maloney's office downtown."

Williams and a fellow agent found Butch sitting in Maloney's office, parked in a chair next to Maloney, his face obscured in the shadows just beyond the soft ring of light cast by a green lamp atop the desk.

"Have your friend wait outside, will you?" Maloney asked, and stood up. He tossed his keys to Butch. "Lock up when you're finished."

Butch settled himself in Maloney's leather chair and leaned back.

"Are you prepared to die?" he asked.

"Are you?" Williams said.

"We know where your mother lives over on Austin Boulevard."

"We know where your mother lives over on Aberdeen," Williams shot back. "Are you going to kill some police officer, just for doing his job?"

"I want you to apologize to Ruthie for what you said," Butch declared.

"No," Williams said. "I won't do that."

The conversation went on for more than hour, a duel of sorts between two aggressive, hard men, neither willing to back off.

Until, at last, Williams had had enough and stood up, preparing to leave. "We're working the case and it's a good case," he said. "We'll be seeing you."

Butch didn't move. His voice came from the darkness.

"Watch your back."

After setting Harry's bond, Judge Suria stepped off the case, citing the potential for a suggestion of impropriety because one of his wife's relatives was distantly related to Harry. When the clerk of the court reassigned the case once more, it was sent back to Wilson, even though Wilson had earlier been rejected by the defense. *Just a mistake,* Iavarone thought, and the first time the case came up before Wilson, Iavarone approached Maloney in the hallway and suggested that as soon as the judge took the bench, the defense team could raise the mistaken assignment.

But Maloney waved his hand. "We're waiving the SOJ," he said.

"That's a surprise," Iavarone said, grateful that his discipline as a trial lawyer kept his mouth from falling open.

"There's another surprise," Maloney declared. "I'm withdrawing from the case. Two or three nights ago, I got a call and I was told to just go to court and do what they tell me to do. It will be taken care of by somebody else. They are bringing in the old man, Frank Whalen, from Florida."

"I thought he was retired," Iavarone said.

"He is, but he's coming back for this one."

"Well," Iavarone said. "This is too bad. I was looking forward to trying this case to a jury against you."

Maloney laughed, a series of short barks, and said, "What makes you think there's ever going to be a jury trial?"

Iavarone practically ran back to the second floor office of his supervisor, Ken Gillis.

"Something is kinky here," Iavarone said.

"Wilson's a state-minded judge," Gillis replied. "He likes us. He hammers people."

"Yeah, if you're poor and black," Iavarone retorted. "Look at what they're doing. They dump Wilson, now he's back. Maloney gets off the case and now they're bringing in Whalen. He hasn't even been working in the last several years."

"Cool off, Nick," Gillis said. "Don't get all upset. Just try your case."

On the advice of colleagues, Iavarone began carrying a gun. Strings had been pulled to arrange for the issuance of police credentials so that he could legally carry a concealed weapon. It had been years since he had fired a pistol and he had started to visit target ranges. One afternoon he dropped into the Belmont Area detective station to take some shooting practice. When he finished, two detectives approached.

"Nick, can you take a few minutes and talk with us?" one asked. Iavarone followed them down the hall and into a room where several officers sat at a table littered with police reports and paper coffee cups. A haze of cigarette smoke floated above. Iavarone saw that some of the men were members of the Central Intelligence Unit. Others were homicide detectives. Belmont Area was the geographical location in which Logan had been killed—as it was for several other men whose deaths were believed to have come at the hands of Harry.

"Sit down, Nick," said one of the detectives. "We've heard about some of the stuff that's been happening, the calls, that fucking van. We don't appreciate that kind of thing."

"Well, I don't appreciate it either," said Iavarone.

There was a brief pause, and then a detective said, "Well, we've been talking about this Logan case. Are you going to put Aleman away?"

"It's not going to be easy," Iavarone said, "but I believe so."

"Are you sure?" another asked.

"Nothing is for sure," Iavarone replied. He looked around the room. Some of the men were staring at the table. One idly picked his teeth. Finally, a burly sergeant broke the silence. He leaned his thick forearms heavily on the table. His voice was flat, unemotional.

"We've been thinking," he began. "Why don't we just kill the son of a bitch?"

Iavarone froze. For the first time since Vietnam he felt a tingling under his shirt collar and hair rising on the back of his neck. These men were serious. Involuntarily, he shot out of his chair. "Forget about this," he said. "Just forget about this."

15

S ome vacation," Bob Lowe thought, sitting in the driver's seat of a
brown Chevrolet as it sped south from Chicago. He looked across the
seat at Fran, who stared out the window at the rolling plains of south central Illinois. The fields flowing by made Bob more depressed than he already
was. Is there anything drabber than a farm in winter, with barren trees and
vast stretches of flat land dusted with snow? He thought to grab Fran's hand,
but in so doing he would have to disturb their two youngest children, who
were asleep between them, tangled up like rag dolls. In the backseat, Tina
used a green crayon to color in the dress of a princess in a coloring book and
Joe looked at a comic book they had bought a few miles back when they had
stopped for gas. Up ahead, in a brown Buick sedan, were three Illinois Bureau of Investigation agents, the family's guardians.

"At least it's quiet," Bob said, surprised to hear the words out loud.

"You say something?" asked Fran, turning her head. There was nothing
pleasant in her tone. "The kids are sleeping. Be quiet."

At least it's quiet, Bob thought.

It had not been quiet for weeks, since the crash of the dishes the day the
agents had moved them from their apartment. They first settled into a small

apartment in northwest suburban Wheeling. Each day, in those days before Christmas vacation, agents drove the children to school and took Bob to work. At night, two agents sat in an unmarked car on the street.

One morning, as Bob was getting ready to leave for work, he looked out the window and saw the agents, heads lolling, asleep in their car. *Screw this,* he thought. *I'll teach them a lesson and drive myself to work.* He walked to the garage and bent down to grab the handle to pull up the door and, as he did, he felt a hand on his left shoulder.

"What the hell?" he shouted, jumping back and snapping his head around, eyes wide with fear. It was a man he had never seen, but he was holding a badge. "Don't you ever sneak up on me like that again!" Bob shouted. "What in the hell are you trying to do? I don't know who you guys are. Nobody tells me who's who. Dammit to hell!"

"Relax, Bob," the agent said. "But can you see how easy it would be for Harry or someone else to get close to you? We need to move you completely. Forget this driving to work and taking the kids to school. You should cut the cord completely."

Stubbornly, Bob refused to compromise, though each day one or another of the agents would give him a variation of the same speech. After only a few days, Bob was chafing at the control the agents were exerting on his life, the scare tactics they were using. *I'm not going to be frightened by them,* he told himself over and over. And, indeed, for the first few days of the family's exile, there were no signs of danger, no mysterious strangers coming into the gas station, no cars following them home. He was convinced that the agents were exaggerating the potential for harm. *They're paid to be cautious,* he thought. As an exercise in self-determination, one day he convinced the agents to allow him to pick up Tina after school. Reluctantly they agreed, but it would not be. On his way to the school, Bob got caught in traffic and arrived several minutes late. He spent a few frantic minutes looking for his daughter, until a school aide told him that Tina had already been picked up and, more ominously, the aide added that a few minutes later, another man appeared and was asking for her, saying *he* was supposed to take her home. Bob sped home to find Tina safe, eating a cookie and drinking a glass of milk at the kitchen table.

An agent was at the table and began talking as soon as Bob burst through the door, saying, "Take it easy, take it easy. I picked her up, I had to. We think Harry's people are getting close. Some of his men have been spotted cruising the area. We don't think they have made you yet, but we think they are getting close."

"They told me at the school that somebody was there asking about her today," Bob said. And at that instant, he realized for the first time that he was scared. Not scared for himself, but for Fran and the children. With that came the crushing knowledge that perhaps he alone could not protect his family, that he was powerless against Harry's shadow world.

"I want to move," he said. "Now."

And so they drove, the two cars cutting through the midsection of Illinois. It was early January when they moved into a rented farmhouse, using false names. For a couple of weeks everything was fine. The house was large and cozy. There was room to roam. But two weeks after the suitcases were unpacked, the property owner received a telephone call. "I understand you are renting a home to a man named Bob Lowe?" the caller, a man with a husky voice, had asked. Unaware of Bob's true name, the man had professed his ignorance and hung up. He then called Williams, the man who'd signed the rent check, and told him about the call. Williams listened quietly, thanked the landlord, and then called the farmhouse. "Get on the road, right away," he told the agents. "Stay in motels. Never more than a few days—a week at the most."

And so again they hit the road, heading south, eating up Interstate 57 as it rolled past Effingham, Salem, and Mount Vernon. They cruised through Marion, the site of a federal penitentiary that would, one day, be the full-time residence of New York mob boss John Gotti; cut over on Interstate 24; crossed the Ohio River at Metropolis; and arrived in Kentucky just before nightfall. Home for the night was a motel on the outskirts of Paducah.

Tired, hungry, and irritated, Fran carried Bobby on her hip as she herded Tina, Tammy, and Joey into their room. She surveyed the two double beds, put Bobby on one of them, and walked into the bathroom.

"No tub," she said, spitting out the words. Brushing a strand of hair from her perspiring forehead, she turned to face the mirror and was taken aback by her image. Fran studied herself in the mirror, pushing at the beginning of bags under her eyes. Her eyes were bloodshot.

"Dammit!" she said.

She ducked her head out of the door. Bob stood in the room, holding a suitcase in his left hand. On the mottled carpet was another suitcase, where it had exploded open when it hit the floor. Speechless, the children stared.

"What are you looking at?" Bob said gruffly. He leaned against the wall. Wide-eyed, the kids said nothing until they noticed the beginning of a smile curling their father's lips.

"Wow, Dad, you made a mess," Tina said, jumping from the bed. "Look at all the clothes. Hey, there's my pajamas." She snatched at a worn pink nightgown.

"I'm hungry," Joey complained. "I want pizza. Can I have pizza? And a Coke? In a can? With a straw? Can I? Dad? Can I?" He turned toward the bathroom as Fran emerged. "Mom, can we have pizza?" he pleaded. "Please, please, please?"

Fran looked at Bob, who just shrugged and began scooping clothes from the floor onto the bed.

"We had that last night, Joey," she said.

"And the night before that and the night before that," Bob muttered. "And the night before that."

"Please, please, pizza," Joey said.

"Yeah, pizza. With green peppers and mushrooms," Tina said.

"Yeah, pizza," Tammy chimed in.

Life as a protected witness was not glamorous but quarrelsome. There always seemed to be a quarrel, between Bob and Fran, Fran and the agents, Fran and the kids, Bob and the kids, Bob and the agents. They quarreled over television stations: sports or sitcoms, *The Waltons* or *CHiPs*. They quarreled over food: too cold, too hot, too stale, too soggy.

Riding in cars brought a sad relief. At least they were moving, traveling east toward the hollows and beleaguered towns of south central Kentucky, then it was on to Tennessee and then Alabama. Motel after motel after cheesy, greasy, carpet-stained, paint-peeled, short-sheeted motel.

"Give it back; it's mine!"

"No, I had it first. Get your own."

"You're not the boss of me!"

"Am too."

At the end of one of the two beds in the room, Bobby and Joey struggled over a toy soldier. They each had been given one, but one was missing. It was likely in one of the many fast-food restaurant parking lots where the car doors had opened and closed so many times in the past two months. The room was a shambles. Food cartons peeked over the top of the wastebasket. Soft-drink cups lined the nightstand, guarding an ashtray overflowing with cigarette butts. In stocking feet, chinos, and a T-shirt, Bob lay on his side on one bed, watching television, seemingly oblivious to the battle raging inches away.

In the corner, Tina slumped in a chair, listlessly watching the flickering images on the television. Fran pulled the brush once more through Tammy's hair, unaware that the girl winced. Fran eyed Bob, but he paid her no attention.

"Tina," Fran said. "What are you watching?"

"Huh?" Tina stared at the screen.

"What are you watching?"

Tina did not reply.

"Tina!" Fran said.

Slowly, Tina turned toward her mother. "What?" she whined.

"Never mind," Fran muttered. She pulled the brush through Tammy's hair just a little harder.

"Give it back," Bobby shouted. He reached over and slapped Joe on the arm. "That's mine."

Fran exploded, screaming, "Joey! Bobby! Stop it! Stop it right now!"

The boys stopped and stared, speechless.

"If you don't stop fighting over that, I'm going to take it away and neither of you will have it," Fran declared. "Is that what you want?"

Two heads shook from side to side.

"Well, then stop it," she said. "Why don't you go outside?"

"There's no place to go," Joey objected. "I hate this place. Why do we have to live here? I want to go home."

"Hate it, too" mimicked Bobby.

"Shoo, all of you," Fran said, rising. "Tina, take your brothers and sister outside. There's a teeter-totter out back. I saw a slide, too. Get some air. Blow the stink off yourself."

"Aw, Mo-om," Tina whined again, but Bobby was already at the door, pulling at the knob. She grabbed his hand and opened the door. Joe shot past her, nearly tripping over the outstretched leg of an ever-present agent who had propped a chair against the wall to read a newspaper.

The door slammed shut. Fran looked at Bob. He had not moved or spoken in more than an hour. She stomped over to the television and punched it off. Still, Bob did not move. Finally, with what seemed to Fran like an exaggerated effort, Bob lifted his eyes.

"What?" he asked.

"Do you hear what's going on in here?" she asked. "Are you paying any attention to your kids?" She felt as if her insides were tied in rage. She felt hot, as if her head was about to explode as all the images fought for space: the claustrophobic motels, the pile of pizza boxes, the damp bathrooms littered with dirty towels, the sniping and quarreling of the kids.

"I am sick of this," she snapped. "Look at me." She stood at the end of the bed, fingering the sleeve of her blouse, a red stain—pizza sauce—on the cuff. "How much longer is this gonna go on?" she demanded. "I am just sick of it. This isn't living. This is barely existing. We gave up a perfectly normal"— she swallowed hard—"normal life. A good life."

She began pacing at the foot of the bed.

"Happy! Did I mention happy?" she snapped. "And this, this is life in one hellhole after another, dammit. We're on top of each other, all cooped up. The kids are piled on top of each other. It's no wonder they're fighting half the time. And you? You spend all damn day lying around, watching the television. Watching TV. Watching TV. Watching TV. Don't you ever get sick of TV?" Her chest heaved. Her eyes welled and tears began to slide down her cheeks. "This is not a way to live, Bob?"

Bob crossed the room and reached out to embrace her. Taking a step back, Fran brushed his arms aside.

"I know, baby," Bob said, undeterred, his voice low and soft. "Any day now. The trial is coming soon and we'll be back home. Come on now, babe."

"This is too much," she said, between sobs. "And what about what we were promised? 'Oh, yes, Mrs. Lowe. Tutors for the children? Absolutely. A new job for Bob? Oh, no doubt about it.' " Her voice dripped in sorrow and sarcasm. "Yeah, right. Well, you can take this Kentucky, Alabama, Tennessee bullshit and shove it. I want to go home." She fell onto the bed. "I just want to go home." Feeling helpless, Bob walked outside, nodded at the agent sitting near the door, and walked over to watch the kids play.

He's gone," said the agent.

"What do you mean?" Williams said. "Who's gone?"

"Bob," the agent said. "Bob's gone."

Seated behind his desk in Iavarone's office, Williams bolted upright in his chair. "Well, look for him, dammit! Find him!" he yelled into the receiver. "I sent you guys down there to watch him, for Chrissake. What the hell is going on down there? You sleepin' down there?"

"I guess he took off in the car—he and Fran—he, uh, well—"

"Just find them, dammit," Williams demanded and slammed down the receiver. He had been receiving regular reports about the Lowes and the family's odyssey, and though he was angry at the news of Bob's disappearance, he wasn't surprised. Williams was learning what the U.S. Army learned years earlier—Bob bridled under close supervision and control.

Shortly after his marriage, Bob had registered for the draft, hoping his status would convince sympathetic officials to give him a pass. They did not and over the following two years there ensued a strange dance between Bob and the Army. Though almost comical in its particulars, it also vividly displayed the mixture of immaturity and stubbornness that was one of Bob's most obvious and perplexing characteristics. He was never sent to Vietnam, but he did go AWOL at least three times, returning each time to Fran, only to be brought back from Chicago in handcuffs later. The last time this happened, his red-faced commanding officer at Ft. Leonard Wood in Kansas shouted, "Lowe, what the hell is your problem?"

"I don't believe in this war," Bob said, though his feelings were more fearful than ideological. "And I don't like taking orders." And so he was discharged.

But this was not the army. There was no way out. The trial was still more than two months away and the street talk buzzed louder every day with word of a $100,000 contract for Bob's death.

And he wasn't the only target. With Harry under indictment for murder, rumors were rife that outfit bosses had imported a hit squad from California to take out Iavarone and Williams. That's what informants were saying, but Williams was aware of the problems with that sort of information.

One of the most difficult tasks a law enforcement investigator faces is sorting out the accumulation of intelligence from a wide variety of sources from society's underbelly: pimps, dope pushers, track-marked junkies, petty thieves, burglars, prostitutes, bust-out gamblers, bookies, and pretend wise guys. These characters prowl a subterranean world where information has real value. It can be bought, sold, and traded for a leg up, for a break, for the chance to make a play, to make a score, to earn a marker that can be cashed in when times are tough. Some play the game just for the money. Some do it to get out of a jam. Some do it just to play cops and robbers. It comes in the form of whispered words in a gangway, a hurried telephone call in the early morning hours—information, disinformation, half-lies and half-truths, sometimes accurate, sometimes not. Even so, a smart man doesn't take chances.

Williams had his own network of informants and he knew firsthand what could happen to the careless. He had learned that on an August night in 1975 when Williams had met one of his regular snitches, Frank Goulakos, a forty-seven-year-old part-time chef at DiLeo's Restaurant on Chicago's Northwest Side. When he wasn't cooking or gambling, Goulakos was hanging out on the fringe of the Taylor Street mob. Williams had cultivated Goulakos for more than two years, meeting on the sly in restaurants, coffee shops, and on dead-end streets. Goulakos was only modestly talented in the information-supply game, but he knew a lot of wise guys and was often able to provide decent and helpful background.

"I met him at DiLeo's," Williams would recall. "We talked for a little while, thirty minutes maybe. He had always been the kind of guy who talked too loud for somebody who was meeting with a cop. I said I had to leave and offered to walk out with him. He took me into the bar and introduced me to a woman that he was dating. He told her exactly who I was, which I thought was really stupid. I said I had to leave. He said he was going to stay."

About ninety minutes after Williams left, Goulakos walked out, alone, to his car, parked on the street in front of the restaurant. He saw the rear tire on the driver's side was flat and bent down to inspect it. At that moment, a car drove up and stopped. The back door opened, and a man stepped out and shot Frank six times in the back.

"I didn't learn until later that Harry did it," said Williams.

Williams and Iavarone learned a lot about Harry, and few facts were as chilling as what they learned after the death of Charles Nicoletti.

In his earlier years, Nicoletti had fashioned a reputation as a hit man for organized crime, but at age sixty, he was, police said, no longer taking contracts. Believed to hold a high-ranking position of power, Nicoletti delegated hits to underlings. However, on the night of March 29, 1977, he was found dead behind the wheel of his car in the parking lot of the Golden Horn Restaurant in west suburban Northlake. There were three bullets in his head.

The hit had the earmarks of a Harry job, prompting reporters to quiz the state's attorney about Harry's possible involvement. "Aleman is out on bond and he is quite proficient," Bernard Carey declared.

They're back," said the agent's voice.

"Where'd they go?" Williams asked.

"Said they went for a drive."

"How long were they gone?" Williams asked.

"Coupla hours is all."

"Let me talk to Bob."

Quietly, but forcefully, Williams reminded Bob of his responsibilities and the danger of going off on his own. After the close call at the rented farm-house, Williams refused to underestimate the reach of those who were try-ing to find Bob.

"When are we coming back, Dave?" Bob asked.

"Soon, Bob. Soon."

"Can we visit my sister for a few days?"

"Where is that?"

"Sipsey, Alabama—it's just north of Birmingham," Bob said. Williams heard him exhale cigarette smoke. "It's my sister, Joetta. It's out in the country."

The white frame house sat on top of a small knoll at the end of a lane and was surrounded by broad cotton fields. Anyone who approached would be easily seen long before they arrived. The suitcases were unpacked, and stayed that way for three weeks. The kids roamed free. Bob and Fran took evening strolls along Burton Creek, which snaked around the bottom of the hill behind the house. The tension eased. Some days, it was possible to for-get the trial and the mob menace in Chicago.

But the pressure wouldn't go away. In April, Detective Rich Law, who was working side by side with Williams, was summoned to meet with a high-ranking police official, who shocked him by demanding to know where Bob was being hidden.

"I have a goddammed right to know where he is," the official thundered. "Your duty is to the police department, not to those assholes in the State's Attorney's Office."

"I can't talk about that, sir," Law replied.

"I can and will bust you back to walking on a fucking street corner," the official snarled.

Law walked out of the office, saying over his shoulder, "You do what you have to do."

Finally, Harry's arm reached out and touched the inner circle of the fam-ily. Williams broke the news, telling Bob, "Word is Harry's people are talk-ing to Fran's sister-in-law Pam and that she showed them pictures of you, Fran, and the kids."

Bob was staggered. "Why—why would she?" he asked.

"She wants a divorce from Fran's brother, George," Williams explained. "She offered to help find you if they'd break George's legs."

Bob hung up the phone. "Pack it up," he declared. "We're going home." Fearing their cover was blown and with the trial approaching, Williams had agreed that they should move back to Chicago, though it was sooner than he had anticipated.

Tight-lipped, they had driven through the night, arriving midmorning. Bob and Fran allowed the agents to check them into a motel, then suggested they make a trip to the grocery store. But they had no such intention. Instead, they drove to Ravenswood Hospital on Chicago's North Side to confront Fran's sister-in-law, Pam, at her job.

Bob wheeled the car into the parking lot and immediately spotted Pam walking to her car. He sped up and screeched to a halt. Behind them, the agents' car pulled into the lot. Fran burst from the passenger seat. Pam was too startled to speak.

"What in the hell do you think you're doing, bitch?" Fran yelled. "You trying to get my family killed?"

Pam began backing up and Fran began walking toward her, fists clenched. Two car doors slammed. A hand grabbed Fran's shoulder and pulled. "Don't, Fran," the agent said. "You can be charged with battery."

"If that bitch is telling where my kids are," Fran shouted, "she's the one who ought to be arrested!"

The agent turned to face Pam. "Go on, home," he said. "Forget about this. And keep your mouth shut."

16

J ury selection in the trial of Harry Aleman was scheduled for Monday, May 16, 1977. As sunlight burst through the windows along the west wall of courtroom 700, spectators were already jammed into the pews and crowded along the walls. The mood was anticipatory, the tension thick, having already triggered a number of flare-ups in the hallways. Extraordinary security precautions delayed the opening of the courtroom, as every person who sought entry was individually searched. Even the judge had been forced to undergo a search—an irritating moment for a man known for his shortness of temper. Shotguns bristling, deputies lined the hallway. Members of the media—reporters, cameramen, and television sketch artists—were angry because, by the time they entered the courtroom, the front rows on both sides were packed with what appeared to them to be Harry's supporters: a cheering section of sorts made up of large, scowling men wearing suit coats and dark shirts. To Iavarone, this smacked of an attempt to intimidate his witnesses, but before he could take action, a police sergeant dressed in plainclothes walked over and stood silently in front of the men. Casually, he pulled his sport coat to the side to reveal a nine-millimeter handgun. He then addressed the men in a voice of controlled fury that was just loud enough to reach his targeted audience and Iavarone.

"If any of you motherfuckers does anything in court—and I mean any-thing, a look, a gesture—you will get a visit at your home tonight," he said, his head swiveling to take in the entire row. "Do I make myself clear?" One or two of the large men nodded. The others just stared as the sergeant pulled his jacket back over his pistol and backed up against the wall where he would remain, arms folded, for the rest of the day.

It was after 10 A.M. when Criminal Court Judge Frank Wilson, black robes billowing, emerged from his chambers and strode imperiously to the bench. Iavarone watched him walk up the steps to his chair, still filled with questions about why Harry's lawyers had agreed to let Wilson preside over the case after first objecting to him.

Iavarone glanced over his shoulder and estimated the crowd in the court-room at nearly two hundred people. He turned back to face Wilson, who was settling in, stacking motions from that morning's trial call into a pile. He was a stern man with an impeccable reputation for honesty on the bench and for his capacity for alcohol when off it. On Friday nights, he was a regular at Jean's, the basement shot-and-a-beer saloon a block north of the courthouse, where defense lawyers, prosecutors, investigators, and judges gathered while waiting for juries to finish deliberations, to kibitz over what they had done and what they should have done, to celebrate victories, or to drown losses. Marriages were ruined and boozy romances were begun in the dark recesses of Jean's. Not infrequently, a volunteer was needed to drive an inebriated Wilson home.

Frank Whalen and his nephew, Ed, flanked Harry at the defense table. Iavarone and his trial partner, Joseph Claps, stood at the prosecution table.

"Both sides ready to proceed?" Wilson asked.

"Yes," Iavarone replied.

"The defendant answers ready, your honor," Whalen said.

"Call up the jury," Wilson told his courtroom deputy.

"Your honor," Whalen interrupted. "The defendant has now advised me he wishes to sign a jury waiver."

At the prosecution table, Iavarone and Claps exchanged a look of shock, but neither spoke.

Illinois was, and still remains, one of a handful of states that permits a defendant, without any agreement by the prosecution, to waive a trial by jury and ask for a bench trial in which a judge decides guilt or innocence. Most states and the federal criminal justice system allow for bench trials only if both the prosecution and defense agree to proceed in that fashion.

"Mr. Aleman, you understand you're entitled to a jury trial in this case?" Wilson asked.

"Yes, Your Honor," Harry said politely.

"Only you can make the decision to be tried by this judge, do you understand that?" Wilson said.

"Yes," Harry replied.

Wilson instructed Harry to sign a jury waiver form. "With that turn of events, does the state have their witnesses available, or did you expect to pick a jury today?" Iavarone said he would be ready by the afternoon. Whalen suggested the following morning.

"I have today set aside for this trial," Wilson said sternly. "One o'clock."

By the time Wilson returned to the bench shortly after 1 P.M., the courtroom was again overflowing. The media had solved their seating problem—they now filled the jury box—and were ready, pens and pencils poised. Their ranks included reporters from the three local newspapers—*Tribune, Sun-Times,* and *Daily News*—as well as national media, including *The New York Times.* The most notable and famous of the reporters present was *Daily News* columnist Mike Royko, who had long delighted in skewering the mob, the police department, politicians, and the judiciary. Typical was a recent offering, which had come in the form of an open letter to the police superintendent. In it, Royko went after the department following disclosures that a secret squad of police officers, the "Red Squad," had spied on activist groups and citizens involved in liberal causes, often infiltrating organizations and taking photos of protesters. One of their targets was 5th Ward Alderman Leon Despres, who had regularly, and almost always as a minority of one, stood up to Mayor Richard J. Daley. Royko noted that twenty-five years of surveillance on Despres had "uncovered" only that he didn't like the Daley political machine. The column was headlined:

A crime-fighting tip:
Keep an eye on Aleman

Not once did your sleuths discover Despres shooting anybody, collecting juice loans, taking bets or hijacking trucks. . . . So it seems to me that maybe you ought to now consider revising your list of people who are followed.

If somebody had been following Aleman the way they followed former Ald. Despres, they might have seen something worth talking about. For example, Aleman and his partner, Butch Petrocelli, seem to be in charge of just about everything lively in the Taylor Street neighborhood.

Your men might see Harry and Butch collecting juice loans, beating people up in alleys, running high stakes poker and crap games, and otherwise earning their livings.

If your men are lucky, they might also see them on those occasions when they wear ski masks. They prefer ski masks to the traditional gray fedoras when they perform a hit.

If you should consider shifting the emphasis of your surveillance to someone like Aleman, you might see him in the company of Chicago policemen.

That's right. Contrary to what you might think, superintendent, Aleman gets along pretty well with some policemen. They help him in some of his projects. They feed him information, stay out of his way when he is busy, and otherwise make themselves useful.

You can't do any worse. The last time I checked, the Chicago Police Department still hadn't solved any of the 1,000-plus syndicate murders in this city's history.

Royko was one of the few in the room who knew Harry, having met him more than a decade before when Harry tried to steal the $82 from a *Daily*

News vending machine. However, all the reporters were intrigued by the defendant's reputation and a certain charisma that was not sullied but rather embellished by the fact that police now believed he had killed as many as twenty men.

Harry did not disappoint. In an era when most outfit characters were trying to keep a low profile, Harry glided into the courtroom, looking and acting the part of a celebrity: Dark and curly hair neatly cropped, sport coat and dark beltless slacks perfectly tailored, shoes polished to a high sheen. He shook hands, slapped backs, and smiled while entering the building, a man knowing that he was the center of all attention, the object of stares and whispers, the subject of the sketch artists and their furiously moving pencils.

In the hallway outside Courtroom 700, he was bold enough to stroll up to Richard Logan, younger brother of the late Billy Logan. This meeting had been inevitable, but it was important to Iavarone that it not happen sooner. When he had called Betty Romo to inform her that Harry was going to be indicted for the murder of their brother, he pleaded with her not to tell Richard. He feared that Richard, who was employed as a trampoline artist with the Barnum & Bailey circus, might try to confront Harry and that that might not be conducive to his health.

"Hello, Richard," Harry said as he strolled past. "How are you?"

Stunned momentarily, Logan answered. "I'm fine. How are you?"

Harry smiled a toothy grin. "I'm OK," he said.

Claps gave the opening statement for the prosecution, a straightforward recitation of the expected testimony of Logan's relatives, Louie Almeida and Bob Lowe. "The evidence will prove that the defendant intentionally, premeditatedly, and in cold blood shot down William Logan in front of that house on Walton on September 27, 1972," Claps said.

Frank Whalen opened for the defense. Veteran lawyers in the courtroom quickly recognized the man who, in the 1940s and 1950s, as one of the most relentless and successful prosecutors in Cook County, was known as "The Voice of Doom."

A rock-jawed man with a stern face, Whalen had convinced five juries in just one year to send defendants to Death Row. He was at his best performing before juries, where his talent for theatrics was most appreciated.

Twenty years earlier, while prosecuting a man accused of raping and knifing a woman to death, Whalen had constantly fiddled with the murder weapon, poking it gently into the wooden jury box rail. Then, during his closing argument to the jury, as he bellowed, "There is no justice left in America unless this man goes to his death, death, death!" he plunged the knife directly into the top of the rail and strode away, leaving the mesmerized jurors staring at the vibrating blade. Whalen won the case.

He had jumped to the defense side of the fence in 1956 when he was subpoenaed by a federal grand jury investigating allegations of ambulance chasing by lawyers. He refused to testify, asserted his Fifth Amendment right against self-incrimination, and then resigned as a prosecutor. As a defense lawyer, he was successful as well, winning acquittals for a number of clients, including some high-ranking mobsters.

Whalen stood behind the lectern and clasped his hands behind his back. In a presentation of less than five minutes, he predicted that Louie's testimony would hopelessly contradict Bob's. "In short, Your Honor, the defendant believes the evidence introduced by the state will be so unsatisfactory that we can only wait and let the court hear the evidence as it unfolds from the stand."

Billy Logan's sister, Betty Romo, was the first witness. Although she had been present immediately after the shooting, she was called as a "life and death" witness, someone who could establish for legal purposes that Billy had been alive and that he now was dead. Though Iavarone led her gently through her testimony, she broke into sobs as she recounted the horror of that night more than five years earlier.

"He was—" she began. But her voiced cracked and she paused, struggling for control. She took a deep breath and began again. "He was laying on his back and I kept calling his name," she said, her voice trembling. "And he turned and I knelt there and I just kept saying his name over and over."

"And did he look any different when you saw him outside than he did when you had last seen him?" Iavarone asked.

"Well, he left the house alive and I doubt he was still alive when I got to him. He was hurt real bad," she said. "I got blood all over me when I knelt down."

"Do you know if the police arrived that night?"

"Yes, they did," she said.

"And did they remove your brother from in front of the house?"

"Yes, they did," she said.

"When is the next time you saw your brother?" Iavarone asked.

"At Salerno's Funeral Parlor," she said. "He was dead."

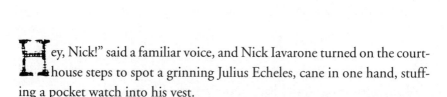

17

"H ey, Nick!" said a familiar voice, and Nick Iavarone turned on the court-house steps to spot a grinning Julius Echeles, cane in one hand, stuffing a pocket watch into his vest.

A veteran defender of criminals, Julius Lucius Hudilio Octavio Echeles was a colorful thread in Chicago's legal tapestry of fiery litigators, backroom fixers, and hallway hustlers. Sworn in as a lawyer in the days when a law degree was not required, Echeles had been sent to prison for taking payoffs to arrange U.S. Postal Service jobs. The conviction temporarily cost him his law license but, once paroled, he used his extraordinary powers of elocution to persuade regulators to give it back.

Echeles used the jail experience to his advantage, fashioning it into a custom-made argument for sentencing hearings. Typically, he would tell a judge about to impose prison on a client, "I know only too well, Your Honor, the pain of prison. And I would urge you to spare my client too many years."

A distinguished-looking man with a salt-and-pepper beard and neatly waxed mustache that curled upward at the ends, Echeles had defended his fair share of mobsters over the years. His clientele included the son-in-law of mob boss Sam Giancana. He was known for engaging in courtroom hi-jinks. Once he secreted a music box in his jacket pocket prior to his cross-examination of a prosecution witness about receiving protection payments, then, as he stood up in court, reached in to flip it open to play the tune "If I Were a Rich Man." On another occasion, while representing mobster Sam "Mad Sam" DeStefano, the trial was halted briefly when his client tossed a roll of toilet paper at a judge to express his opinion of justice.

"How's the trial going, Nick?" Echeles asked in his familiar clipped, stac-cato voice.

"I'm working my ass off," Iavarone said.

"Ahhhh, Nick," Echeles said. "Don't knock yourself out."

"What do you mean?"

"You'll see," Echeles said. "And one day, it will all even itself out. They'll make you a judge." He laughed.

"Get lost," Iavarone said, trotting up the steps and into the courthouse.

The second day of the trial began with the testimony of Dr. Edward Shalgos, a pathologist who had, in the course of his tenure with the Cook County Coroner's office, conducted thousands of autopsies. In the cold, sterile rooms of the morgue, he had cut open chests, weighed organs, peeled back scalps, and counted wounds. He had probed bodies to dig out bullets, knife blades, and shards of glass.

Just a few hours after Billy Logan was pronounced dead, Shalgos had stood over the body and commenced his examination, beginning with a sim-ple external appraisal. Then, carefully, he made a long incision down the cen-ter of the chest and abdomen and began to remove, measure, and weigh Billy's heart, liver, intestines, lungs, and spleen.

While Billy's sister established her brother's life and death, Shalgos de-scribed just how he had died. "The abnormalities on William Logan were those of grouped projectiles with a large particle shotgun identity," Shalgos testified. "The appearances were those of a passage through the body of similar-sized multiple particles with severe damage on vital structures. There were two major groups. One of the groups was present on the left side of the chest. The second grouping was on the front and high aspect of the arm, shoulder and chest of the subject on the right side."

He said the wound to the right shoulder appeared to have been the first shot, and the pellets had failed to strike any internal organs, though one had penetrated Billy's jaw and lodged in his back. The second blast, he said, had virtually destroyed Billy's heart and left lung.

"From your examination and your experience," Iavarone asked, looking down at his notes on the lectern before him, "do you have an opinion as to what caused the death of William Logan?"

"The death of the subject was related to lacerations of vital structures, specifically the heart, aorta, pulmonary artery, and both lungs, with related major internal bleeding."

The first time Iavarone saw Louie Almeida was in a federal prison hospital in Springfield, Missouri, where Louie had been taken for a psychiatric examination. He initially had been put in a cell in the general prison population, but Louie was so afraid of getting killed (there were Kansas City organized crime members housed there) that he was moved.

"I found him in the psych ward," Iavarone later recalled. "It was horrible. There were these cells, each with one guy in it. And there were people screaming, people just rocking back and forth, people curled up on the floor."

Louie was in his cell. Sitting on the floor in front of his bunk were six one-gallon cartons of ice cream, melting, puddles of black-and-white liquid congealing on the tile.

"What the hell is going on here?" Iavarone asked.

"He asked for ice cream," said a guard.

"He has nothing to eat it with," Iavarone protested.

"Inmates in psych can't have silverware," the guard replied, and walked away.

Iavarone scanned the cell. No shoes, no belt, but six gallons of ice cream going uneaten. Louie smiled weakly and shrugged his shoulders.

"How can I help you?" Iavarone asked.

"They took my books," Louie said.

"Anything else?"

"Get me out of here?"

Iavarone raised hell on the telephone with the U.S. Department of Justice when he returned to Chicago and, after weeks of haggling, Louie eventually was moved to the Cook County Jail. Iavarone saw that Louie got his books. They were third-grade primers; he was teaching himself to read.

As he walked into the courtroom to testify against Harry, Louie was flanked by three deputy U.S. Marshals. Louie had traded his continued cooperation to cut his ten-year prison term in Ohio to a five-year sentence and admission into the federal Witness Protection Program, where he would receive a new identity and be relocated to another state. Now, the marshals were part of Louie's permanent entourage whenever he left his prison cell. After Louie settled into the chair, spelled his name, and gave his age, Iavarone got right to the point. "Have you ever been involved in any murders?" Iavarone asked.

"Yes, sir," Louie replied.

"How many?"

"One."

"One murder?" Iavarone asked.

"Yes."

"Whose murder were you involved in?"

"I was involved in the Billy Logan murder," Louie said.

"Was anyone else involved with you in the Billy Logan murder?"

"Yes, sir."

"Who else was involved with you?"

"Harry Aleman."

Iavarone backed away from the lectern, nearly to the first pew of spectators. "Mr. Almeida," he said. "I would like you to look around the courtroom and tell the court if you see Harry Aleman in this courtroom today."

"Yes, sir, I do," Louie said, looking directly at Iavarone. His eyes didn't move.

"Would you please point out Harry Aleman in court?"

Louie swiveled the witness chair just to his left and gazed across the room to the defense table. He raised his right hand and gestured toward Harry. For the next hour, Louie dutifully recounted, with Iavarone's guidance, how he had grown up with Harry, and became a thief and ultimately a personal assistant of sorts for Harry. "I got tires for his wife's car, took his wife's car to the garage on Taylor Street to have it fixed, took it back home, go and get him and his friends a hot dog."

For a man with a sixth-grade education, a $100,000 price on his head, and a burning fear that someone was bound to collect it, Louie was remarkably calm and self-possessed on the stand, providing a lucid account of the murder; all of the preparation conducted by Iavarone and Claps in their courthouse office was paying off. Louie started the murder tale with Harry's request to follow Billy, detailed the failed attempt, and then came to the night of their success.

"We parked the car two houses from the corner. Harry jumped in the back seat," Louie said. "He rolled down the window and he put shotgun shells in the shotgun."

"Who saw William Logan first?" Iavarone asked. "You or the defendant?"

"Harry Aleman," Louie said.

"How do you know that?"

"Because he told me, 'Get ready,' " Louie said. "I pulled out and Harry told me to put my lights on. When I pulled up, I made sure that the back door was directly in front of the path where Billy Logan was going to walk off onto the street."

"What, if anything, did Billy do when you pulled up in front of him?" Iavarone asked.

"He jumped back onto the curb," Louie said. "He stepped back and then Harry hollered out his name: 'Hey, Billy, come here.' Then Harry shot him."

The courtroom was silent, except for the rustling of reporters' notebooks and the scratching of pens. All eyes were trained on the witness stand. At the defense table, Harry leaned back in his chair, his face emotionless and his legs crossed, the only movement from him the slight twitching of a tasseled black loafer as his foot moved to some silent rhythm.

"Did you see Harry shoot?" Iavarone asked.

Louie's voice never wavered. "Yes, sir. I seen Harry shoot him. Billy flew back four or five feet, laying down. Around a second or two later, Harry shot him again."

"At any time," Iavarone asked, "did Billy ever say anything?"

"Yes, Billy hollered out, 'Oh, my God,' " Louie said.

"What, if anything, happened after the defendant shot Billy the second time?" Iavarone asked.

"Somehow he crawled on his hands and knees to the side of his car," Louie said. "Then he opened up the door of the car."

"Who opened the door of the car?" Iavarone asked.

"Harry Aleman," Louie said. "He went to step out of the car. I just seen him go halfway out of the car. At that time a car turned the corner up ahead and I was worrying about that."

"Why were you so worried about that car?"

"Well, I didn't know if it was a squad car or a plain car and I was trying to look above the car to see if it was a squad car or what so I could drive out of there," Louie said.

"After the defendant opened the door, what, if anything, happened next?" Iavarone asked.

"Well, five or six seconds later, I heard another shot," Louie replied. "And then the car door slammed and I started to take off in a hurry. Harry shouted, 'Drive slow, he's gone,' so I slowed up. I asked him if he was gone, and he said, 'Yes, there is no way that he could live through that.' "

Iavarone led Louie through the circumstances of his arrest in Ohio and decision to cooperate.

"At the time you were arrested in Ohio, were you associating with the defendant?" Iavarone asked.

"No, sir," Louie replied. "I stopped around February of seventy-four."

"Would you tell the court why?"

"Object, Your Honor," said Whalen, rising to his feet.

Wilson said nothing. He rose and gestured toward his chambers, then walked off the bench, followed by Iavarone, Claps, Whalen, and his nephew. This was the first of what would be several intense legal arguments conducted behind Wilson's closed chamber door.

A few murmurs rippled through the courtroom spectators, but were shushed by sheriff's deputies. Louie looked toward the jury box, crammed with reporters, then shifted to look at the defense table and found himself staring directly at Harry. Seconds became minutes and neither man would break away. Finally, Harry slowly put on a pair of sunglasses but kept his gaze at Louie, whose face broke into a nervous smile.

This staring contest ceased when Wilson and the lawyers returned to the room. Iavarone had lost his legal battle. He had hoped Wilson would allow Louie to testify that he stopped associating with Harry because he feared for his life. "We have no more questions," Iavarone said.

Whalen began his cross-examination on Wednesday with a painstaking probing of Louie's arrest in Ohio, his decision to cooperate, his subsequent suicide attempt in prison, his many statements to federal and state investigators, and his failure to remember exact dates and times.

Whalen barked at Louie and snapped at Iavarone. He shuffled through his notes, lost his place, misquoted reports, misread dates, and, at times, seemingly confused himself with his own questions.

"The first statement was in March of seventy-five, am I correct, Mr. Witness?" Whalen asked, standing next to Harry at the defense table.

"Yes," Louie said.

"Well, as a matter of fact, Mr. Witness, you had made a statement on the sixteenth day of April 1975, had you not?"

"In Toledo, Ohio?" Louie asked.

"I'm asking *you*, Mr. Witness," Whalen said, sarcasm dripping. "I'm asking you. You just testified that the first statement you gave was . . ." Whalen paused, apparently at a loss for words.

"In March," Iavarone said, finishing his sentence for him.

"In March," Whalen repeated, glaring at Iavarone, who grinned and fired right back. "April comes after March as far as the calendar is concerned," Iavarone said.

"Let me conduct this," Whalen snapped.

"Well, if we can understand your questions, we'll be happy to," Iavarone retorted.

At times, Whalen's questions and Louie's responses sounded as if one, or both, was deaf. The cross-examination was so excruciating that it was difficult for spectators to watch.

"How many statements have you given to police, authorities, or prosecutors up until the present time, from March of 1975?" Whalen asked.

"From March of seventy-five?" Louie asked.

"Yes."

"Statements?" Louie asked.

"How many?" Whalen said, his voice rising. "How many times were you interviewed by officials either of the police, government, or prosecutor's office?"

"A number of times," Louie said. "I don't remember."

Though some in court assumed that the sixty-six-year-old Whalen was suffering from sad mental lapses, his seeming befuddlement was actually part of a complicated strategy to confuse Louie, to turn him around in his chair, and to slowly undermine his credibility.

"Mr. Witness," Whalen began. "You understand what a statement is: when you give an interview to the police authorities. Is that right?"

"Not really, no," Louie said. He began to fidget in the chair, clearly uncomfortable.

"You don't understand that?" Whalen asked with feigned incredulity.

"No," Louie said stubbornly.

"Well, you told us that on many occasions you were questioned by various authorities, is that right?"

"Yes."

"And they were writing down what you told them at that time?"

"Yes, sir."

"On how many such occasions did that happen?" Whalen bellowed. "How many times? A simple question, Mr. Witness."

"A number of times, sir. I don't know," Louie said, feeling confused and exasperated. "They interviewed me a number of times. I don't know."

Whalen took a step toward the witness stand. "Do you have a bad memory, Mr. Witness?"

"Objection, Judge," Iavarone snapped.

"Don't argue with the witness," Wilson said, casting an eye toward Whalen.

And so it went that afternoon, with Whalen trying mightily to chip away at Louie, and Louie occasionally giving it back as good as he got. Some exchanges resembled a legal adaptation of Abbott and Costello's famous "Who's on First?" routine.

"Was there any long-barreled weapon in this car at the time of the shooting?" Whalen asked.

"Long barrel?" Louie asked back.

"Long-barreled weapon," Whalen said.

"No," Louie said.

"There was no long-barreled weapon in the car?" Whalen asked again.

"A long barrel?" Louie repeated.

"A long barrel—L-o-n-g, Mr. Witness."

"Yes, there was a long barrel, yes," Louie said. He smiled.

"What was the long-barreled weapon?" Whalen asked.

"It was a shotgun," Louie said.

"And how long was that?"

"Eighteen inches long."

"Eighteen inches long," Whalen said, pursing his lips. "And you consider that a long-barreled weapon?"

"No, sir," Louie said brightly. "That's a short barrel for a shotgun."

Whalen looked at the ceiling.

"So then," he said, "I'll ask you the question again. Was there any long-barreled weapon in the car?"

"Was there any long-barreled weapon in the car?" Louie repeated the question.

"Yes," Whalen said impatiently.

"Yes," Louie said. "One."

"Which one was that?" Whalen asked.

"The shotgun," Louie replied.

"How long was the barrel?" Whalen asked.

"Eighteen inches," Louie said. He smiled again.

"Do you consider that a long-barreled weapon?"

"Objection," Iavarone declared, his patience likewise exhausted.

"Objection overruled," Wilson said. "He said he saw a long barrel. Now he says it's a short barrel. I'm confused. Let's straighten it out."

Whalen tried again. "Do you consider that a long-barreled weapon?"

Louie's answer was a non sequitur: "There was two guns in the car."

"There were two guns in the car?" Whalen asked.

"The gun that had the long barrel was the shotgun," Louie said.

"You mean one was a handgun and the other was a shotgun?"

"A handgun—a forty-five, yes," Louie replied. "And the other was a Browning automatic twelve-gauge shotgun."

"By that, you mean the shotgun had a longer barrel than the handgun, is that right?" Whalen asked.

"You said long barrel," Louie said. "I'm just answering what you said."

Whalen exploded. "Do you understand what I'm saying, Mr. Witness?"

"Objection!" Iavarone barked.

"Overruled," Wilson said.

Whalen began again: "I'm asking you if there were any long-barreled weapons in the car. Yes or no?"

"Long-barreled weapon?" Louie asked back.

"Yes," Whalen said.

"Just a shotgun," Louie said.

"And was the shotgun a long-barreled weapon?" Whalen asked for what seemed to those listening the hundredth time.

Louie sat, motionless, as if he had not heard the question. He did not respond.

"Did the shotgun have a long barrel?" Whalen repeated.

Louie paused before saying, "Not that long. No."

It ended, mercifully for all of those in court, more than three hours after Louie entered the courtroom and he was excused and walked out with his small band of heavily armed protectors.

Ella Jo DeMarco was still in the process of spelling her last name when Whalen bounced to his feet and requested a meeting in Wilson's chambers.

This woman was potentially more trouble than Louie. Whalen knew that DeMarco's testimony, if allowed, could be devastating to Harry's defense. Whalen had to convince Wilson to bar it.

DeMarco lived at 5922 West Walton Street, less than seventy-five yards from where Billy was shot. In early December, before Harry was indicted, she began receiving telephone calls from an old boyfriend, Harry's brother, Anthony. He was asking a lot of questions: "Were you a friend of Billy Logan? What did you see that night? Did you see a car drive away?" He insisted that they meet, but she declined. Even before any indictment had been handed down, she had already been contacted by prosecutors who were planning to call her to testify about what she might have heard or seen the night Billy was killed. When she heard from Anthony Aleman, she called Iavarone, and, on his advice, the next time Anthony called, Ella Jo agreed to a 7 P.M. meeting at Tofinetti's Restaurant on Randolph Street near downtown Chicago. Three of Iavarone's agents positioned themselves at tables in the restaurant and watched as Ella Jo arrived and was seated. But Anthony never showed.

Three days before Christmas, after Harry was indicted and taken into custody, Anthony called again and arranged a meeting at La Margarita, an upscale Mexican restaurant. Agents staked out the restaurant again. But, again, Anthony was a no-show.

A third meeting was set—this one for December 29 at a subterranean downtown bar and restaurant called the Brasserie. Dave Williams took up a table near Ella Jo, who arrived with some friends. Shortly after 8 P.M., Anthony walked inside, but refused to approach her table. He stood in the vestibule and waved Ella Jo over. Speaking in a hoarse whisper, he said, "I heard you picked my brother's picture out."

"That's not true," Ella Jo said.

His hand shot out and gripped her chin.

"If my brother is convicted," he snarled, "you will be looking over your shoulder for the rest of your life." He twisted her chin in his hand, staring into her eyes, then turned on his heel. A rush of cold air from an open door smacked Ella Jo in the face as she watched Anthony bound up the steps that led to Michigan Avenue.

Six days later, he called and said, "What you should do is testify for my brother."

She said nothing.

"You could say that you saw somebody else, not Harry, get into the car after the shooting," Anthony suggested.

Ella Jo hung up the phone. He called again, on the morning of January 7, the day Harry's case was up before Judge Suria. "You really should think about testifying for Harry," he insisted. "I can make it worth your while." Again, Ella Jo did not respond.

He called again later that day, after Ruth had posted Harry's bond and he was released from the county jail.

"Harry wants to talk to you," was all that he said. She said, "No."

Four days later, the telephone rang again, and, when she answered, she heard an unfamiliar voice say, "Do you know who this is?"

"Who is this?" Ella Jo asked.

"This is Harry Aleman," the voice said. "Anthony, my brother, suggested you might want to talk to me."

"About?"

"You might want to help me."

She said nothing.

"How does $10,000 sound? All you have to do is say you saw someone get into the car and it wasn't me," said Harry.

Ella Jo hung up. Now Iavarone wanted to put Ella Jo on the stand to testify about it all.

Whalen was ranting before anyone could take a seat in Wilson's chambers.

"This is clearly inadmissible," he declared. "We move that it be suppressed."

"Motion sustained," Wilson said. "Nothing will be allowed."

Iavarone protested, saying, *"People v. Gambony* says that any threats made or any offers or bribes made to a witness can be proven by circumstantial evidence." He added citations from two other cases.

"Additionally, Your Honor," Iavarone's partner, Joe Claps, said, "at the time of the conversations, the number of people who were aware of the fact that the defendant would be identified by any witness as either getting out of a hit car or getting back into it were very, very, *very* limited. It shows by circumstantial evidence that the individual who called on that last phone call was Harry Aleman."

"I am trying to keep error out of this," Wilson replied. "It would be very prejudicial. It's hearsay. It will not be allowed in." He stared hard at Claps and Iavarone. "That is my ruling."

18

Courthouse veterans could not recall ever seeing a witness afforded more security than Bob Lowe as he was escorted into the building to testify against Harry Aleman.

Friday morning, minutes before nine, three dark blue vans were waved past the security shack inside the ten-foot-tall chain-link fence that surrounded the judge's parking lot on the north side of the courthouse. Immediately, twelve Illinois Bureau of Investigation agents and an equal number of Chicago police officers surrounded the vehicles. One of them slid open the side doors and Bob emerged. Because he didn't even own a suit, he had borrowed one, a four-button navy blue leisure suit that he wore over a loud polyester double-knit shirt. With his head down, and his collar-length brown hair swaying gently against his long sideburns, Bob stepped into the swarm of protection.

Jammed together between temporary barricades on the other side of the fence, reporters gawked and motor-driven cameras chattered. As if on cue, the agents and cops drew their pistols and, holding them at their sides, the scrum headed toward the side door. The lobby had been cleared and an elevator waited. Bob felt sweat dripping down his ribcage as he rode to the seventh floor, where more security awaited to sweep him down the hall to the witness room behind the courtroom. Iavarone was waiting and motioned toward a wooden chair at the head of an oak table. Except for a canister ashtray in one corner and a green metal wastebasket in the other, the room was bare.

"You all right?" Iavarone asked.

Bob nodded and said, "Yeah, I guess so."

There was tightness in his gut. It started on the afternoon before his scheduled appearance in court. It started as he sat down for dinner with Fran and the kids. He had lifted his fork to his mouth, and then dropped it back on his plate. "I can't eat, babe," he said. "I'm sorry."

"You should eat something, Bob," Fran insisted. "Try to settle yourself down a little."

Bob smiled weakly. Under the table, the force of his grip on his thighs turned the backs of his knuckles white. "I'll be okay, I guess," he said.

But he wasn't. Fran was awakened just after dawn by a choking sound. She turned in the bed and found it empty. She lay there, listening, and heard the choking again, the sounds of the man who, in their nearly ten years of marriage, had wanted little more from life than a solid roof over his head, a steady job, a loving family, and the financial wherewithal to take a vacation once a year. And for all of the pain, the quarrels, and chaos of the last few months, she felt something beyond sympathy. She shoved aside the covers and went to the kitchen to make coffee. The four agents living with them would be up soon. As she shuffled to the sink and filled the pot, Bob stood behind the bathroom door, retching.

The courtroom was a blur at first as Bob kept his eyes focused solely on Iavarone, who stood behind the lectern next to the prosecution table, and began to speak. "Mr. Lowe, calling your attention to September of nineteen-seventy-two, will you please tell His Honor where you were living at that time?"

"Fifty-nine-oh-three West Walton." Bob's voice was tight. He took a sip of water from a paper cup next to the microphone.

"Are you still living at that address?"

"No, sir."

"Would you please tell the Court when you moved?"

"Winter of seventy-seven."

"And who moved you?"

"The State's Attorney's Office."

"And did you move at that time into a home or an apartment?"

"Apartment."

"Do you know how much the rent is on that apartment?"

"Two-hundred seventy-five dollars a month."

"Who has paid the rent since you moved in there?"

"The State's Attorney's Office."

"Mr. Lowe, do you currently have a job?"

"No," he said.

"When did you quit your job?"

"In March, seventy-seven."

"Why did you quit your job?"

"The State's Attorney's Office asked me to."

Bob explained that he had been earning $247.41 a week working at the gas station, but was now receiving a weekly $250 check from the state. And he said the state had paid the family's expenses while they traveled through the South, as well as the rent on the home in which they were now living in Twin Lakes, Wisconsin.

"Did you request to be moved, Mr. Lowe?"

"No, sir," Bob declared.

"Did you want to move?" Iavarone asked.

"No, sir," Bob said, his voice loosening at last. He unclenched his fists and wiggled his fingers. He sucked in a long breath, then let it out, beginning at last to relax slightly as Iavarone moved to the night of the shooting. He traced his footsteps out the door with his dog, Ginger, and as he spoke, the images of the night came rushing back.

"Where was William Logan when you saw him?" Iavarone asked.

"Walking down his walkway."

"What did you do when you saw Mr. Logan walking toward his car?" Iavarone asked.

"I started toward him," Bob said.

"Why did you start toward him?"

"I wanted to talk to him."

"What were you going to talk to Mr. Logan about?" Iavarone asked.

"He had mentioned he wanted to buy my dog—" Bob began, but was cut off.

"Objection," Whalen said. It was the first of more than one hundred objections he would make during Bob's testimony as part of his strategy to deflect, diffuse, and disrupt him. Some were valid and some clearly were not. Wilson thought this objection was proper, though, and barred the testimony as hearsay—a rule of evidence that prohibits a witness from recounting an out-of-court statement.

"Objection sustained," Wilson ruled. "That will be stricken."

Bob stepped off the witness stand and stood before a blown-up map of West Walton Street. Iavarone handed him a marking pen.

"What, if anything, happened when you started to go across the street?" Iavarone asked.

"A car pulled up," Bob said, adding that he had seen the car parked on the corner with its engine idling when he first came out with Ginger.

"Could you draw an X showing where you were at the time this car pulled up and stopped?" Iavarone asked. "Put your initials next to that X, please."

Bob recounted how he saw Billy put the brown sack on his car and said, "I heard a noise like somebody hollering."

"Was it Mr. Logan's voice?" Iavarone asked.

"No, sir."

"After you heard a voice call out, what, if anything, happened next?"

"I heard a loud noise," Bob said. "He flew back."

"How far did Mr. Logan fly back?"

"About four or five feet," Bob said. Then, he said, he heard another gunshot and saw what appeared to be a rifle or shotgun being pulled in through the rear passenger window.

That rear car door then opened, he said. "I seen a man get out."

"What did he have with him?" Iavarone asked.

"It was a handgun."

The man, he said, made a bending motion toward the curb. "Then my dog lunged for the car," Bob said. "I lunged for my dog."

The tension in the courtroom had steadily built to this moment. There were no courtroom murmurs. No one moved.

"And after you grabbed your dog, what, if anything, happened?" Iavarone asked, his voice calm, controlled.

"Well, me and that man stared at each other," Bob said.

"How far away from that man were you?"

"About four feet."

"Did you see that man's face?"

"Yes, sir."

"How were you able to see the man's face?"

"There was a streetlight above us." Bob tried to lick his lips, but his mouth had gone dry. He continued to stare only at Iavarone. It was then, and just then, that he realized that he was no longer nervous. He was not afraid. It was for this moment that he had uprooted his family, quit his job, and put himself, his wife, and his children in jeopardy.

"How long did you look at that man?" Iavarone asked.

"Four seconds."

"What was that man doing?"

"Looking at me."

"Mr. Lowe," Iavarone said. "I'd like you to look around the courtroom and see if you see that man in court today. Do you see him?"

Finally, Bob allowed himself to look away from Iavarone. Slowly, he turned toward the defense table and came face to face with Harry, and he realized that the face he was looking at was the face that had been roaming through his nightmares for so many months.

"Yes, sir," Bob said, without hesitation. He lifted his left hand to point. "The man in the blue shirt and tie, a blue suit, wearing glasses."

Across the courtroom, Harry, his eyes invisible behind tinted glasses, sat impassively next to Whalen. After pausing for a beat, then two beats,

Iavarone continued. "After you stared at this man, what, if anything, happened?"

"I ran," Bob said, dropping his arm. "Across the street. Jumped behind some shrubbery, trees that had been cut down the same day." He said he heard another shot, then a car door slam.

"I heard it drive away," he added.

The rest of Iavarone's questions and Bob's answers went quickly. Bob described Harry's clothing as "dark" and recalled how he had picked out Harry's photograph right after the shooting and then again four years later.

Iavarone flipped through his notes one last time, then gathered them, stacked them neatly, and looked toward Whalen.

"Your witness, counsel," he said and sat down.

After a short recess, Whalen pounced and the verbal battle began.

"Mr. Lowe," he said, "have you changed your story between what was previously given and what you testified to here today?"

"No, sir," Bob said, a note of surprise in his voice.

"On September twenty-seventh, nineteen seventy-two, Mr. Lowe, you made a statement to the investigating police officer right after this occurrence," Whalen declared. "And at that time, Mr. Lowe, did you tell the officers that shortly after eleven o'clock, you had let your shepherd dog out and that you saw two occupants in a nineteen-seventy or nineteen-seventy-one Mercury Cougar or Montego parked in front of your house?"

"No, sir."

"Is it your contention that the interviewing officer would put down something that you didn't tell him?"

"Objection," Iavarone said.

"Objection sustained," Wilson declared.

"Did you tell the officer that the car was of a dark color, possibly black, and that you saw the car drive west on Walton and then heard three gunshots in succession?"

"Objection," Iavarone repeated.

"Overruled."

"Yes," Bob said, "that I seen a car drive west on Walton, but not the part that I heard the gunshot blasts."

"Did you tell them that you saw a man getting into the suspect car and then saw the car pull away at a high rate of speed?"

"No."

"You did not?" Whalen said, brandishing a sheet of paper. "Any reason why the investigating officer would put something in there that you didn't tell them, Mr. Witness?"

Iavarone objected again. "He is taking it out of context, Your Honor."

"Sustained."

Whalen paced behind the lectern. "Well, we'll take it one by one, Mr. Witness. We'll find out which one they didn't take down properly."

"Objection, objection," Iavarone snapped.

Wilson shot a warning look at Whalen. "All right," the judge said. "That last remark will be stricken from the record."

Whalen plunged ahead, asking questions about what Bob had told the police, carefully crafting his questions to include a minute piece of incorrect information so that Bob would have to deny making the statement. Bob, a man inexperienced in the ways of the courtroom and fearful that he would be caught in a lie, felt hamstrung by the literal truth and became increasingly uneasy as Whalen picked at his every word.

"You said you were employed at a gas station, is that right?" Whalen asked.

"Yes, sir."

"How long had you worked at that gas station?"

"I don't know, sir."

Now Whalen turned to face the jury box, apparently forgetting it was filled with journalists, not jurors. "You don't know how long you worked there?" he asked sarcastically. "Prior to that job, where did you work?"

"Oscar Mayer," Bob said, recalling his work for the meat-processing firm.

"And before the job with Oscar Mayer, where did you work?"

"I don't remember," he said.

"You want the court, Mr. Witness to believe—"

"Objection," Iavarone interrupted.

"—to believe that you can remember an identification, a face—" Whalen barreled forward, but Wilson stopped him.

"Objection sustained."

"I was moving around, trying to find a steady job that I liked," Bob said, ignoring Wilson. "I worked at quite a few places."

"Well, Mr. Witness," Whalen said, puffing himself up, "do you have a bad memory?"

"Objection, judge," Iavarone said.

Wilson paused. "He can answer that. Overruled."

The judge turned to face him.

"No, sir," Bob replied, his irritation growing. Whalen's demeanor was rude and sarcastic. His questions were insulting. Bob looked at the prosecution table, searching for Iavarone's eyes, but the prosecutor had his head down, scribbling notes on a yellow legal pad. To Bob, this lack of visual contact was because he was doing so badly on the stand. But to Iavarone, it was his way of not giving Whalen cause to suggest that he was in any way influencing Bob's answers. Still, it was awkward for both men.

"How much money, goods, and services has been rendered to you by any official of this state, the State's Attorney's Office, the state of Illinois, or the federal government?" Whalen asked.

"About four thousand dollars."

Using a list supplied by Iavarone prior to trial, Whalen then launched into a series of questions designed to elicit each individual benefit Bob had received: rent payments, replacement salary checks, the per diem when he was out of state, and the payment for a life insurance premium.

"Mr. Witness," Whalen said. "You testified that you had received about four thousand dollars. I advise you that you have now testified to receiving seven thousand five hundred seventy dollars. And I ask you, which is the correct amount?"

Bob spoke slowly, trying to control his growing anger at Whalen. "I guess the second would be accurate. I didn't know for sure. I was estimating."

"Well," Whalen snapped, "have you been estimating throughout your testimony here?"

"Objection, judge!" Iavarone stood up.

"Objection sustained," Wilson said.

It didn't matter, though. Whalen was accomplishing his objective: Bob was simmering. Whalen pounded at the financial issue further, suggesting that Bob decided to become a state-paid witness because he was deeply in debt.

"Yes, I owed money, but not great sums," Bob said.

Whalen pointed out that Fran's stay for gallbladder surgery at Augustana Hospital, where police officers Mudry and Law had found him the previous October, had generated a bill of $2,240.

"When your rent is being paid and you are receiving one thousand dollars a month in cash from the State's Attorney, did you ever take any of that money over to Augustana and pay them what you owed them?"

"No, sir," Bob replied.

"Did you beat them out of the money?" Whalen asked.

"Objection!" Claps and Iavarone said in unison, both rising from their chairs like twin jack-in-the-boxes.

"Sustained."

Unbowed, Whalen tried again. "Your conditions improved after you made your negotiations with the State's Attorney, did they not, Mr. Witness?"

"No, sir."

Whalen totaled aloud and asked Bob to confirm other debts: $1,300 to a furniture store, $300 to a carpet store, $1,100 on his car. He also owed money to three personal loan companies, but couldn't remember the amounts. By now, Bob was reeling on the stand. Whalen was painting him as an opportunist who leaped at a chance to duck his debts and start a new life on the government dole. Skillfully, Whalen had managed to skirt the truth—that the debts were not erased. Instead, Williams and Iavarone had negotiated a temporary suspension of Bob's debt payments until after the trial, when he could get back to a normal life.

Whalen gestured toward Harry at the defense table. "This man, you say he stared at you?"

"Yes, sir."

"But you told the agents at that time that you were collaring your dog," Whalen said. "Where was your dog at this time?"

"When I ran, I let go of the dog," Bob said. "And I don't know where she went."

"How was this man dressed that you stared at for four seconds?" Whalen asked.

"I was looking at his face," Bob replied.

"Well, it was a brightly lighted area," Whalen retorted, feigning indignation. "It was bright enough to see good, wasn't it, Mr. Witness?"

"Yes, sir."

"And you can't tell the court what the man was wearing?" said Whalen, sounding incredulous.

"I wasn't looking at anything but his face."

"Was he wearing a sweater?"

"I didn't notice—" Bob began, but Iavarone cut him off with another objection. Wilson swatted him down again: "Overruled."

"Was he wearing a coat?"

"I don't know, sir," Bob said, his voice hinting at the snarl of a cornered, wounded animal.

"Was he wearing a windbreaker?"

"I don't know, sir."

"Was he wearing an overcoat?"

"I don't know, sir," Bob repeated.

Whalen stepped to the jury box—proving that old instincts die hard, as there was no jury, only the press—and in a tone that had long ago earned him the nickname "Voice of Doom," said, "You want the court to believe that you stared at a man for four seconds, and you can't tell me one thing as to his apparel?"

Iavarone objected, but was, again, overruled.

"All I had on my mind was his face," Bob declared and fired back a shot of his own. "I'll never forget that face as long as I live."

Whalen gave it right back. "I'll ask that that be stricken, Your Honor."

"It will be stricken from the record," Wilson intoned. "It was not responsive."

Like a prizefighter who senses his opponent is damaged and ready to hit the canvas, Whalen unleashed a flurry of questions.

"Well, did this man see you?" he asked.

"Apparently, yes," Bob replied.

"Did he raise his gun and point it at you?"

"Not to my knowledge."

"Did he shoot at you?"

"Not to my knowledge."

"Did he smile at you?"

"No, sir."

"Did he talk to you?"

"No, sir."

"What color were his shoes?" Whalen demanded.

"I didn't look at his shoes, sir," Bob said.

The question-and-answer session continued with Whalen hammering at Bob's finances, and Iavarone frequently, but unsuccessfully, objecting. Finally, Whalen turned his back on the witness stand and said, "No further questions, Your Honor."

Iavarone's best attempts to rehabilitate Bob—to undo whatever damage the defense examination might have done—were rebuffed by Wilson, who repeatedly sustained Whalen's objections.

"Mr. Lowe," Iavarone asked, "are you testifying here today because of the money the state gave you?"

"Objection."

"Sustained."

"Mr. Lowe," Iavarone asked, "did your father want you to testify?"

"Object."

"Sustained."

"Did your wife want you to testify?"

"Object!" Whalen shouted.

"Sustained," Wilson thundered. "The last three questions will be stricken from the record."

"Your Honor—" said Iavarone, weakly.

"Sustained," Wilson repeated angrily.

"Your Honor, I'm just trying—" Iavarone began.

"Counsel," Wilson snapped, "you know it's improper. I have stricken them from the record."

Iavarone tried again. "Are you close to your father?"

"The same objection," Whalen said. He had stood up to make his first objection and remained standing, poised to object as soon as the words were out of Iavarone's mouth.

"Sustained."

"Has your and your family's life been pleasant the last—"

"Objection, Judge."

"Objection sustained."

"Why do you remember the defendant's face?" Iavarone asked.

"Object," Whalen said.

"Sustained," Wilson said. "The objection has been ruled upon. Be seated."

"Will you ever forget that face?" asked Iavarone.

Whalen jumped up again. "Objection."

"Sustained," Wilson said. "Leading question. It's improper. It will be stricken from the record."

Defeated, Iavarone sat down, saying, "No further questions."

19

"Would you state your name, please?"

"Mrs. Ruth Aleman," the woman said, folding her hands before her.

Blonde, with long, manicured fingernails and a husky smoker's voice, Ruth looked toward Harry at the defense table and was comforted by the small smile that he gave her. She then focused on Whalen, who stood at the lectern in the middle of the courtroom. Though this was her first time on a witness stand, Ruth displayed none of the nervousness common to such debuts.

"Are you the wife of the defendant, Harry Aleman?" asked Whalen.

"Yes, I am," said Ruth.

"How long have you been married?"

"Thirteen years."

"Do you have any children?"

"Yes, we do," said Ruth. "Four."

Under Whalen's polite questioning, Ruth explained that on the night of September 27, 1972, she had driven Harry to Golf Land, a public driving range less than ten minutes from their home. "It was around seven o'clock," she said. "I talked to the boys that he played golf with—Joe Gizzi, Dennis Colucci, and Anthony Padavonia."

"Did you leave the golf range?" Whalen asked.

"Yes," Ruth replied. "I went back home." She went on to explain that she had returned sometime after 10 P.M. "I parked my car, got out of my car, walked over to where my husband and Joe Gizzi were hitting a bushel of balls, and sat there as they continued hitting balls. When they got done, we all sat at a table and talked."

"What time did you leave the driving range?" Whalen asked.

"I would say around midnight, a little before or a little after," Ruth said.

Whalen turned to Iavarone and Claps and, in what they considered a smug tone and exaggerated formality, said, "You may inquire, gentlemen."

"A few questions only," said Iavarone, rising to his feet.

"Mrs. Aleman, do you love your husband?" he asked.

"Yes, I do," said Ruth.

"Do you want to see your husband go to jail?"

"Definitely not," she said.

Whalen next called James Griffin, one of the Chicago police officers who had interviewed Bob on the night Billy was killed. Griffin was a veteran detective who had conducted hundreds of homicide investigations in his twenty-year career.

"You have taken many statements," Whalen began. "You put down what you are told and you do not omit or add to those statements, is that true?"

"Objection, leading question," Iavarone said.

"Let's get to it," Wilson replied. "Let him answer the question."

"I have incorporated in my reports statements the witnesses or defendants have told me. Yes, sir."

"And you didn't add anything that they didn't tell you, did you?"

"No, I haven't," Griffin said.

"And you didn't omit anything that they told you either, is that true?" Whalen asked.

"That is true."

"Officer Griffin," Whalen said. "I call your attention to the night of the twenty-seventh of September nineteen seventy-two, or the early morning hours of the following date. Did you interview one Bobby Lowe?"

"Yes, sir," Griffin said. "I did."

Waving a copy of Griffin's report, Whalen looked at the officer. "Did the witness, Bobby Lowe, on that night, tell you that he was eye to eye with a man, that he stared at him for four seconds, and that his dog lunged at the man and that he then fled and hid in some bushes? Did he tell you that, Officer Griffin?"

"No, sir, he didn't," Griffin said.

The rustle of reporters' notebooks was audible from the jury box. Heads down, they began writing furiously.

"Did he tell you in that statement that he was one foot away from the suspect's car?" Whalen asked.

"No, sir, he didn't," Griffin said.

Whalen turned to face the prosecution table. "You may examine," he said, and sat down.

Rising from his chair, Iavarone asked, "Officer Griffin, where did you interview Bobby Lowe on that night?"

"At the hospital," Griffin said.

"Now, when you interviewed Bobby Lowe, didn't he express to you that he was fearful of retaliation?"

"Yes, sir," Griffin said. "He did."

"Didn't he also request his name not go to the newspaper or be circulated to anyone?"

"Yes, he did," Griffin said.

"Did you ask Bobby Lowe whether or not he could identify the person who got out of the car that night?" Iavarone asked.

"Specifically, no, sir," Griffin replied.

"What were you interested in that night?"

"In what he saw and the vehicle and the man that got out of the car," Griffin replied.

"Why were you interested in the vehicle?" Iavarone asked.

"For registration on the vehicle—to see who the owner was," Griffin said.

"And isn't that what you concentrated your questioning of Bobby Lowe on—the vehicle?"

"Yes, sir, I did."

"Officer Griffin, that night, did you push Bobby Lowe for details?"

"Objection," Whalen said.

"Sustained," Wilson declared.

"Did you ask Bobby Lowe to go into the details of everything he did?" Iavarone asked.

"Objection," Whalen said again.

"Sustained," the judge said.

"I have no further questions," Iavarone said.

Whalen next called the manager of a finance company, who testified that Bob had borrowed $560 in 1972, but the loan had been written off because the company couldn't locate Bob. Under cross-examination, the manager admitted that Bob had repaid the loan, a few days before the beginning of the trial.

Next up were Harry's driving range buddies, one after the other. All swore under oath that they had been hitting golf balls with Harry at the time Bill Logan was gunned down. Colucci added that he particularly remembered that night because he had seen a newspaper account of Billy's murder the day after the shooting.

Iavarone and Claps were unable to poke holes in their stories and each witness answered questions with obvious animosity in their voices. The best the prosecutors could do was force each to admit that they were Harry's long-time friends. Gizzi recalled that he and Harry had split a bushel of golf balls and launched into a discussion of driving range economics. "There is different sizes," he said. "This was a big bushel. The reason we always split a big bushel was because we always get two or three extra baskets."

He further recalled that Ruth had dropped Harry off and come back, remaining with them until the range closed. "We kind of sit around and kibitz until they close or kick us out. It was after twelve o'clock."

Claps pressed Gizzi on his reasons for testifying, saying, "You wouldn't want to see anything happen to Mr. Aleman, would you?"

"Absolutely not," Gizzi said.

"And when did you first learn that Mr. Aleman was charged with the murder of William Logan?" Claps asked.

"When it broke out in the papers," he said.

"And at the time, did you go to any members of law enforcement or State's Attorney's Office and tell them that Mr. Aleman was with you on September twenty-seventh, nineteen seventy-two?" Claps asked.

"Why should I?" Gizzi said, belligerently.

"Would you answer my question?"

Gizzi leaned forward in the witness chair and said again, louder and almost threateningly, "Why should I?"

That prompted Wilson to bark, "Just answer the question. You don't ask them."

"Yes or no?" said Claps.

"He'd already been charged with the crime," Gizzi said.

"Just answer the question," Wilson said.

"No," said Gizzi.

He was the last witness called in the trial.

Because the prosecution has the burden of proof, it is allowed to give two closing arguments sandwiched around that of the defense. Claps led off and, as is typical for prosecutors, gave a low-key, factual summary of the case, devoting a large portion of his remarks to Bob's testimony.

"Bobby Lowe finds himself face to face with the murderer, with Harry Aleman," Claps said. "He sees the forty-five in his hand. He has lost sight of William Logan, but he knows he is behind the car somewhere. And for a moment, for four seconds, they are face to face under that light.

"I would suggest to Your Honor that those four seconds—face to face with the man with the gun, face to face with the man who Bobby Lowe just saw shoot down William Logan—is an eternity. Bobby Lowe observed Harry Aleman and Harry Aleman observed Bobby Lowe. For over four and a half years, Bobby Lowe has been waiting to see that man, knowing that he was an eyewitness. He could never forget his face." Claps concluded by branding the defense case as "completely unbelievable" and "nothing more than a lie."

Whalen rose from his chair and strode to the lectern. He paused for a full minute.

"Judge Wilson," Whalen said.

The judge nodded.

"Gentlemen of the prosecution," he continued, casting a glance toward Iavarone and Claps and then turning to look directly at Wilson.

"In my opening statement, I told the Court that the evidence adduced by the state would be in such absolute hopeless conflict that no man could be found guilty under that evidence. With the opening testimony of Mr. Almeida, the Court witnessed an attempted miscarriage of justice."

He assailed Louie as a professional criminal and would-be assassin who was so psychologically unbalanced that he attempted suicide while in prison. "He's going to do anything and say anything to get out," Whalen declared.

He tore into Bob, ridiculing his testimony about picking Harry's picture out of the mug-shot book in the days after Logan was killed. "If he had picked out the photo of Harry Aleman and said, 'This is the man that I saw commit the murder,' Mr. Aleman would have been arrested the next day," Whalen declared. "That is perjury, Your Honor. Rank perjury. There is no record of him picking out any pictures of the defendant. And, Your Honor, that should be enough. I should be able to rest this case right now."

But he didn't. Instead, Whalen continued in rousing fashion. Even the press was riveted. "The case rests upon the tainted, perjurious testimony of Almeida, plus the tainted and impeached testimony of the witness Bobby Lowe."

He urged Wilson to study the record of Bob's finances. "It shows further what type of liar he was," he said. "We take a man here—he is interviewed after four years—hopelessly in debt. Hopelessly in debt, and they promise him a new identity and work if he will become a witness."

Whalen had worked himself into a lather and now the "Voice of Doom" was resonating through the courtroom, impressing even the most jaded reporters. "And they are paying him one thousand dollars a month, plus his rent—two hundred seventy-five dollars—plus vacation trips," he thundered.

"Mr. Lowe expects and hopes that this case is continued for a year so he can continue on. And then, if he gets that new identity, he can't be found and he escapes all these creditors."

"In closing—"

Motion from the right corner of his eye caught Whalen's attention and he stopped. At the defense table, Harry waved him over. Whalen bent at the waist and lowered his head next to Harry's face. After a few seconds of whispering, Whalen nodded and returned to the lectern, where he noted that he had been reminded that he was about to omit his characterization of the gunshot evidence.

Shotgun pellets, he told Wilson, had killed Billy. Bob had testified to hearing three shots. Billy's body bore no powder burns from the close-range discharge of a gun. No bullet was found. Therefore, he argued, Bob had lied about a third shot.

"Let me say this, Your Honor," Whalen said. "You, sir, have witnessed an attempt at a miscarriage of justice. The state has utterly failed to prove the defendant guilty beyond a reasonable doubt."

Speaking without notes, Iavarone counterattacked in rebuttal. "The defendant has tried to shift the blame or shift the attention to every other witness put on the stand, and that isn't going to work. The reason is because Harry Aleman stands out. He is a cancer on the soul of humanity. That man doesn't look at human beings as vibrant individuals, alive with emotion, but merely as targets, just as he saw William Logan—a target to be cut down using his shotgun, that special sickle of death that he brought with him in that work car."

Methodically, Iavarone ticked off twenty-eight points of Louie's testimony that had been backed up by other evidence. "This man has been corroborated by every single occurrence witness that took the stand. We know something else. We know that the name called out was Billy. Every other witness here testified that this was William Logan. That's how they referred to him—Billy, a name out of childhood."

Heads swiveled as now Iavarone raised his arm and pointed directly at Harry. "And that man grew up with him in the same neighborhood," Iavarone declared. Harry sat silently in his chair. He did not move.

"Then we look at Bobby Lowe, a man who has no motive at all to lie, a man who Mr. Whalen tried to vilify," Iavarone said. "If Bobby Lowe had done anything illegal, Mr. Whalen would have shown it. All he has done is try, by innuendo, to destroy the credibility of a witness whom he could not shake. What has Bobby Lowe gone through? On the night of the killing, he said he saw the man. He could have said he didn't. Officer Griffin said he was frightened, that he was fearful of retaliation. And who wouldn't be? Four years later, Bobby Lowe could have said, 'I don't want to get involved.' But Bobby Lowe got involved. And Bobby Lowe stood up for everybody in this courtroom.

"He quit a job that he liked," continued Iavarone, leaning on the lectern. "He has moved away from his family, his relatives, his friends. He has lived out of a suitcase. His life has changed and will never be the same again. Why did he go through that?"

"He did it for you, Your Honor, so that you could hear what happened that night when he saw that"—Iavarone pointed at Harry again—"cowardly killer strike down William Logan.

"Everything that Bobby Lowe testified to has been corroborated," Iavarone declared. "When Mr. Whalen asked him, 'Do you ask the court to believe you don't remember the clothing?' he answered, 'I'll never forget that face.' And, Your Honor, I ask you to look at the face and those eyes." He gestured toward the defense table. "For there sits evil itself. And you would not forget it, either, if you had stared at that man, face to face for four seconds, after he brutally murdered another human being."

Reporters feverishly took notes as Iavarone paused to draw a white handkerchief from inside his suit jacket and wiped at the sweat streaking the sides of his face. "Bob Lowe has gone through an ordeal for four years for us," he said. "We cannot desert him now. If that killer walks out of this courtroom, we'll be deserting Bob Lowe. And we'll be deserting every other potential witness that ever witnesses a crime.

"Each and every one of those alibi witnesses only came in because Harry Aleman told them to. And you had better do what Harry Aleman says. William Logan didn't do it, and he's dead."

Whalen couldn't take it any longer. "Objection, Your Honor," he shouted. "This is so prejudicial."

"Overruled," Wilson said. "Let him proceed with his argument."

"We seek justice and no more than justice," Iavarone said. "We believe that with this overwhelming evidence, Your Honor, that justice requires one verdict and one verdict alone—that he be found guilty. That Harry Aleman not be allowed to come into this courtroom and ask the system of justice to validate his hunting license. We must no longer allow him to stalk his prey in the streets of Chicago like he did William Logan." He dropped his voice to a near whisper. "We ask for justice. We ask that he be found guilty. Thank you, Your Honor."

"Pull over. Pull this damn thing over now," said Bob Lowe. Tom Petersik, the agent driving the dark blue van, flicked on his turn signal and eased the vehicle onto the shoulder of Interstate 290, then glanced at the agent sitting next to him before turning around to face Bob and Fran in the back seat.

"I want to hear this and we ain't moving this thing until I hear the verdict," Bob declared. He pulled a pack of Marlboros from his left shirt pocket, shook one out, flicked his lighter, and inhaled deeply.

They were headed to the northwest suburbs—house hunting, looking for a permanent living arrangement for the family after the weeks and months of living out of suitcases, cramped into tiny, dingy motel rooms, apartments, and condominiums. Now, according to the radio bulletin, Bob and Fran were about to learn if it had been worth the discomfort and disruption.

"Turn that up, will ya?" Bob asked. The voice on the radio was urgent.

. . . case of reputed mob hit man Harry Aleman. After five days of trial, Judge Frank Wilson has retired to his chambers to make a decision. If Aleman is convicted, criminal justice experts say it will be the first time

in Chicago history that an organized crime hit man has been found guilty of one of his murders. We will go live to our correspondent outside the courthouse when we have a verdict to report.

Four long days had passed since Bob had been ushered from Frank Wilson's courtroom. Iavarone had spoken with him briefly in the vestibule behind the courtroom on his way out, offering words of thanks and encouragement. But he had been brisk, already moving on to the next witness, the next exhibit. Drained, Bob had shaken his hand and slipped into the river of security that swept him down the elevator and out of the building to the van and the ride back to his family.

Bob tapped his cigarette on the armrest before lighting it as the all-news radio station moved on to a report about the stock market. "What's taking so long?" Bob said.

Not long before, after hearing the closing arguments, Wilson had declared a recess while he went into his chambers to study his trial notes, promising to return before 1 P.M. The spectators and press kept their seats and traded opinions on whose argument had been the most effective, the most dynamic.

The hiss of traffic became louder as Bob opened the window of the van and flicked another cigarette out into the stream of traffic.

"How much longer can it be?" Fran asked.

"I don't give a damn, I'm not moving until I know," Bob said. He flicked his lighter again. Fran noticed that his hand trembled ever so slightly as he held it to the cigarette and inhaled deeply.

Iavarone realized a verdict was near when a platoon of sheriff's deputies flooded the courtroom, flanking the spectator seats and blocking the side and rear entrances. Seconds later, Wilson was settling into his chair. He held several pages from a legal pad in his left hand and he cast a stern look about the room. "When I announce my decision, I will not tolerate any outbursts by anybody in this courtroom," he declared. "The deputies have been so instructed. I wish nobody to leave this courtroom until after I have finished reading my few remarks."

He thanked the prosecutors and Whalen for their hard work, their punctuality, their preparation, and for the minimum of bickering between sides.

"I have sat in this courtroom for almost ten years," Wilson said. "I have presided over one thousand cases. I have had tough cases, easy cases, long cases, short cases. In fact, from this same bench, I have sentenced two different defendants to the electric chair."

The courtroom was tomb-quiet. No one coughed. No one whispered. Iavarone and Claps sat at the prosecution table, their eyes on Wilson. Whalen and Harry sat side by side. Neither spoke. They, too, watched the judge.

"Although this case has created a certain amount of public interest, it is not a particularly difficult one," Wilson continued. "The case took only one week to try and the facts are not that involved. I have listened to all the witnesses in the case, examined the exhibits, and heard the final arguments of counsel. I will not at this time go into each witness's testimony. The main issue is the credibility and the weight to be given to the state's two main witnesses, Louis Almeida and Bob Lowe. Also the pathologist, Doctor Shalgos. He testified that there was not any evidence of handgun bullet wounds on the body."

The reading of a decision from the bench is a curious exercise in frustration and body language. As a judge reads, his audience watches and listens, straining to discern from his words, his tone, and his posture what his final decision will be. Opinions sway as first the words hint at conviction, then bespeak acquittal. Wilson tipped his hand almost immediately. He said Louie had been impeached. He said Bob had been exposed as a man whose story of that night improved dramatically in four years. And Wilson discarded any explanation that Bob had either been too fearful or the police had failed to ask the right questions in that first interview at the hospital.

"It is well established in the field of evidence that the first story told, when the memory is more recent and when less time for the play of influence has elapsed, is inherently more trustworthy than the testimony from the stand," Wilson said. "It goes back to the old saying: Is he telling the truth now or was he telling the truth then? We all know that Lowe did not tell the truth on the witness stand last Friday. The fact that Lowe lied on the witness stand must naturally cast a cloud over his entire testimony. My job here is not to say whether the defendant is innocent and I do not say at this time that he is innocent. That is between him and his God. It is my duty to rule whether the state has carried the burden of proof in proving the defendant guilty beyond a reasonable doubt."

Wilson looked up momentarily, and then continued to read, "My decision may not be a popular one. But for those who disagree, I wish to state that every defendant, and I mean every defendant, no matter who he might be, is entitled to a fair trial and must be proven guilty beyond a reasonable doubt, whether it is a gang shooting or the mere stealing of a bicycle." He began to speak quickly. "Because of the variance of the testimony, the lack of evidence of a bullet wound in the body of the victim, and because of the credibility of Bob Lowe, so badly shaken by the unbelievable number of impeachments, and Mr. Almeida, as an accomplice under the grant of immunity, whose past criminal record, as well as impeachment, puts great doubt upon his testimony—I find the state has fallen far short of their burden."

Wilson paused.

"The defendant is not guilty."

There was silence for several beats, then a burst of motion as reporters leaped from their seats and headed for the doors. At the defense table, Whalen pumped Harry's hand. The spectator section behind him was a riot of hugs and kisses. At the center was Ruth, who turned and smiled broadly at Harry. He nodded and smiled back.

A minute later, the news reached the van parked on the side of the road. Bob was in shock as he listened to the voice of a radio reporter.

Harry Aleman and his lawyer are being mobbed by the press as they come out of the Criminal Court building. They are not stopping to answer questions. I repeat: Judge Frank Wilson has just acquitted Harry Aleman of the murder of William Logan. In reaching his decision, the judge said he could not believe the two prosecution witnesses. The men—one a

neighbor who said he saw the shooting, the other a convicted felon who
said he drove the murder car—were not credible, the judge ruled.

Without warning, Bob slammed a fist into the seat of the van. "Turn this
goddammed thing around," he roared. "Take us back!"

Fran, her face ashen, said nothing. She stared at Bob as she would a
stranger. The agents turned toward him.

"Now, Bob—" Petersik started to say.

"Dammit," Bob shouted. "You heard me! Turn this fucker around. I want
to go home. Not Twin Lakes. Not a fucking motel. Home. This is bullshit!
I just sacrificed my life for nothing. Just take us home. Take us back to Walton Street, right goddammed now."

The agents exchanged a look.

"Bob," Petersik said, "you can't go home"—he paused—"ever."

The verdict was plastered across the top of the next morning's newspapers.
"Judge acquits 'hit' suspect," the *Chicago Tribune* blared, streaming the headline above a photograph of Harry, tight-lipped and wearing his aviator-style
tinted glasses, and Ruth leaving the Criminal Courts building, surrounded
by a pack of reporters, television cameras, microphones, and curious eyes.

State's Attorney Bernard Carey and Chicago Police Homicide Commander Joseph DiLeonardi were quoted in the papers, expressing outrage and
demanding that legislators close the loophole that allowed a defendant to
waive a jury trial without agreement of the prosecution.

"I have never seen a stronger case," Carey declared. "I only wish a jury
could have heard this case. We will never have a better case involving a gangland assassination unless the police catch the killer with the smoking gun in
his hand standing over his victim's corpse."

Any discrepancies in Bob Lowe's testimony, he said, were minor and did
not mar the substance of his testimony. "The unrehearsed truth often has
minor discrepancies," Carey said. "Usually, a judge's suspicions should be
aroused when a witness's testimony is too smooth."

"Without people like Bob Lowe, there is no way in the world we in law enforcement can break up the animalistic organization called the crime syndicate," Police Commander DiLeonardi declared.

On the floor of the Illinois legislature, Wilson was vilified as a "craven judge." The *Tribune* labeled the verdict a "tragedy." The *Sun-Times* quoted legal organizations that called Wilson "unqualified" to be a judge.

Joanna Dietrich, one of Billy Logan's sisters, was inconsolable, weeping as she left the courthouse. "If they let him walk the streets, they'll let anybody walk the streets," she said between sobs. "There will never be any witnesses coming to Criminal Court. Never again."

Carey disclosed for the first time that Wilson had forbidden Iavarone and Claps from introducing the attempted bribery of Ella Jo DeMarco into evidence at the trial. Further, Carey noted that Wilson had impounded the transcript of the legal debate that had taken place in his chambers.

"The judge would not allow us to present evidence that would have been very important in this case," Carey said. "It involved a bribe attempt and a threat on a witness. Evidence was presented to the judge, but he would not allow testimony."

He also explained that, although police officer James Griffin did testify that Bob was frightened and only gave a sketchy account of the killing on the night of the incident, Wilson had forbidden the prosecutors from eliciting, on cross-examination, testimony that Griffin had not pressed Bob to elaborate.

Wilson, disregarding the unwritten rule of judicial silence following a verdict, fired back. He issued a statement defending his decision and denying as rumor a newspaper report that he had been the target of threats before the trial that included the receipt of a doctored photograph depicting mutilated bodies of his family. Wilson reiterated the final portion of Whalen's argument (the portion that Whalen almost forgot until Harry interrupted his closing remarks) that related to the missing bullet from the third gunshot. "If a handgun was used, where is the bullet, the bullet wounds, or expended cartridge case if it was a forty-five-caliber automatic?" Wilson asked in his statement. "This lack of evidence was just another factor that created reasonable doubt."

Finally, Wilson ridiculed Carey for his comments about DeMarco, saying her testimony would have been "rank hearsay. Every lawyer who took a course of evidence in law school would know that."

Carey fired right back, branding Wilson's explanation silly and absurd. "We wanted her to testify in open court. Why was this kept secret? There was no jury to influence. From whom was he hiding this? The public? The press? Judge Wilson himself has convicted and sentenced to long prison terms many defendants on far less evidence."

Wilson found himself standing nearly alone in the court of public opinion, as lawmen united to tear at his decision. One of his few supporters was William Murphy, an assistant public defender who frequently worked in Wilson's courtroom. In a letter that appeared on the editorial page of the *Tribune*, Murphy accused the press of attempting to "coerce and influence Judge Wilson into finding Aleman guilty without regard to the strength of the prosecution's case. Judge Wilson's decision," Murphy wrote, "was a profile in judicial courage."

Bob awoke with a painful hangover. In anticipation of a conviction, Dave Williams had previously arranged for Bob and Fran to spend the evening of the verdict's delivery in a suburban Marriott resort as a reward for the months of inconvenience. But what was to have been a celebration became a wake. Joined by Fran's brother, George, and sister, Patty, they began with dinner, but Bob refused to eat, saying he wasn't hungry. The truth was, he was afraid he wouldn't be able to keep any food down. Instead, he began ordering drink after drink after drink. And as the night went on and the group moved to the hotel bar, the Jack Daniel's went down easier and easier, and his simmering anger began to boil.

"Here's to nothing," Bob declared, raising his glass in toast.

"Bob, it's almost two A.M., let's go to bed," Fran said. "You've had enough."

"There ain't enough for me to drink," Bob said. "Let's drink to getting away with murder. That's what happened, babe. Harry got away with murder."

"You did the right thing," Fran said.

"Bullshit," he retorted. "You didn't see what that lawyer did to me in there. You weren't in that courtroom. I was the one that was on trial, not Harry. Damn." He drained his glass. "Barkeeper, another Jack on the rocks."

"Shhhh, not so loud," Fran said, aware of the irritated looks from patrons at the other end of the bar.

"One more," Bob said, slurring the words. "Make it a double, goddammit." He stared at Fran. "Don't you get it? Don't you see what happened? Harry won. I lost. What do we get? Months of shit, living out of suitcases, driving all over hell. Did you like that?"

Fran sighed. "You know how I feel," she said.

"We got a life insurance policy. So what? I got to get killed for that to mean shit," he said. "I got no job. We got no home. This is the last time we're ever going to see my family, your family. Harry? Shit, he gets to go home, to his home, goddammit. And where are we? Did the right thing? I don't think so. I've been beat. That's what it is. I've been beat."

They did not stay the night in the hotel, but returned to the cabin in Twin Lakes, where they had been living for the past two weeks. Bob staggered into bed and passed out immediately.

Now, with the sun breaking through the pines that circled the far side of the lake, Bob bolted awake, sweat-covered and tangled in the sheets, tasting the cigarettes and booze. In his dream, he had been walking Ginger on West Walton Street and stopped to watch the dark Plymouth pull up. Harry got out and looked over at him, smiled, and aimed the shotgun at him. He had looked for the branches to hide behind, but they were gone. In his dream, he had turned and tried to flee, but found himself in the nightmarish sea where sleepers cannot move. As he struggled to dig in his toes, the shotgun roared, and he awoke.

He lay there, eyes stinging, heart pounding, and through his groggy haze, he began to feel the bitter sensations of anger and fear. Anger at himself for believing Iavarone and Williams that Harry would be convicted. Anger at Wilson and Whalen for calling him a liar. Anger at having to give up close ties with his parents and relatives. And fear of the unknown, in the form of questions he could not answer. Would Harry seek revenge? Would a friend of Harry's take him down to curry favor with the outfit? Would they find him and wait for him, early in the morning, a morning such as this? Would he walk to his truck and be dropped by a sniper's bullet? Would he turn the key in the ignition and go up in a fiery explosion?

And the dreams—how long would he be tortured by these images of blood and guns and Harry and Billy? The dreams had gradually receded early in 1973, in the months after Billy was cut down. Booze had helped him then on those sleepless nights when he had found himself staring out of the living room window onto Walton at the spot on the curb where that dark Plymouth had waited, engine idling, the night Billy died. But while alcohol brought sleep, it could not always keep away the nightmares.

Carefully and quietly, so as not to wake Fran, Bob eased out of bed, pulled on a pair of pants, and walked down a quiet path and to the end of a worn wooden pier that stretched thirty feet into the lake. As the sun glistened off the nearly still water, a cardinal sang in the high reaches of a pine bough. Bob lit a Marlboro, took a deep drag, and coughed. He remembered the first day they had arrived and borrowed a rowboat, piled in all the kids and Fran, then promptly swamped it at the edge of the pier.

He recalled the afternoon he had offered to grill hotdogs and hamburgers, but had succeeded in nearly causing a forest fire when he squirted almost an entire can of starter fluid on the charcoal and then dropped a lit match through a smoke vent in the lid. The explosion had singed his eyebrows and launched the barbecue lid twenty feet into the air.

Standing on the dock, he smiled, remembering the day that Fran and the kids had gone to a movie for the afternoon and he offered to make barbecued ribs for the security team. Before long, beers were opened and a stag film was playing on the kitchen wall. And at that moment, Fran had surprised them by returning early. "What the hell is this? Bunch of perverted bastards!" she had screamed, sending the pack of grown men scurrying outside and into the surrounding woods, leaving Bob to sheepishly shut off the eight-millimeter projector.

"I want that wall scrubbed!" Fran shouted. "I'm not gonna eat in a kitchen where that filth has been!"

Overhead, a hawk wheeled. Bob inhaled one last drag and flicked his cigarette into the water, walked up the pier and into the cottage. Inside, he crawled beneath the covers and tried to sleep.

With the end of the trial, the daily protection was dropped. There was no less danger, but the government would not provide lifetime security at taxpayers' expense. There would be no more escorts to and from the grocery store, to drop off and pick up the kids. From now on, Bob realized, they would be on their own.

Out of a combined sense of professional and personal obligation, Dave Williams did what he could to help. Through a contact at St. Paul Federal savings and loan, he arranged for a mortgage and Bob and Fran bought a home thirty-five miles northwest of West Walton Street, in Carpentersville, a small but growing suburb in Kane County. It was a cozy three-bedroom house a dozen years old and priced at $29,000. Here, under the names Jane and Joseph Reese, Bob and Fran would try to blend in, pick up the pieces, and find another life. But Bob immediately discovered the flaws and inadequacies of the witness protection program. He and Fran were given driver's licenses, but no birth certificates for them or the kids. No job history. No school history.

He was no longer Bob Lowe, but who was he?

When he met a neighbor, he could not tell the person about the man he used to be, about the dog, Ginger, that he missed, and the other dogs he raised, or about his father and mother, who he also missed but could not even call on the phone.

He needed a job but how could he get one? He ran away from his first job application when he learned he would be required to take a polygraph exam, knowing that he could not even give his new name without sending the polygraph needle off the chart.

The promises of relocation and a new life, which had sounded so mysterious and exciting, had become a reality that was complicated and fearsome. A man not accustomed to idleness, Bob turned his attention to fixing up the house, as Williams arranged for the state to temporarily continue replacing his lost salary of $250 per week. Some of the money went to pay for the mortgage, groceries, electricity, and the telephone bill. And some of it, always some of it, bought a bottle or two of Jack Daniel's. He would sit sipping the booze every night while watching TV. "It's nothing to worry about, babe," he would tell Fran, when she mentioned that the bottles were being emptied with increasing dispatch. "Just takes the edge off a little, helps me relax." It was more than that, he knew. It was not relaxation he was after, but peace. The Jack Daniel's was becoming an essential companion, something he needed just to feel normal again. It helped comfort his mind, as a blanket might warm his body on a chilly night. "Just one more, babe," he would say, as Fran headed off to bed.

Just one more, he would think, *and I can sleep. Just one more and the nightmares won't visit.*

In the months after the verdict, Bob Lowe floundered. The five days immediately following the verdict set the stage. They were a blur of booze and anger, overshadowed by feelings of humiliation and self-doubt. Why hadn't he listened to his father? Why hadn't he kept his big mouth shut? *They were all laughing at me,* he thought to himself when struck by a rare lucid moment. *They were all laughing at me: the reporters, Harry's friends, the lawyers, the cops—all of them. Especially Harry, sitting in the court, his eyes hidden behind tinted glasses.*

Bob was glad that Fran had not been in court, but that was only a fleeting comfort. She would not have been laughing, he knew that. But what was she feeling now, after those months of motels and hiding, of strange new towns, and fears now of an uncertain future? Did she still love him? How could she love a man who was beginning to hate himself?

Dave Williams had suggested Bob try to find work as soon as possible, so every day he would begin with just that intention. He would turn on the TV, spread out the newspaper ads, and pour himself a glass of Jack Daniel's. But as soon as the alcohol kicked in, the urgency eased and the importance of finding a job flickered away. He was getting nowhere.

In November, he thought he caught a break. It came in the form of a letter Williams passed on from a man named Otto Lang. It began:

The June 6th issue of Time *magazine carried a brief account of your
totally innocent involvement with a Mafia murder case. Not knowing
anything about your background, your wife, and children, I was very
much taken by the "human interest factors" of this happenstance and how
one man's life and that of his family could be so completely turned
around.*

Tell me about it, Bob thought as he read.

*It also occurred to me that this sort of a nightmare could happen to any-
one taking a casual stroll and suddenly finding oneself pulled inexorably
into a vortex of criminal vengeance, simply by having been an eyewitness to a violent crime. As a film producer and director, this story ignited
my imagination that it might possibly provide the basis for a gripping
and worthwhile motion picture.*

Bob read on, of how Lang had successfully produced the 1948 movie *Call
Northside 777,* a haunting black-and-white film in which James Stewart
played an investigative reporter for a Chicago newspaper who helps save the
son of the cleaning woman after he was wrongly convicted of murder and
sentenced to life in prison. Based on the real work of *Chicago Daily Times*
reporters Jack McPhaul and James McGuire, the film used then novel doc-
umentary techniques and featured many Chicago locations.

Bob had seen the movie, but couldn't recall many details.

With each paragraph of the two-page letter, Bob became more excited,
more hopeful. Certain sentences seemed to leap off the page:

*We would want to use your name and conceivably the title of the film
could be:* The Bobby Lowe Story!

    *Step No. 1 is to get permission to adapt your story into a screenplay.
No. 2 is to arrive at a sum of money, which would compensate you and*

your family for the rights to use your story. I propose a sum of $10,000—
off the top of my head and pending the approval of financial backers—
if and when they can be found.

Bob read the letter a dozen times, at least. For the first time since the trial he felt the flush of self-confidence. This man in the letter, this Otto Lang, with his big flourish of a signature, not only seemed to understand what Bob had put himself through, he seemed to admire it and, more to the immediate point, was willing to pay Bob to tell his story.

"A movie, babe," he said to Fran. "A movie about us."

"I don't know," she said.

"And ten thousand dollars," he said. "Almost a year's pay. That could get us on our feet."

"I just don't know," she said.

Bob was dismayed by her initial lack of enthusiasm, but he had always been able to convince her to bend his way. Optimistically, he called Williams and detailed Lang's offer.

"No way, Bob," said Williams. "It's too dangerous."

Bob was stunned. "But it's—here, listen to what else he says." He began to read from Lang's letter. " 'At no time would you ever be asked to appear in public in connection with this film, nor have a photograph of your present likeness be shown to anyone. The same restrictions would apply to all the members of your family. Your personal safety and that of your family transcends the importance of any film and should be one of your prime considerations.' You hear that, Dave? It's not going to be dangerous."

"Bob, you just can't do this. There's no way we can let this happen," said Williams. His voice was firm. "Tear up the letter. It's not going to happen. Harry's out there. You try to throw this in his face, he's not going to let that happen."

Bob tried to argue, but it was useless. After a few days, he stuck Lang's letter in a drawer and went back to reading the want ads, watching his TV, and drinking his Jack Daniel's.

Of course I felt bad for him," Williams said later, recalling the months following the trial. "I felt I had an obligation to Bob. He had stuck his neck out for us and we had forced him to give up his home, his job, and his close ties with his parents. He was sitting out there without a job, and this was a guy who needed work in his life."

With money getting tight, Bob found work at a gas station twenty miles from his house, but the work was boring and, for the first time in his life, he began drinking while on the job. Often he was so drunk by the end of his shift that after locking up the station at night, he would lie down behind the counter in the office and pass out. In the mornings, head pounding and full of guilt, he would look through the want ads, searching them desperately, as if for salvation.

And then he found it, or thought he had, in an ad for a muffler shop. It was available for "Little Money Down," with the offer to "Run Your Own Business." He called Williams and, as close to begging as he felt he had ever come, pleaded with him to see what he could do.

The muffler shop was in Janesville, a city of 50,000 in south central Wisconsin that relied for much of its economic health upon a General Motors Chevrolet plant and a Parker Pen Company factory. Williams acted as Bob's attorney. It was not a difficult deal to arrange, since it called for only $1,500 down; a monthly franchise fee was to be based on a percentage of receipts. And so Bob took over the business and began making the seventy-five-mile commute from Carpentersville. Most nights, after closing the shop and before driving home, he would wander over to a cinder-block tavern less than one hundred yards from the shop. There, he could have a couple of drinks and some conversation without worrying about people asking questions. Most of the patrons were male and minded their own business. They talked about work, bitched about their wives, and idolized the Green Bay Packers. Bob fit in easily and if you had asked the regulars about him, all they might have said was, "Joe Reese. Owns the muffler shop. Good guy."

By mid-1978, Bob had convinced Fran to make the move to Wisconsin, arguing persuasively that his commute was too long. They sold the house in Carpentersville and moved to Orfordville, a sleepy little town sixteen miles west of Janesville, settling into a three-bedroom home. For a time, things were good. The commute was a breeze, a twenty-minute drive through rolling farmland, past the corn, soybean, and alfalfa fields and dairy farms with names such as Shady Maple, Morning Glory, and Haberdale Heights.

Business was steady at the muffler shop and it fueled Bob's ambitions. He found a shuttered gas station in nearby Walworth and convinced the Union 76 Company to advance him the fuel in the ground against future sales. He installed a manager at the gas station and began turning a considerable profit. Fran and the kids enjoyed the new setting, too. She was visibly more relaxed and the kids liked their new school, the new friends. The four kids had gotten used to their new names faster than Bob and Fran. To them it was like a game and they played it without worry. Bob and Fran were closer than they had been in more than a year. Laughter and love returned to their lives. A few months after moving to Wisconsin, Fran gave Bob some news: She was pregnant with their fifth child.

Bob worked hard and drank even harder. The nights were still terrifying, filled with nightmares, but the booze sometimes helped dull them. Despite the success of his businesses and relatively calm home life, a bottle of Jack Daniel's was still always within reach: on a shelf, in his pocket, nestled on the passenger seat of his car. He drank to keep away the nightmares and he was convinced that unless he drank, he could not sleep. He had tried without the whiskey, crawling into bed and closing his eyes, and then the images would begin to play—Harry and Billy and blood. When he drank there were no images, only darkness. He would emerge from these black nights filled with a combination of remorse, guilt, and self-pity. Some mornings he promised himself he would stop, but he usually broke that promise by late afternoon.

On Thanksgiving in 1978, with the shop and station closed for the holiday, Bob began drinking after breakfast. By noon, the air thick with the smell of roasting turkey and stuffing, Bob broke the rules. He called his parents. "What are you doing for Thanksgiving?" he asked.

"Nothing," his father said. "Just sitting around."

"You having turkey dinner?"

"For just the two of us? No, your mom will just fix us a sandwich or something," Joe said.

"That ain't right," Bob said. "I miss you, Dad."

"We'll be all right, Bob," Joe replied. "I miss you, too. You doin' OK? Fran? The kids?"

"We're great and I'm gonna show you," Bob said. "You just sit tight. Don't go nowhere."

"Now, Bob, don't do anything foolish," his father said.

"You just sit tight," Bob said. He hung up the phone and walked into the kitchen and excitedly said to Fran, "Pack up the dinner. We're going to Chicago."

"What are you talking about?" Fran asked.

"Mom and Pop are alone and they aren't having turkey dinner," Bob said. "So we're gonna take it to them."

"We're not supposed to go back there," Fran said.

"To hell with that," Bob said. "How the hell is anybody gonna know?" Fran stared at him in surprise, then grinned. "OK," she said. "Let's get this together."

Within the hour, they had the dinner packed in the trunk of their car and were speeding toward Walton Street. Soon, for the first time in more than a year, Bob was home, and for a few hours, it was bliss. Amid the hugs and food and laughter, it was possible for the family to pretend (and even believe) that their world had not been shattered by what had transpired six years before when Billy Logan had been blown across his lawn. But, back in the car, driving in silence through the night to Wisconsin, Bob realized that he could not put his wife and kids in jeopardy like that again. It was too risky. At that moment the illusion of happiness or normalcy seemed just a dream.

That winter was particularly cold in Orfordville. Bob spent most of it in a drunken fog. Often, conscious he'd had one too many and embarrassed of his drunkenness, he would not go home, sleeping instead on a mattress he dragged into the muffler shop office. Just as often, though, the liquor would fill him with a sudden sense of self-righteousness and he would pile into the battered Lincoln Continental and weave home, where he would berate Fran over trifling or imagined problems. His behavior scared the children.

On one of those nights, speeding west toward home after spending the evening at a tavern, he failed to negotiate a curve and cut a furrow deep into a cornfield, half-burying the Lincoln in mud. The mud was packed so tightly in the undercarriage that after it was towed into town, he spent the better part of a week knocking out the dried loam with a crowbar.

Tiffany, their third girl and fifth child, was born on March 9, 1979, in Mercy Hospital in Janesville, and Bob got drunk. He was up to as much as two fifths of Jack Daniel's a day. Fran felt helpless.

Late that summer, for the first time, after he had been gone for two days and nights without a word, Fran locked him out the house. He discovered this when, shortly after 4 A.M., he hurtled the car to a stop behind the house. He staggered across the lawn and into the attached garage. He fumbled for his house key, dropped it, picked it up, and tried to ram it into the door-knob. But he could not make it fit.

"What the hell is this shit?" he mumbled. The keys slipped from his hand and hit the floor. "The hell with it," he said. He clenched his fingers into a fist and banged on the door. "Open the damn door," he yelled. There was no sound from inside. His fist slammed into the door again. "Open this door, dammit," he thundered.

Silence. And then, he heard steps, and Fran's voice saying, "Bob?"

"Bob?" he said, cruelly mimicking her voice. "Of course, it's Bob. Who in the hell else would it be? Just open the door."

"No, Bob," Fran said, her voice defiant. "I've had enough—too much—of your drinking. Just stay away."

At first, he could not understand what he was hearing. Slowly, his fogged and benumbed brain acknowledged what was happening. "Open the door, Fran," he said, his voice low and hard, his words slurred. "Just open the door."

"No."

He pounded on the door and threw all of his weight against it. Inside,

Fran jumped back, fearful the door would give way. Her heart racing, she screamed. "Get away from here! I don't know you anymore, Bob! You're a drunk! I can't take this anymore!"

Outside, Bob leaned against the doorframe. He lit a cigarette and slowly slid down until he was sitting on the garage floor. He began to mumble, his words nearly incoherent. He pulled the bottle of Jack Daniel's from his jacket pocket. "I don't know who I am anymore. I ain't Joe, I ain't Bob. Maybe I'm Tom or Frank or Jerry." He took a long pull on the bottle, letting the booze dribble from the corners of his mouth. He wiped at himself with the sleeve of his jacket and, with great effort, hoisted himself to his feet, staggered to his car, and crawled into the back seat, where he closed his eyes and fell into the familiar and dangerously comforting black sleep.

Fran refused to budge. She had finally reached the end with Bob and insisted that she would not live with a man whose life seemed to begin and end with a bottle of booze.

Bob thought a change of scene might be a solution, might provide a fresh start. So he took money from the muffler shop account and purchased a home in Streamwood, Illinois, a suburb just west of Chicago. He rented a truck and packed up their furniture and moved Fran and the kids into the home, then put the Orfordville home on the market and rented himself a cheap cottage on the western shore of Lake Geneva, Wisconsin. It was a resort town, the lake itself circled by the Victorian mansions of industrialists and old-money families, most of them from Chicago. But the streets of the downtown business area were dotted with galleries, souvenir shops, restaurants, and bars—lots of bars. This was a party town and, in the summers, it attracted hordes ready to let loose. And Bob was always ready to let loose. He split his days between the muffler shop and the gas station and spent his nights curled up next to a bottle of Jack Daniel's. When the booze didn't give him enough kick anymore, he began smoking marijuana and snorting an occasional line of cocaine. The rush of cocaine made him feel confident, but it was a transient feeling, only made better by more cocaine.

Every few months or so, he would appear on Fran's doorstep, seemingly sober, and try to convince her to take him back. Sometimes she would let him in—he still gave her money and he was ever loving to the kids—and there were times when he was able to stay sober for a week or even two, but it always ended. She would find a bottle and toss him out.

Each time he came back, increasingly disheveled and, in her eyes, pathetic, he promised to straighten out. Each time he broke his promise. Each time, she ordered him out and with every such event she felt her sympathy for him wane. She now had to struggle for some meaning, some justification for why this man she had once loved had vanished.

Yes, she thought, *Harry's acquittal was devastating.* Yes, Bob was fearful about the possibility that Harry or someone wanting to impress Harry would figure out that Joe Reese was actually Bob Lowe, track him down and kill him. Yes, she understood that Bob was still haunted by dreams of the killing; she could recall the many nights in bed when she had been awakened by his screams.

But no, none of that was an excuse for his behavior during these years. Harry and the dreams were no longer his trouble. His problem was booze and dope, not bad memories. Fran now had trouble recalling the early days of their marriage; she could not evoke the way she felt when Bob had taken a needle and thread and a bottle of ink and stitched her name—a homemade tattoo—on his right bicep. She tried to remember his tender words of love and his easy nature. The way he played with the kids and read them stories. She tried to summon these images of a man, but all she got was a ghost. The man she once knew was gone.

One night, Bob got behind the wheel of his car and took off for Streamwood, but never made it. High on cocaine and whiskey, he drifted off the road and hurtled into a ditch, where the car became mired in the mud. He slumped over onto the passenger seat and passed out. He woke up in the morning, rocked the car back and forth until it was freed from the muck and drove back to the cottage where he cracked open a fresh bottle of Jack Daniel's, poured himself a drink to straighten out, and passed out again on the bed.

Six months later, his businesses failing, Bob locked the front doors, packed up his clothes and drove out of Wisconsin. He was too drunk to know where he was going and too drunk to care.

In December 1984, Bob found work at a Checker Oil gas station. It was the latest in a series of gas station jobs he had gone through in the past few years. It was easy to find work at a gas station—he had spent most of his life pumping gas, changing tires, and checking oil. He knew the business and he talked the language. Perhaps most important for those hiring him, he was willing to work nights, a time when help was hard to find.

He started at Checker working the 3 P.M. to 11 P.M. shift. On his second day of work, Melinda Craig, Bob's relief, arrived to find the station deserted and locked. Bob was gone. And, according to an audit, so was $5,621.

Meanwhile, without a steady source of cash, Fran had been unable to make the mortgage payments on the house and the bank foreclosed. She and the five kids moved into a small apartment at 1140 Peachtree Lane in Elgin and she found work as a nurse's aide and receptionist in a home for senior citizens. They barely got by.

Eleven days before Christmas in 1984, a man walked up the sidewalk to the apartment building on Peachtree Lane. He rang the buzzer and waited.

Fran came to the door and asked, "Can I help you?"

"I'm looking for Joe Reese," the man said.

"Who are you?" Fran asked.

"I'm George Wick, detective for the DuPage County Sheriff's Police," he said. "Are you Mrs. Reese?"

"That's right," Fran said.

Wick waited, but Fran offered nothing more.

"I'm looking for your husband," he said.

"What for?"

"I have a warrant for his arrest."

"What now?" Fran asked.

"He stole five thousand dollars from a gas station, a Checker station over on Devon Avenue in Itasca where he was working," Wick said.

"I don't know anything about that," she said. "I didn't even know he was working."

"Do you know where he is?"

Fran sighed. "No, I don't," she said. "He doesn't live here. He used to stay here sometimes, but he isn't here anymore. He stops by sometimes to see the kids—we got five—but I have no idea where he is."

Wick handed her a business card. "If he calls or comes by, tell him to call me. Tell him there is a warrant out for him."

Fran stared at Wick as he walked to the street, climbed into an unmarked detective car, and drove off. She looked at the card in her right hand, then slipped it into her pocket and closed the door.

She was not surprised.

Several days later, Wick was sitting at his desk when the telephone rang. "This is Joe Reese," the caller said. "I understand you have a warrant out on me?"

"That's correct," Wick said.

"My wife told me you came to her house looking for me."

"That's correct," Wick said.

"I want to come in and take care of this tonight."

"I'll be here," Wick said.

Three hours later, Bob sat across from Wick's desk and listened as Wick read his Miranda warning and said, "Want to tell me what happened?"

"I decided to keep the money from my shift," Bob said. "I was supposed to drop it into the floor safe, but I just kept it."

"How much did you take?"

"It was two thousand, six hundred eighty-four dollars," Bob said.

"That's not what they say at Checker," Wick said.

"What do they say?"

"That you took the money on both nights that you worked and it's more than five grand," said Wick.

"They're lying," Bob said. "I didn't even go to work the second night. I called and asked what time was I supposed to be at work. And they told me I was already late. I figured they had found out the money was gone, so I kept on going."

"Why did you do it?" Wick asked.

Bob shrugged. "I needed money. I didn't have any. It was a lot of money. I guess something just snapped."

Wick booked Bob and led him to a cell where he spent the night. Wick did not attempt to resolve whether Bob had stolen one or both day's receipts; he would be charged with a felony in either case.

The following morning, Bob was released on bail. Before he surrendered, he had taken the remaining cash to Fran and she had used it to post his bond. As bad off as Bob was, she could not stand the thought of him spending time in jail. Outside, he begged her to let him stay with her. Reluctantly, she agreed. *Maybe this trouble,* she thought, *will scare him straight.*

It did not. Three days later, Bob wheeled his car into the circular drive at the senior citizens home. Wobbling, he slammed the car door shut and shoved through the revolving door. No one stopped him as he barreled down the hall and stopped abruptly in front of Fran's desk.

"Hey, sweetie," he said, a tight smile pasted on his face.

"What do you want?" Fran snapped.

"Ooooh, baby, why is it you think I want something?" Bob purred.

Her eyes narrowed. "Because I know you, that's why," she said.

"Well, actually, I could use a loan."

Fran frowned and leaned back in her chair.

"Only a couple hundred, babe," Bob said. "I'll pay you back next week. I got some money coming in. Really."

"Get lost."

"Now, Fran—"

"Get out!" Fran shouted. "I don't want to see you. You got no business coming here."

Bob stared at her. "Well," he said. "If that's the way you're gonna be—" She never saw it coming. His hand smacked into her cheek, sending her spilling out of her chair and to the floor. This was the first time he had ever struck his wife but, in his mind, sizzling on cocaine, it didn't register. He was gone, like a wild animal going for a kill, and in an instant, he pounced behind the desk and began rifling her purse.

"Ohhhh," Fran moaned, clutching her face, rolling to her side.

"Dammit, where is—ah," Bob said, holding up a wad of $20 bills. He tossed the purse onto the desk, stuffed the cash into his pocket, and hurriedly strode out of the building. Fran was still struggling to rise. She felt tears on her cheeks and tasted blood in her mouth as she heard car tires squeal out of the driveway.

In March 1985, Bob answered an advertisement for a night cashier at the Gas & Grub, a service station on Larkin Avenue in Elgin.

"My name is George Sampson and I need a job pretty bad," he told the manager. "I just got back in town from Lexington, Kentucky."

The manager cast a critical eye. Blue jeans, brown, long-sleeved shirt, greasy brown boots. She would later describe him to police as ugly and dressed "on the scummy side." He had the beginnings of a reddish beard and long sideburns. His shoulder-length brown hair had been bleached to a dingy shade of blonde and was combed straight back.

"Got any experience?" she asked.

"Yeah," Bob replied. "I managed a Martin station in Hanover Park, but it went bankrupt. That's when I went back to my hometown, Lexington, to look for a job, but couldn't get anything."

It sometimes amazed him how good he had become at lying, how efficient a thief he was becoming. *They called me a liar in court,* he would think to himself, *and a liar I am. My life's a lie and I'm taking my share of what's out there. Harry gets away with murder. What's a few robberies? No one's getting hurt.*

And it was so easy. Give a fake name, plead poverty, offer to work the night shift. Two or three days later, grab the cash and disappear. His memory vaporized by the drugs and alcohol, he had already lost track of how many stations there had been.

"You have to take a lie detector test," the Gas & Grub manager said.

"No problem," Bob said, displaying his gap-toothed grin.

He was hired even though the results of the lie test were deemed "questionable." The polygraph examiner had advised that he not be left alone, but the station manager was not worried, later saying, "His knowledge of the business was greater than usual and he had a charismatic personality."

Bob started on a Friday and was assigned to work the evening shift. That day, shortly after Bob began work, the manager took $11,000 out of the safe, arranged it in piles on a table in a back room, counted it, stuffed it into a bank bag, and placed it in a floor safe. Several times Bob interrupted her counting to ask seemingly innocuous questions about his work routine. After the manager left, Bob and a coworker, Dawn, were left in charge.

A few hours later, Dawn's husband drove in and asked if she could take him home so she could have the car to get home at the end of her shift. She asked Bob if he would mind handling the station alone for a few minutes. Bob agreed and the moment she was out of sight, he locked the station door. He walked into the back room and pulled a gram of cocaine from his back pocket. Sniffing deeply and muttering "stupid bastards," he pulled the key to the safe from the hook on the wall. He stuffed the cash into a garbage bag and relocked the safe. Then, casually, he walked to his car and put the garbage bag into his trunk.

A half hour later, Dawn returned to find Bob sitting behind the cash register. Smoke swirled from a Marlboro 100 resting in an ashtray.

"Hey, how's about I pick up the trash outside?" he asked.

"Fine by me," she said.

Ten minutes passed. Dawn looked out the window, but could not see

Bob. His car was gone, too. At that moment, the station door opened and two Elgin police officers walked in to buy coffee.

"Did you see a guy picking up trash out there?" she asked.

"No, ma'm," one said. "Why?"

"We hired a new guy and he said he was going to take the trash out and pick up the garbage and that was, like, ten minutes ago," she said. "I don't know where he went. His car is gone."

"Were you here the whole time?"

"No, I was gone for about an hour driving my husband home," she said.

"Check the register."

Dawn punched a button and the cash drawer opened.

"No, looks all here," she said. "Ain't that weird?"

"Call the manager," one officer advised.

She did and the manager told her, "Get the key and open the safe. See if there is a money bag in there."

Wake up." The voice seemed far away. Bob burrowed his face deeper into the pillow. "Bob Lowe? Wake up."

The voice was deep. Bob's eyes snapped open and focused immediately on a gun barrel inches from his face. In an instant, his mind flashed to the image of Harry at the defense table.

"Don't move, Mr. Lowe," the voice said. "Take your hand out from under the pillow. Nice and easy. Put both your hands out where I can see them. Slow. And do it right now."

Precariously close, the gun barrel rested almost on his nose.

"There are men outside. We have a warrant for your arrest, Mr. Lowe— or should I say Reese?"

Bob held out his hands and was immediately cuffed. Three police officers, guns drawn, stood around the bed. Behind them, in the doorway, Fran watched silently. He had stopped by the night before and tried to convince Fran once more that he was going to get straight. He explained that he had flown to Alabama to visit his parents, who finally had given up struggling to make a living on Chicago's West Side. The Austin neighborhood had changed too much, Joe told his son.

"It's too damn dangerous," he said. "People are getting robbed and the dope is all over."

But Joe saved his harshest words for his own son, excoriating him for his drinking. "You're drunk all the time," Joe snapped. "Look at your family, son. Look at what you've done to them. What do those kids, my grandkids, think when they see you like that? Stinking, clothes raggedy, all boozed up?"

Shamed, Bob had cut the visit short and stopped to see Fran. He dropped several thousand dollars onto the table, and convinced her to let him spend the night. Fran had relented and gave him her bed while she slept on the couch. When the officers arrived with the warrant, she allowed them inside, knowing what they would find in the bedroom. And she said nothing as the police led him out into the August sunshine and to a waiting police car.

Bob used his only telephone call to reach out to Dave Williams, but Williams was nowhere to be found. When Williams showed up at the Kane County Jail four days later, he was shocked by what he saw. Withdrawal from booze and drugs had turned Bob into a quivering mess. Wracked by diarrhea, pounding headaches, insomnia, and delusions, Bob was gray, alternately shivering and sweating.

"They're trying to put sixteen gas station jobs on my ass," Bob said. "That's not right. I did some of these, but not all of them. They're just trying to clean up their cases with my ass."

"You broke the law," Williams said.

"You know what else? They ran my prints and found out my real name," Bob said. "So they got me in here as Bob Lowe. Not Joe Reese. You have got to get me out of here."

"I can't do that," Williams said.

"What the hell?" Bob demanded. "You got to help me. What if somebody in here finds out who I am? Then I'm dead. If it ain't a friend of Harry's, then it'll be somebody who wants to try to get in with Harry."

Williams listened, but said nothing.

"Dave," Bob pleaded. "After what I did for you guys—I wrecked my life, I ruined my wife and kids' lives—you just gonna forget me?"

"No," Williams said. "But I can't make all this go away. I helped you get a mortgage and helped you get a business. But you did this to yourself. There's nothing I can do."

Like many fights, this one started innocently enough as Bob sat at a table in the day room, the common area where inmates were allowed to commingle. He had only been in Kane County Jail for two days. He was weak and sick from the symptoms of withdrawal, trying to stay away from the other inmates. He kept his head down through hours of playing solitaire.

"Hey, new boy," he heard a deep voice say. He did not look up. He flipped another card onto the pile on front of him.

"Hey, white boy," the voice said, deep and with a trace of Mississippi accent. "I'm talking to you." The voice was standing next to him now, in the person of a large black man. Bob flipped another card, but prepared for the worst, dropping his right hand below the table and sliding it toward a vacant chair next to him.

"I know you hear me," the inmate said. "What's the matter? I got something for ya, new boy. But you'll have to give me something."

The man's large black hand touched the table, then slid over to nudge one of the piles of cards. Silently, Bob rearranged the pile. But before he could draw back his hand, the black hand gripped his wrist.

Bob didn't think. He reacted. With his right hand, he grabbed the empty chair and, with surprising strength, whipped it across the table and upward, smashing the inmate squarely in the chest and face.

"Jesus!" the man shouted, staggering backward. "What the fuck's with you, man?"

Bob was on his feet now, dwarfed by the man, who stood at least six inches taller than his own five-foot, eight-inch frame and outweighing him by perhaps seventy-five to one hundred pounds. Bob shoved himself back from the table and squared off, crouching, the chair now a weapon held in both hands.

"Don't touch me!" he yelled.

Cries of "fight!" echoed through the room and down the corridor. An alarm was sounded. Other men—black, white, and brown—encircled Bob, along with the other inmate, blood trickling from under his right eye.

The men formed a tight ring around the pair to try to keep the guards from immediately getting through to break up the fight. "Fuck him up!" someone shouted. "Fuck him up good!" There were other voices, filled with rage, as the boredom of confinement and the suppression of violent urges erupted in a bloodcurdling chorus that angered and terrified Bob.

"Kick that motherfucker's white ass!"

"Beat his ass!"

Bob slashed the chair back and forth as the men tightened the circle.

"Come ahead!" he roared. "Ever' last one of you! Come on! I don't give a shit what happens to me! Let's go to it!"

Suddenly, a hand clamped on his shoulder. He turned and was engulfed. Hands on his face. Hands yanking his arms back. The chair was wrenched free. An arm wrestled his head back. He began to choke from a hand pressed against his windpipe. He struggled, but could not move.

"Hold still!" a voice shouted. "It's over, man! Hold still!"

Bob tried to focus, but the room was beginning to spin. Then he realized these assailants were guards and he allowed himself to be half dragged, half carried from the cellblock.

"Hey, asshole," one of his escorts said. "You know where you're going?" Bob said nothing. "Solitary, that's where. That's where we put assholes who can't behave. Punks like you who gotta fight somebody."

Solitary confinement is the absolute isolation of a human being in a tiny room, no bigger than a small bathroom. The toilet is a hole in the floor. There is no window. The bed is a steel platform. Known as "The Hole" or "The Tombs," solitary confinement is the destination for inmates who are deemed dangerous, disruptive, or a potential target of other prisoners.

"Welcome to the system," Bob said, as he was tossed into the hole.

Bob emerged from solitary after five days. He returned to the day room, found a chair, and sat down to watch television. Almost immediately, the same inmate he had slammed with the chair sat down next to him. Bob saw the healing wound on the man's cheek and tensed.

"Hey, man," the inmate said.

Bob turned to face him and was surprised to see a smiling face.

"Man, what'd you hit me for?" the man asked.

"You grabbed me," Bob said. "You said you had something for me, but I had to give you something. I got to defend myself."

"Shit, man," he said. "I was just gonna offer you some of my smokes. I seen you throw away your last empty pack. We smoke the same brand, Marlboro. I was gonna sell you some of mine. That's all."

Bob exhaled slowly. "Well, speak English, dammit," he snapped. "How the hell was I supposed to know that? You come up to me like that, grabbing me? I don't back down to nobody. Not in here. Not nowhere."

The inmate stretched out a meaty, scarred hand.

"Virgil," he said.

Bob took his hand and said, "Bob. Just call me Bob."

On December 12, 1985, Bob pleaded guilty to the thefts at the Gas & Grub and Checker Oil, part of a deal in which those two crimes were bundled together with three other gas station robberies in exchange for a sentence of two years in the Illinois Department of Corrections. He was prisoner #N54398. He went into the system at the Joliet Correctional Center.

Joliet is the oldest of four maximum-security prisons in Illinois. As well as serving as "home" to more than 1,200 adult males serving time for crimes ranging from robbery to murder, it also functions as a processing center, where new inmates are received and classified for assignment to one of the more than a dozen prisons in the state. It is here that the finality of a prison sentence begins to take permanent hold. Inmates arrive by bus and are led, handcuffed, into a receiving cell. Over several days, they are subjected to a psychiatric exam, given a physical exam, and evaluated by counselors who study their backgrounds, their crimes, and their sentences. Then, inmates are designated to an institution to continue serving their time.

In December 1985, when Bob arrived at Joliet, he had already chipped a few months off his two-year term. His time spent in jail in Kane County was counted as time served and brought him that much closer to his eventual release. After five days at Joliet, he was designated for Vandalia Correctional Center, a minimum-security prison for men located eighty-five miles southeast of the state capital of Springfield. Originally designed as a prison farm, the facility provided other state prisons with beef, pork, Polish sausage, lunchmeats, corned beef, milk, and juices. While there, inmates harvested corn, soybeans, wheat, and sorghum, and also tended a garden several acres in size.

Bob was assigned to work in the meat-processing plant and, following the lead of more experienced inmates, began to smuggle out an occasional steak that he steamed in a plastic bag propped on a radiator or sold to other inmates. He traded pieces of meat for vegetables from the prison garden and made his own soup.

In time, his pasty complexion was replaced with a tan. Muscles he had not used in years began to harden. He began to settle into the routine. But trouble dogged a man like Bob and trouble soon found him. One afternoon, slouched against the side of the building in the exercise yard, Bob watched a guard approach. He stubbed out his cigarette and steeled himself.

"Lowe," the guard said. "There's ten pounds of hamburger missing."

"So?" Bob said.

"Word is you took it."

"The hell I did."

"Sit up when you're talking to me," the guard snapped.

"Fuck you," Bob said. "I'm not in the damn military."

"No," said the guard, "you're in damn jail."

Bob spent that night and two more in solitary confinement. And he was back in solitary a week later, after getting caught sneaking a cigarette in a nonsmoking area. That night a jail counselor visited him and suggested that he straighten out or face a transfer to Stateville, a maximum security prison filled largely with Chicago street gang members convicted of murder and surrounded by a thirty-three-foot high concrete wall.

"Fine, send me there," Bob said. "I don't give a shit."

"You stole meat; you smoked. You are not following the rules. You are losing days of good time. Your time is getting longer," the counselor said.

"I didn't steal any hamburger," Bob protested. "I might have lifted a steak or two, a filet mignon once in a while. What the hell would I do with ten pounds of hamburger? It would rot before I could eat it all. And I don't even like hamburger."

He was not disciplined, but transferred. Instead of Stateville, he was sent to Jacksonville, a two-year-old facility thirty miles west of Springfield. It was far more modern than Vandalia or Joliet and the grounds consisted of twenty-four acres within the fence, surrounded by another forty-six acres of empty land.

Bob had barely settled in when he was offered a drink.

"Take a slug of this, brother," said another inmate, holding out a plastic cup half-filled with a murky liquid. "This'll do you right."

"No," Bob said, holding up his hand. "That done me a lot of wrong."

Bob was determined to maneuver through the rest of his prison term without serious incident, so he refused all offers to drink homemade prison booze, a nasty concoction that smelled like turpentine but carried a wallop. He turned away from the marijuana and pills that were smuggled in. Assigned to a two-man cell, he smashed a portion of the top bunk so it could not be used and he would not have to share his space with a stranger whose attitudes, habits, and desires he did not know. He kept to himself and refused to be bullied or pushed around.

Bob wanted his time there to be as uneventful and plain as the land he could glimpse while exercising in the yard, but he kept his guard up. There was always a possibility that Harry would learn of his incarceration, and Bob knew it was perhaps easier to kill a man in prison than on the outside. A homemade knife—a shiv—could be fashioned from a variety of materials accessible to inmates. He himself had made such a weapon—a toothbrush he had painstakingly filed on his cell floor until it bore a point as sharp as an arrow. He kept it hidden in his cell. He was willing to use it if he had to.

Don't try to visit me. Don't bring the kids," Bob had told Fran after pleading guilty but before being sentenced, fearful that he could receive the maximum sentence of sixty years. "Forget about me. Just leave me be."

But he could not forget about her. At age thirty-seven, Bob was alone for the first time in his life and it hurt. Not a man given to introspection or self-analysis, Bob had lived most of his life from day to day, from paycheck to paycheck, and, in the eight years since Harry was acquitted, from bottle to bottle. Jail gave him time to think. His head clear for the first time he could remember, he found himself almost overwhelmed by the anger, humiliation, and hopelessness that he had so desperately tried to bury. The long hours of work, the hundreds of bottles of Jack Daniel's, the marijuana, and the cocaine, he saw clearly now, were not any help. They had only masked the pain and had been transformed into the sharp implements of self-destruction.

And as his head cleared, this realization also came: He was not afraid of dying and not afraid of Harry anymore. If Harry had wanted him dead, he would be dead, wouldn't he? *Why,* he wondered, *had Harry not killed him immediately after Billy Logan?* Surely Harry must have suspected that he could identify him. But hadn't Iavarone discovered that the police had buried the investigation? *That was it,* Bob realized. Harry didn't need to kill him—not when he could beat the system in his own way.

As he surveyed the bare walls of his cell and the emptiness of his life, he came to understand that he was not a lesser man just because Harry had beaten the system and Judge Frank Wilson had branded him a liar. In jail he had begun, uncharacteristically, to write down his thoughts. It was his halting attempt to make sense of his life, to restore to it some meaning, to start to heal. His pencil scratched slowly across pages of notepaper, often in the middle of the night when he was unable to sleep.

Everyone is here, yet I'm not.
I'm alone, even in a crowd.
Even though there's light,
I'm in the dark.
I've cut myself off from life.
There are exceptions.
Moments of love, perfect solitude.
Where I could make peace with myself.
But contradictions that remained in my life
I remained indifferent, unseen, unfelt and unfeeling
I learned disillusionment, anger, rebellion, and loneliness.
But what I learned, I could not understand.
I felt like a tree, a rock. Without feeling.
But then I entered my own soul.
And therefore, remain alone.

The words poured out, a sort of fuel for what he felt was a new determination, not merely to survive but to somehow recapture the man he once was and in so doing gain back the love of his family, their trust and respect.

He wrote to Fran, composing poems and letters that spoke of his feelings and thoughts. He sometimes grasped for the right words but was not embarrassed when he couldn't find them. What he was writing was something truer and deeper than right, it seemed to come from deep within.

Loving

The nights feel so cold and bare,
Now that you're not with me.
Sharing my days and nights,
Loving and sharing our dreams.
For my heart is empty now,
A space only your love can fill.
For without your love, I know,
I could never be able to love again.
Those nights and days were ours.

Now is a time we can't share.
But soon to be over for us.
To find our place again.
Loving each other in all our days and nights.

Love,
Bob

In letter after letter, Bob asked Fran to forgive him, to consider giving him another chance. He promised to renew his love for her and for the children. He had bottomed out, he wrote, and was on the upswing—if only she would give him a chance. These letters and poems had the desired effect. Fran came to the prison on visiting day.

Not surprisingly, the reunion was awkward.

"I liked the letters, Bob," she said.

He just nodded.

"We'll just have to see," she said.

"I'm gonna make you proud," he said. "We paid a price. I made you pay. But it's not too late, baby. I swear."

She wanted to hear more but she still felt the sting of promises never kept. So she started a monologue, giving the details of her life. It was not a happy speech. She told him she had lost her job because of a staff cutback. The car had been repossessed. Unable to pay the rent on the Peachtree Lane apartment any longer, she had moved in with a sister, Patty, who lived in a two-bedroom apartment on Albany Avenue just north of Addison Street on the Northwest Side of Chicago. "The kids and me are staying in one room," Fran said. Her hair was brushed and tied up neatly and she had put on makeup, but Bob could see the weariness in her eyes.

"One room?" Bob said. "Where do you sleep?"

"On the couch in the living room," Fran said. "The girls are in the bed and the boys are on the floor."

"Is she charging you rent?"

"No," Fran said. "But I have to do all the cleaning and the dishes. Mostly, we eat pizza from Little Caesar's—you know, two for the price of one."

They sat there for a few minutes in silence. He wanted to hug her, to hold her hand, to tell her everything was going to be OK. Visiting time was almost over.

"Fran," Bob said. "Don't visit me no more."

"Why?" she asked in surprise.

"This is too hard," he said. "It's too hard to see you go."

"That's it, people, time to go," a guard yelled.

And Bob watched Fran walk out of the room, joined by the wives and lovers and sisters and mothers of the other inmates, all of them carrying fragile promises and hopes.

Hey, it's me," Bob said.

"What's wrong?" Fran asked, as her hand clutched the phone tighter.

"Nothing," he said. "What are you doing Thursday night?"

"Same as always—nothing."

"How about you and I go on a date Thursday night?'

"Don't play with me like that," Fran said.

He laughed. "I'll call you back."

On Thursday morning, August 27, 1987, Bob was handed a new pair of shoes, $100, and a train ticket from Springfield to Chicago. He rode the bus to the train station in Springfield with several other inmates who also were going home. As soon as they hit the train station, all of them went directly to the nearest bar and ordered drinks, including a beer for Bob.

He took a sip and stopped. "What the hell am I doing?" he muttered. *Are you gonna drink again? Are you an idiot?* he asked himself.

He slipped off the barstool and boarded the train. Arriving at Chicago's Union Station four hours later, he went outside and hailed a cab.

"I only got ten bucks," Bob said. "It's all yours to get me to Addison and Albany." His heart began to race and the passing scenery was a blur. In what seemed like only minutes, he was walking up the front steps and ringing the doorbell. Eight-year-old Tiffany answered the door.

"Hi, there, Tiff," Bob said, smiling broadly. She stared and then she began to cry. Bob stepped inside and embraced her. Across the room, Fran was paralyzed in disbelief. "Is it you?" she asked. "Really you?"

"Yeah," Bob said. "It's me."

"Oh, my God!" she screamed. "Oh, my God!"

Bob kissed his wife. It was not merely the kiss of a man who had been away in jail for two years, it was that of a man who had been away for more than a decade. They all but melted into each other.

When I get out, I'm walking straight. How many times had he told himself that in prison? Two days after being released he had a job hauling furniture for a moving company. He walked to work, trekking the three miles each way from their apartment on Albany Avenue to North and Milwaukee avenues. When he got a $20 tip from a customer, he splurged and took the bus.

The family still ate pizza, but in so doing they were soon able to save enough to have a car and rent a house in the northwest suburbs. And Bob found a better job, driving a truck for Sears, Roebuck & Co. The job paid by the delivery—more deliveries meant more money—and he hustled. Soon he was taking home as much as $1,000 a week. Within a year, Bob and Fran, who had found work again as a nurse's aide, had set aside enough to make a down payment on a house.

Bob was staying sober. He slipped for a few months after he began working for Sears, but Fran did not notice. She was too busy putting back together the pieces of their family, too busy working and fixing up the house. She wasn't even concerned that Bob had buried Joe Reese and had returned to using his real name, while she and the kids continued to use the name provided to them so many years before. Bob also was trying to reintroduce himself to the kids, to be a real father. It was easier with the youngest, Tiffany, and the other girls, Tina and Tammy; they were quicker to give him their trust than were the older boys, Bobby and Joey, but he could feel them warming once again to him. And always, he remained cautious, though the memories of Harry began to fade and the nightmares subsided.

"The past is gone, babe," he told Fran. "We only got the future now."

On the day of his acquittal, Harry walked hand-in-hand with Ruth down the steps of the Criminal Courts Building. There were dozens of reporters and half a dozen television cameras waiting for them. "How's it feel, Harry?" "What are you going to do now?" "Mrs. Aleman, are you happy?" But the couple ignored them all. They stepped into a waiting car and headed home for a celebratory dinner and a good night's sleep.

But domestic peace was not long lasting. Furious over the acquittal, federal prosecutors thrust Louie Almeida before the grand jury and asked him to detail the home invasion ring he said Harry directed. Louie complied.

In July—two months after Wilson's verdict—Harry was indicted along with Lenny Foresta on federal charges of conspiracy, racketeering, and interstate transportation of stolen furs, jewelry, and cash. "If they couldn't convict him in state court, we figured we would get him in federal court," one lawman said.

While Harry remained free on bond pending his trial, investigators began leaking information to the press in an attempt to heighten the pressure. One news account reported that federal agents were focusing on Harry as a suspect in a series of gangland killings in Kansas City, including that of David

Bonadonna, who had been shot five times at close range in July 1976, and then stuffed into the truck of his car. Federal investigators said he was slain because he refused to buckle to pressure from organized crime to bring go-go girls and nightclubs to a fashionable strip along the Missouri River known as River Quay. The murder was just part of a bloody series of bombings and arsons and killings that investigators said were the result of a struggle for control of the Kansas City crime syndicate.

Locally, another news account reported that Harry was a suspect in the 1975 murder of Frank Goulakos, a chef at DiLeo's Restaurant on Chicago's Northwest Side who was shot to death as he walked to his parked car after work. Goulakos paid the ultimate price for failing to pay his gambling debts and for becoming a part-time informant.

As damning as the news stories may have seemed, many knowledgeable observers believed Harry to be untouchable as he arrived in U.S. District Court in the spring of 1978 for another confrontation with Louie. Harry had just turned thirty-nine but looked years younger. He was, as usual, dressed smartly, in a dark sport jacket and dark slacks, with a razor-sharp crease. Ruth took up her familiar spot in the first row of the spectator's benches, occasionally whispering encouragement or expressing her disgust with the testimony. One morning, just before the jury was ushered in, she stomped out of the courtroom, saying, "I'm going outside to smoke a cigarette. I'm getting crazy from this garbage."

As Louie and the other witnesses testified, Harry tilted his chair against the walnut-veneered wall, scratching pages of notes on a yellow legal pad. "I gotta pay attention," he told a reporter. "It's my life, right?"

His demeanor hadn't changed much from a year earlier when he sat in Judge Wilson's courtroom. He winked and nodded to friends and relatives who slid into the first two rows behind the defense table. He stared at the spectators, looking for acquaintances or perhaps enemies. He watched the witnesses, laughing if one of them made a humorous remark. He looked at the jurors, sometimes with a hint of a smile, at other times with no expression at all.

He seemed bored by Louie's testimony. After all, this was a man he called mentally retarded and a moron. Once, according to a newspaper columnist, Harry turned to his attorney while Louie was testifying and gestured with his hands open as if to say, "How could he say such things about me?"

But Louie was not flustered. He told the jury how Harry had instructed him and Foresta to carry nine-millimeter Browning semiautomatic pistols because, "It's a better gun to shoot. It doesn't jam. . . . It had fourteen rounds and you could carry a couple of extra clips and have more firepower." He recalled that he, Foresta, Harry, and a friend of Harry's from New York City had gotten a tip that an elderly couple was hoarding $70,000 in gold coins in their house; how Foresta flashed a sheriff's badge when the homeowner, William Djidich, answered, and then smacked him in the head with a pistol; that Djidich and his wife were tied up and left on the floor while the house was ransacked. Louie recalled that as the gang drove away, "Harry apologized to me that there wasn't any money in the house and Lenny said he ought to shoot the tipster in the head for the tip."

To combat Louie's testimony, Harry's lawyer, Raymond Smith, adopted a strategy that was similar to Whalen's approach at the Logan murder trial. He called Louie "scum," a career criminal, and a perjurer. He accused him of concocting false stories about his old friend to cut his prison sentence from ten years to five for the Pittsburgh murder plot. Foresta's defense consisted largely of testimony by his wife, Theresa, who married him twenty days after her first husband was killed while participating in a home invasion in March 1973. She said that Louie had been in love with her and swore revenge after she spurned him.

On May 5, 1978—forty-nine weeks after Harry was acquitted of Billy Logan's murder—the jury reached a verdict: Both men were guilty. It was a stunning, surprising victory for the prosecution.

Ruth began to weep and was escorted from the courtroom. "They had scum up there telling lies," she snarled through her tears. Across the room, Harry remained inscrutable in his chair at the defense table.

U.S. Justice Department prosecutor Robert Rose immediately asked that both men be held without bond, arguing that Harry was responsible for numerous murders and announcing that the federal government intended to seek a judicial finding that Aleman was a "dangerous special offender," a finding that could increase his maximum sentence from fifty years to seventy-five years.

"Harry Aleman is a killer and we are prepared to prove it," Rose declared, adding that Harry was a threat to prosecution witnesses and kept an arsenal of weapons in his home.

"Mr. Aleman is not going anywhere," Smith retorted. "And he poses no threat to society."

Rose scoffed. "If there ever was a case involving organized crime and all its dangers posed to society, this is such a case."

Judge Stanley Roszkowski set bond for Harry at $200,000—which family members immediately posted. Foresta wasn't going anywhere. It was his eleventh conviction and he was already serving an eighteen-year prison sentence for a home invasion in Indianapolis.

This is a man who kills human beings in cold blood. Chicago should not be the headquarters for organized thugs and hoodlums," Rose declared a month after the verdict, at the sentencing. He argued that Harry was responsible for numerous murders. He invoked the names of Richard Cain and William Logan. For the first time in a courtroom, Rose accused Harry of killing gamblers Anthony Reitinger and Orion Williams, as well as murdering Robert Harder, the informant who had helped solve the killing of police officer Anthony Raymond. Rose disclosed that shortly after Reitinger was slain, investigators found a car matching the description of the vehicle that his killers had used. A warranty book in the glove compartment bore Harry's thumbprint, evidence linking him to the car, if not tying him directly to the murder.

If there was any doubt about what was at stake, Rose cleared it up almost immediately as he urged Roszkowski to impose the maximum penalty. Harry sat quietly, expressionless, and with his hands folded.

"The people of Chicago are watching you with the hope they'll be protected from this man," Rose said, speaking directly to the judge. "He has made no expression of remorse or guilt or acceptance of responsibility."

When it was his turn to speak, Smith countered by saying Harry would not admit guilt to something he had not done. His voice raised in anger, he railed at Rose for singling Harry out for exceptional treatment based on allegations of murder, even though Harry had never had been indicted. "It's the decision to start making exceptions that provides the crack in the judicial system that could lead to McCarthyism or to the Spanish Inquisition," Smith declared.

He urged Roszkowski to be lenient toward Harry, saying, "He has a loving family. He's been dedicated to his family. He's raised four kids."

Harry declined to speak on his own behalf.

The judge was brief, but to the point. "People have a right to feel safe in their own homes," he declared. "I sentence you to the custody of the U.S. Bureau of Prisons for a term of thirty years."

Audible gasps were heard from the front two rows, where Ruth and other family members sat, clutching hands for support. But there were no other demonstrations of emotion. Harry, it seemed, had prepared them for the worst, and the worst had not come. With time off for good behavior, Harry could be back home in twelve years, perhaps as early as 1990.

At the defense table, Harry calmly stood up, turned to face his family, and smiled. Two deputy U.S. marshals approached to escort him to the lockup. As he walked toward the lockup, Harry passed by the prosecution table, where FBI agent Jack O'Rourke, the lead investigator on the case, stood, watching what, for him, was a very sweet moment: the incarceration of Harry Aleman.

Harry broke his stride ever so briefly. "Agent O'Rourke," Harry said. "I just want to tell you: no hard feelings."

Initially, Harry was sent to the maximum-security prison in Marion, Illinois, but was later transferred and the medium security federal penitentiary in Oxford, Wisconsin, became his home. Despite the image portrayed by law enforcement, Harry was, in the words of one of his lawyers, "a gentleman. He got along with the inmates and the guards. He signed up for college courses. He began to paint again. Harry was a good inmate."

Later that summer, Jimmy Inendino, Harry's pal who had helped bring Vincent Rizza into Ferriola's stable of gamblers just a few years before, was sentenced to twenty-five years in prison for running a theft ring that specialized in semitrailer trucks. Prosecutors contended that Inendino had accompanied Harry on the murders of Robert Harder and Orion Williams.

With Harry and Inendino both behind bars, Joseph Ferriola entrusted Butch Petrocelli with day-to-day responsibility of his criminal empire: gambling, prostitution, and auto salvage yards where stolen cars were "chopped" into parts and resold. Petrocelli immediately engineered a strict crackdown that generated payments from bookies of more than $400,000 in just three weeks, and then delivered the money to Ferriola.

Meanwhile, every two weeks, Ruth piled the kids into the car and they endured the nearly four-hour drive from Melrose Park to Oxford to visit with inmate #03792-164. They brought the books he had requested and audiotapes of classical music, soothing sounds that he played while he painted landscapes in his cell. "Those visits were hard," Ruth later recalled. "He kissed the kids and hugged them. He asked each one how they were doing in school. He gave each one individual attention. I would not cry in front of him. I didn't want him to see me cry. The leaving was hard. Walking out the door—walking down the hall. I told the kids I never wanted Harry to see me cry because it would hurt him. We would get outside and the tears would be rolling down my face."

Despite the fact that he was behind bars, Harry was still a dangerous man. That became clear in late 1980 when Petrocelli disappeared. On the morning of December 29, he had been seen playing handball at the YMCA in suburban Oak Park, and later he left his home in west suburban Hillside, driving his red Ford sedan to a meeting with friends in the nearby suburb of Cicero. He was never seen alive again. His body was found three months later when a pedestrian walked by a red Ford parked on a side street on Chicago's Southwest Side and noticed a sleeping bag on the floor of the back seat—with two feet sticking out. Police cut open the sleeping bag and made a grisly discovery: Petrocelli was fully clothed, his wrists were taped to his chest and his ankles bound with rope. Surgical tape covered his nose and mouth. He had been stabbed twice in the throat and his face had been burned beyond recognition. Two cans of lighter fluid were found in the car, but the burns appeared to be the work of a blowtorch. An autopsy showed that Petrocelli actually died of suffocation, suggesting to investigators that the stab wounds and the burning were the result of torture at the hands of his assailants.

The media and law enforcement speculation on the cause of Petrocelli's demise varied. Some believed underlings, angered by Petrocelli's rise in Ferriola's organization, were chafing under his rough ways and had taken matters into their own hands. Others suggested that Petrocelli had been caught holding back as much as $100,000 from Ferriola. But those who had followed Harry's career most closely felt, in a theory that was at once chilling and almost surreal, that Harry had orchestrated the hit on his lifelong friend from behind bars, believing that Petrocelli was about to become a government witness.

"He may have been behind bars, but that doesn't mean he can't order someone to handle a job for him," said Dave Williams, in one of the many variations of warnings he would give to Bob Lowe during the years of Harry's imprisonment. "And don't think that there aren't a few guys out there who wouldn't whack you in a second if they thought it would please Harry. You can't let your guard down for a second."

25

On April 28, 1989, nearly eleven years after Roszkowski handed down the thirty-year term, Harry was paroled. Ruth and their seventeen-year-old grandson, Sam, walked him out of the prison doors. They did not return to Melrose Park, but instead he and Ruth moved in with their daughter, Frankie, and her husband, Edward Strong, in their home on Forest Glen Lane in Oak Brook, a wealthy enclave of million-dollar homes. Founded by millionaire Paul Butler, Oak Brook had come to be favored by the polo crowd, as well as by members of organized crime. This group included Joseph Aiuppa, the man who became top operating boss of the Chicago mob when Ferriola died in March 1989. Ferriola himself had lived in a fourteen-room mansion on a tree-shaded corner, a few steps away from the Strong home.

Within a week of his release, Harry met with Ernest Rocco Infelice, a longtime underling of Ferriola. Infelice was a short and stocky balding man who had been a paratrooper in World War II, had served time for heroin trafficking two decades earlier, and emerged from prison to begin a slow, steady rise in the hierarchy of organized crime in Chicago. After Petrocelli was killed, Infelice had moved into a position of power under Ferriola and had been assigned to handle gambling collections. After Ferriola's death, he had taken over gambling throughout Chicago. The meeting was brief but profitable for Harry. Infelice delivered $100,000 in cash that had been left behind for Harry by Ferriola.

Harry went to work at his son-in-law's concrete cutting business, handling personnel matters, but he spent most of his time with his family, particularly his six grandchildren. "We had just gotten through probably the hardest eleven years of our lives," his daughter Terry later said. "We made it and we stood together because of the love and the total commitment that my father has always given freely and without reservation. We are as dedicated to him as he is to us."

For Harry, coming home meant spending time with Sam, who had been seven when his grandfather went to prison. Until then, they had been nearly inseparable. Now, Harry found himself nearly overcome with happiness as he watched Sam graduate from high school.

When another grandson, only three and one-half months old, needed surgery, it was Harry who stayed at the hospital around the clock until the boy could come home. And then, Harry spent virtually every moment with the boy.

Three weeks later, his daughter Frankie became ill and required three separate surgeries. "My father was with me every second," she later recalled.

Each morning before Harry left for work, he made breakfast for Frankie's eleven-year-old daughter before she went to school. He picked her up after school and drove her to her piano and viola lessons. He listened to her practice, attended parents' night at school, and he did not miss any of her concerts. It was, Ruth would later recall, the most joyous time ever for the Aleman family.

But soon the family was back in court. Harry had been indicted again in February 1990. A federal grand jury charged him, Infelice, and eighteen others with racketeering and conspiracy arising from the operation of the gambling rackets during the 1970s. Shortly after 6 A.M., federal marshals appeared on Harry's doorstep. Quietly and without a struggle, he surrendered once again. At a bond hearing three months later, Justice Department prosecutor Jeffrey Johnson demanded that he be kept in jail as a flight risk.

"If convicted, Mr. Aleman faces the possibility of life imprisonment," he

declared. "This man has no substantial employment history. There is no evidence of his employment before his incarceration in nineteen seventy-eight
and upon his release last year he was hired by his son-in-law. We know nothing about the stability of that employment. This man owns no real estate.
He has no bondable assets. Mr. Aleman lives in a home owned by his son-
in-law and daughter. It's not his home. If he flees, he forfeits nothing. They
are not dependent on him—he doesn't provide or even contribute to their
welfare. Most importantly, this man has the financial ability to take off. The
evidence was that in May nineteen eighty-nine, he received one hundred
thousand dollars from Infelice. In many countries—South America,
Greece—one hundred thousand dollars goes a long way."

Johnson ticked off several murders—Reitinger, Logan, Harder—and
dredged up the home invasion conviction as well. "This man is a menace to
anyone who might have anything to do or to say about the charges in this
case when it comes time for trial," he declared.

In response, Harry's family once again rallied behind him.

"I am the eldest daughter of Harry Aleman," said Terry Amabile, speaking emotionally. "It is in this capacity that I wish to speak.

"In the past few months, my family and I have been subject to the pain
of his absence from our lives. There has been the question of whether or not
my father, if released on bond pending his trial, would try to flee. Well, let
me assure you that I find this question completely ridiculous.

"There is no force on this earth that would make him run from us. From
the time my son was old enough to walk, he was at my father's side. A great
love grew between them—a love that has withstood the test of time and hard-
ship. My father spends hours with my son and just as much time with my
daughter: always giving of himself, never too busy to lend an ear or a helping hand, always wanting the best for them and teaching them to strive for
the best in their lives.

"Throughout my life, my father has been there for me and for my family. No matter what the time of day or night, if it was in his power, he was
there. He is a man of his word and I have never known him to say one thing
and do another. It is with these truths and many more that I say to you that
my father will not flee, that he will be in court with his family beside him."

After daughter Terry's plea in front of Judge Ann Williams, daughter Frankie took the stand as well, saying, "He would never, never give up his wife, his children, his grandchildren, his father, his brothers, aunts, uncles, cousins, and friends. My father is loving, warm, gentle, and caring of his family and friends. He is a man of his word. He has honor and pride."

That pride was evident as Harry himself stood up and began reading from a typewritten sheet of paper: "Contrary to what the prosecutor said about me, I am a human being. I'm also a lucky man. I have a wife who has stood by my side for thirty years. I have two daughters, both married, two sons and six grandchildren. That is my immediate family. I also have aunts, uncles, cousins, brothers, brother-in-laws, sister-in-laws and my father, who is seventy-five and still with me. We are all close, and all supported me while I was away for the last decade.

"Beyond family, I am blessed with friends in the community and any number of them are more than willing to vouch for my character and reliability. I love my wife and kids, and that is my stability and predictability. There isn't enough money in the world to make me run away from my family. Throughout my years in prison, I survived for my family and they have stood by me, never knowing when I was coming home with the thirty-year sentence that I had.

"When the man of the household is gone, everything starts to disintegrate. But my family remained strong because there is a bond that just kept growing year after year. I can never, ever flee and leave my family. If you believe anything at all, believe this."

He scoffed at the prosecution's suggestion that he was a threat to their witnesses. "Who can protect them better than the government?" he asked. "I am no threat to any witnesses. I am appealing to you as a judge and as a human being. Do not forget that all humans in our country should be presumed innocent until proven guilty in a court of law. Today, an allegation is one of our evils, along with the omnipotent news media that can make your name a household word, which can affect a potential juror. I'll abide by any conditions you make for bond and I'll keep up my end until we finish this trial."

Bond was denied. Harry would stay in jail to await trial.

On October 28, 1991, Allan Ackerman, Harry's attorney, addressed the court, saying, "I feel very much like a three-year-old thoroughbred at the Kentucky Derby who's withdrawn at the post. Personally and professionally it makes me uncomfortable to do this. I work for Mr. Aleman." He was visibly upset. After nine months of preparation, Harry, on the eve of trial, abruptly decided to give up the fight to prove his innocence and plead guilty. In exchange for avoiding a possible life sentence had he gone to trial and been convicted, Harry decided to accept a twelve-year prison term.

Ackerman continued to address Judge Williams, "Mr. Aleman sits here. He will answer the court's inquiries. This is for the benefit of his family and himself. It's what he wants."

And so, during a lengthy hearing before Judge Williams, Harry admitted to extorting money from Rizza as well as Anthony Reitinger, though he adamantly refused to admit that he had killed Reitinger.

"Why don't you just tell me," the judge asked, "what happened with respect to the extortion of Rizza and the other gentleman, Reitinger."

"What do you want me to say, specifically?" Harry replied.

"What were you to do in connection with them?" she asked. "How did the collection thing work?"

"I extorted Vince Rizza," Harry said.

"And what does that mean?" the judge pressed.

"What does that mean?" Harry repeated. "Take money from him."

"And what about Reitinger?"

"I extorted Reitinger," Harry said, his voice a monotone.

"And what were the extortionate payments for?" Williams asked.

"For sports bookmaking," Harry said.

Williams would not let him get off easily. "And what were they? Were they bettors?"

"They were both," Harry said. "Bettors and bookmakers."

"Why did you have to extort?" Williams asked. "Were they late on payments?"

"It's really hard to explain," Harry replied. "Bettors and sports bookmakers all get together somehow, some way. They owe. They don't owe. They bet. If they don't pay, you get the money. You just ask them for the money."

"And that was your job, to get the money?"

"Yeah," Harry said.

Justice Department Prosecutor Mitchell Mars interjected: "These particular bookmakers, Rizza and Reitinger, were independent bookmakers at the time and they were required to pay a street tax—a percentage of their profits per month—to be allowed to continue in the bookmaking business. Some of the individuals that Mr. Aleman was involved with at this time were Joseph Ferriola, William Petrocelli, who is also known as Butch, and James Inendino."

"Is that right, Mr. Aleman?" the judge asked.

"Yes," Harry replied.

"And was there anybody that you were directing to go out and collect things from other people?" she asked.

Harry paused. This was a question he had hoped not to hear. He was willing to plead guilty, but he would not rat anyone else out. "Yes," he said, hesitantly.

"And who were those people you directed?" the judge asked. "Do you remember their names?"

"I buried all that, Your Honor," Harry replied. "A dozen years passed by. I'm not going to contest what Mr. Mars said, but I'm just vague."

"You don't remember the names?" Williams said, her tone meant to suggest disbelief.

"I don't remember," Harry insisted.

"OK," she said. "But you would agree that there were people you sent out to collect?"

"Yes."

"All right," Williams said. "What is your plea, Mr. Aleman? Guilty or not guilty."

"Guilty," Harry said.

Harry listened as Judge Williams imposed the twelve-year prison sentence. Then he smiled and asked to be returned to Oxford, where the surrounding pine forests with the abundant deer and other wildlife were the focal point of his artwork. His request granted, Harry settled in to do his time. With luck, he would be released in the summer of 2000. By then, the statute of limitations would have expired for the 1970s and he would be free for good. But while he looked toward the future, Harry was unaware that ghosts from his past were up to potentially damaging mischief.

A rguably the most corrupt attorney in the history of Chicago, Bob Cooley was born on the South Side and joined the police force in 1962 at age 20, following in the footsteps of his grandfathers, uncles, father, and four brothers. He abandoned the honest life of a cop shortly thereafter, taking $5 and $10 "gratuities" from motorists he pulled over for traffic·violations. He got his first real lesson in the unique Chicago system when he pulled over 10th Ward Alderman Edward Vrdolyak for making an illegal left turn at 87th Street and Stony Island Avenue. Cooley didn't immediately recognize the alderman but once he did, the pair exchanged pleasantries as they stood outside of their cars. The conversation over, Vrdolyak walked over to Cooley's squad car and placed some bills on the back seat.

By that time, corruption in the Chicago police department was a surprise to no one. During the 1960s, police protection rackets flourished in several police districts, including Austin, the neighborhood where Billy Logan was killed; Chicago Avenue, the district encompassing the topless bars and sleazy nightclubs along Rush Street, and the Far South Side district where Cooley worked. Tavern owners joined the "$100-A-Month Club," making regular payoffs to police, who in return promised not to ticket patrons who parked illegally, broke up fights without penalizing owners for overserving customers, and generally did not harass the owners or threaten their most valuable asset—their liquor license.

After Cooley was cut in on that action, he learned how he could earn fifty dollars each time he would massage the truth during testimony on drunken driving cases in Traffic Court.

As he spent more time in the courts, Cooley realized that the stream of bribes available to police officers was a mere trickle compared to the river of money available to lawyers. Thus inspired, he enrolled in night courses at Chicago-Kent College of Law, graduating in 1970. Two days after he was sworn in as a lawyer, he handled and won his first drunken driving case in Traffic Court. When he left the courtroom, the bailiff approached and told him bluntly: "That one was free. It's going to cost from here on out if you want to get the results you want."

The court system at the time was heavily populated by former prosecutors and city attorneys who had been selected to run for office on the basis of fealty to the powerful Democratic Party rather than for their legal acumen.

With little or no Republican opposition, Democratic candidates easily won elections. And with a clean, crisp set of judicial robes, they were sent immediately to traffic court to learn the ways of judging in a setting where the crimes were less consequential and mistakes of temperament and decision less significant. In Cook County, this indoctrination also included learning which lawyers paid bribes and which lawyers didn't, which cops could be trusted to take a dive, and which court bailiffs could be trusted to handle cash deliveries discreetly.

It was a time when judges who played it straight were separated from those who played along. Some honest judges were quickly isolated—much as an ailing steer is culled from a herd of cattle—and dispatched to remote courtrooms with heavy workloads and few challenges. That is not to say that all good judges were exiled. Some had such impeccable reputations that they were left alone. But judges who accepted the corruption found they were quickly promoted to handle more serious crimes, such as murder, rape, and robbery, where even more money could be earned for delivering a favorable verdict.

It was a system controlled by creatures such as Judge Richard LeFevour, who had devised a test for determining the honesty of those newly named to the bench. He would send his cousin, a police officer named Jimmy, into courtrooms and chambers to offer judges money to toss out a traffic case. Judges who accepted the money passed the test. Judges who didn't failed. There was no middle ground.

It was a system that spawned such men as Lucius Robinson, a courtroom bailiff who signaled to a judge that the bribe had been delivered by sitting in a particular spot in the courtroom when the case was called, as well as a cadre of crooked criminal defense lawyers such as Dean Wolfson, nicknamed "The Dream" because he achieved results that most other lawyers could only dream about. And so did Cooley.

His first year out of law school, Cooley raked in more than $100,000 from his law practice, paying bribes virtually every day he came to court. A man with an engaging personality and a quick wit, Cooley mixed well. He befriended court clerks, policemen, prosecutors, and judges.

Cooley began carrying $1,000 to $5,000 in his pocket (as he became more successful, he would feel naked if he did not have at least $10,000 to $15,000 in his pocket at all times). He never carried credit cards. Plastic left a trail for the Internal Revenue Service. And, anyway, cash was flashier, more powerful. He bought lunches, dinners, and drinks, and became a familiar face in hip disco joints along Rush Street, taking up a station where he could nurse his Dewar's and water and observe the women on the dance floor. He wore expensive suits, a gold chain around his neck, and, almost always, a hat—to cover his balding head.

With a sudden influx of cash lining his pocket and no significant expenses—he was single, lived in a modest but well-appointed apartment, and had no legal staff to support—Cooley began to gamble heavily. This provided the adrenaline rush that he couldn't get in court. How could he get excited over trials, the results of which he knew, which he had bought? He bet the thoroughbreds at Arlington Park or the trotters at Hawthorne or Sportsman's Park. He played poker and occasionally took trips to Las Vegas. But his preference, he discovered, was to bet on the outcome of sporting events, particularly football, baseball, and basketball.

It was not long before he was gambling every day. Soon he began to take bets from other police officers and place them with his bookmaker and before long, he had begun taking bets himself. As he became a familiar player in the world of high-stakes gambling in Chicago, it was natural that he would ultimately meet a man such as Marco D'Amico, the mob's overseer of gambling on the Northwest Side and western suburbs. According to investigators, D'Amico was second in command of a mob crew controlled by John "No Nose" DiFronzo and operated out of Elmwood Park, a western suburb.

Marco demanded that Cooley pay protection money—$2,000 a month—for the privilege of taking bets from his friends and passing them through D'Amico's stable of bookmakers. Cooley paid happily. To him that kind of money was chump change.

Cooley organized poker and blackjack games in his law office. He kept his cash in safety deposit boxes. Money meant little to a man who had a lot of it. After a successful night at the poker or blackjack table in his office, he would impulsively hop on a jet to Lake Tahoe or Reno and spend the day at the tables. He sometimes won as much as $200,000 or $300,000 in a single week. More often, he lost it. But winning or losing was only a way to keep score—the action held his interest.

He bought a suburban restaurant named Greco's, which he turned into a hospitable spot for outfit bosses and hangers-on. Heavy on the pasta, and festooned with fake ivy and twinkling lights, Greco's was decorated to give the feel of sitting in a backyard somewhere in the hills of southern Italy. It regularly catered to some of organized crime's top glitterati and their entertainer friends—Accardo, Aiuppa, LaPietra, DiFronzo, and up-and-coming hitmen such as Joseph "The Clown" Lombardo and Anthony "Tony the Ant" Spilotro. Occasionally, when he was in town, Frank Sinatra dropped in to be wined and dined.

D'Amico was impressed with Cooley's engaging manner and self-assured style, and they became friends. And so, along with financial ties to the mob, Cooley became a member of the outfit's social circle. Legal business was shifted his way—from D'Amico, at first, then from other mob associates. By day, he roamed the halls of the Cook County courts, representing gamblers, mob musclemen, and an assortment of shady characters, dishing out bribes ranging from as little as $100 for a traffic violation to as much as $5,000 for a more serious beef.

By night, he still hit the Rush Street joints, but now he sat at the spot at the bar that was reserved for the same men every night—men who made no secret of their ties to organized crime. They hung out in Faces, the most garish and glitzy of the Rush Street spots, the places where Cooley was able to rub elbows with visiting celebrities, prominent locals, and the most beautiful young ladies. "We had one corner and that was the fun corner," Cooley recalled later. "If a stranger would come over and even stand around, we would make the person feel very uncomfortable. It would get very quiet. Everybody would stare until the person would walk away and leave us. That was *our* corner."

He began dropping in on a nightly, closed-door dice game near Chinatown, just south of Taylor Street. And he often dined in Mama Sue's, an Italian restaurant in the Taylor Street neighborhood and in which Harry Aleman was a silent partner. He knew of Harry by reputation as a man to be feared. He knew Harry killed for a living.

Across from Chicago's City Hall was a restaurant named Counsellors Row, a watering hole for political movers and shakers—aldermen, fixers, and ward heelers. But even they knew better than to try to sit at the table in the back. That was the only reserved spot in the house, set aside for the bosses of Chicago's 1st Ward, a Democratic power base that stretched westward from Chicago's downtown to encompass Taylor Street, Greektown, and Chinatown. The men who ran the ward were John D'Arco Sr. and one of his closest friends, Pasquale "Pat" Marcy, whose ties to organized crime went back to associates of Capone.

In the spring of 1977, D'Arco summoned Cooley to the restaurant. They had met through D'Amico and it was soon afterward that D'Arco proposed to Cooley that he share office space with his son, Illinois State Senator John D'Arco Jr., and other influential 1st Ward lawyers. Even for a high roller like Cooley, this was heady company.

"Pat's coming down," D'Arco said. "I want you to talk to Pat. He wants to talk to you about something."

A few minutes later, as Cooley waited patiently, Pat Marcy walked through the front door and motioned for Cooley to step into the hallway outside the restaurant's rear entrance. D'Arco joined them and made the formal introductions. Marcy got to the point immediately, saying, "I have a very important murder case over at Twenty-Sixth Street. Do you have somebody that can handle it?"

"What's the case?" Cooley asked.

"Harry Aleman," Marcy said, his voice dropping to a near whisper.

"Well, I don't know," Cooley said, momentarily staggered by the significance of what he was hearing. By that time, Cooley had handled hundreds of cases, but mostly misdemeanors and lesser felonies—batteries, illegal gun possessions, traffic violations and drunken driving arrests, and assorted narcotics busts. He had never been involved in a murder case.

"Look," D'Arco interjected, "if you have somebody, that's fine. If you don't, let us know because it's very important. If you don't have somebody, we'll go someplace else."

Cooley was smart enough to realize the importance of the opportunity being laid in front of him. If he could successfully orchestrate this complicated and dark bit of legal work, he would attain a special, rarefied status among the outfit characters who were influential in Chicago's political and judicial circles—and the money and power that would go along with it.

"I have a few people in mind," Cooley said. He didn't blurt out the first name that came to mind. A case like Harry's was going to attract media attention, and success required precise planning. If he were to engineer an acquittal, he knew the judge on the case would need something—even if it were to be just a small kernel of evidence—to justify the result. In the world of the fixer, this was known as having "something the judge can hang his hat on."

"What I'd like to get before I find somebody is the police reports in the case so I can see what type of case it is, how good it is or isn't," he said.

"I'll get the reports," Marcy promised. "If you have somebody to do this, fine. If not, don't say you can. We can get somebody else. This is very important. These are very dangerous people you're dealing with."

As he read over the reports of the initial interviews on the street and at the hospital where Logan was pronounced dead, he noticed that the only witness of any significance was a man named Bob Lowe. Cooley was encouraged by how little information the reports contained. Lowe's description was sketchy—two white men in a dark car—and there was no indication he had seen either man well enough to identify them. And as he perused the reports and considered whom to approach, one name kept coming back to him. A drinking buddy. A gambling pal. A man he could trust. A judge named Frank Wilson.

As he lingered over his hot tea and the police reports in his South Side restaurant, Cooley became increasingly convinced that Wilson was the right man for the job. He knew the man well, though he couldn't remember exactly when and where they had first met. It could have been at Jean's, the basement tavern a block from the Criminal Courts Building. He certainly remembered having to drive Wilson home from Jean's more than once after the judge had been overserved. Those experiences formed the foundation of a friendship that had expanded over the last two years, as the two of them had begun to gamble together, jetting to Las Vegas on junkets and staying in rooms at the MGM Grand Hotel.

Wilson often let Cooley use his chambers as something of a second office; Cooley dropped in almost every day to pick up messages and return phone calls. Such visits would have to stop, Cooley knew, if their plot took wing. But there were still places where they could see each other and talk without raising suspicions. Wilson was a frequent patron at Greco's, and they were often seen there together sharing drinks and dinner.

But friendship alone would not be enough to persuade a judge to take a bribe to throw a murder case. There had to be other reasons, and Cooley knew those too: the judge had a lot of extra expenses, such as a country club membership and a daughter in college, stretching his $42,000 salary to the breaking point.

Yes, Wilson was the man. His reputation was perfect, that of a prosecution-minded jurist not loath to return guilty verdicts in tough cases. He was, in the language of the courts, a "banger," a judge who had no qualms about imposing long prison terms. Before the U.S. Supreme Court set aside the death penalty in 1972, Wilson had sentenced two men to die in the electric chair. If and when Wilson acquitted Harry Aleman, there would surely be heat from the media and law enforcement but if the facts of the case were sufficiently shaky, Wilson's no-nonsense reputation would keep the "temperature" at a comfortable level.

But would he do it? As well as Cooley knew the judge, there was no certainty. He had, as far as Cooley knew, never taken a bribe. Would he risk it all for a friend with an envelope stuffed full of money?

Cooley determined that the best way to broach this delicate subject was when Wilson had a drink in his hand, which he often did. In that manner, were Wilson to be offended or outraged enough to go to the authorities, Cooley could contend that the booze had led Wilson to misinterpret the conversation.

The opportunity came sooner than Cooley had expected. Two days after he had been approached by Marcy, Cooley walked into Greco's and saw Wilson and three other men eating dinner. He recognized the men's faces but didn't know them. He thought they might be Wilson's golf buddies. After waving to the judge from the bar, Cooley slowly drank a Dewar's and then walked casually over to the judge's table. He shook hands with the other men and told them dinner was on the house. Amid the thanks and toasts and casual conversation that followed, Cooley managed to draw Wilson away from the table and to a quiet corner at the end of the bar.

"Frank," Cooley said. "I've been approached by some people to handle a murder case."

"The Aleman case?" Wilson asked.

"That's right," Cooley said, surprised and wondering if Wilson had heard something or if he was merely guessing.

"You know I was SOJ'd on that case?" he asked, referring to the motion filed by Harry's lawyer, Tom Maloney, to substitute the original judge on the case, James Bailey, and to reject any assignment to Wilson.

"No, I didn't," Cooley replied, surprised again. The case file supplied by Pat Marcy had not included any substitution of judge motion. So immediately he changed the subject and steered Wilson back to his table. *That was that,* Cooley thought. It was unlikely, if not impossible, to get the case shifted to Wilson now that Maloney had already filed a motion that, in essence, said Harry could not get a fair shake before Wilson.

But he was encouraged in one respect: Wilson hadn't flinched when the subject of Harry's case had been raised. That meant Wilson might be willing to deal under the right circumstances, or in some future case.

But the circumstances were far from right and Cooley told Marcy so the next day in the hallway outside of Counsellors Row.

"Pat," he said. "I talked to somebody and I think he might be interested in handling the case but—"

"Who?" Marcy asked.

"Frank Wilson."

"Fine," Marcy said. "That's fine."

"But there may be a problem," Cooley said. "He said there was an SOJ filed and he was named in the SOJ. We can't get the case back to him."

Marcy seemed unfazed. "If he wants to handle the case, I'll get the case back to him," he said.

"Well, if you can, what do I offer him?" Cooley asked. "How much? I've never been involved in a case of this magnitude. What's fair?"

"See if he'll take ten grand," Marcy said.

"What are you drinking, Frank?" Cooley asked.

"Scotch and soda," Wilson replied. Cooley gestured to the bartender.

"Judge, I talked to my people," Cooley began. "If we can get the case back to you, will you handle it?"

"I don't think you can," he said.

"They say they can."

"What kind of a case is it?" Wilson asked, sipping the drink that he had taken from the bartender before he could set it down. "How good?"

"They have a couple of witnesses," Cooley replied. "They have one, somebody who was picked up on the way to go whack somebody else. So his credibility is not going to be very good. Then they have a second guy who is identifying Harry now, three or four years afterwards and that's not gonna hold up. That's all they basically have." He took a long pull on his drink. "It's a real weak case."

"I still don't—" Wilson began.

"Judge," Cooley interrupted. "You have to understand that this is a very serious matter. You can't say you're gonna take it if you're not gonna take it. You can't change your mind because *you* will have a problem and I will have a *serious* problem."

Cooley paused, expecting Wilson to say something, but Wilson was silent. Cooley continued, "So what I would like you to do is think about it before you decide whether you want to or don't want to. Think about it and I'll get back to you in a day or so. If you decide you want to do it, fine."

"What's it worth?" Wilson asked.

"If you do decide to handle it," Cooley said, "it's worth ten G's."

He lifted his glass, then set it back down.

"Judge, I don't want a response now," he said. "You think about it, because if you take it, neither one of us can back away."

Two days later, Cooley called Wilson at his chambers at the courthouse and invited him and his wife to dinner. The judge accepted and Cooley, with one of his many girlfriends in tow, confidently walked into Greco's. After the waiter took their drink orders and some small talk was exchanged, Cooley motioned to Wilson and they walked into the bathroom. The room was empty, so they stood before the mirror, side by side, and talked softly.

"Judge, do you want to take this case?" Cooley asked.

"You can't get it to me," Wilson said. "Not with that SOJ."

"Look," Cooley said, "I've been told we can get the case to you. If you want to take it, fine. But—as I said before—if you do, you can't back away later."

Wilson stared into the mirror, then at Cooley.

"OK," he said. "I'll take it."

Cooley didn't hesitate. He reached into his pants pocket and pulled out a wad of money. "Here's twenty-five hundred dollars," he said, thrusting the bills into Wilson's outstretched hand.

"You'll get the rest when the case is over. You understand, once you take this money, you can't back out." It was a statement, not a question.

"I have conditions," Wilson said, putting the money into his pocket. "First, you can't try the case. Too many people know we're friends."

"That's fine," Cooley said. He never intended to handle the case.

"Tom Maloney can't handle it either," Wilson said. "He filed the SOJ. I want him to come to court. I want him to say that he filed the SOJ, that he wants to waive it, and he has to have Aleman there to waive it, too. And then Maloney has got to withdraw from the case."

"I see," Cooley said.

"But I don't think you can get it in front of me," Wilson repeated.

"If we can't, you can keep the money," Cooley said, accompanied by a nervous laugh. "How's that?"

Both men were smiling when they returned to the table. Three hours later, when the check arrived, Cooley happily took care of it.

You did what?" Marcy asked angrily. "Why did you give him money? I hadn't given you any money."

He glared at Cooley as they huddled in the hallway outside Counsellors Row. "How much did you say you gave him? Twenty-five hundred? Why did you give it to him already?"

"I wanted to lock him in," Cooley said. "I don't want him trying to back out of this later."

"All right," Marcy said, finally. "I'll get your money back."

Cooley began to explain Wilson's conditions.

"No, no, no," Marcy said, shaking his head. "Tom Maloney has to handle the case. It's his case. He has to handle it. You better talk to this judge. Change his mind."

"I'll see what I can do," Cooley said, "but he was pretty adamant."

Two days later, Marco D'Amico telephoned Cooley and summoned him to the King's Inn, one of the many flashy nightclubs that formed a faux Vegas strip along Mannheim Road near O'Hare Airport.

"What's this about, Marco?" Cooley asked.

"Harry Aleman wants to meet with you," he said, motioning Cooley to follow him. "He's gonna meet us in the office upstairs."

The office was empty when they arrived and D'Amico said, "You have a bizarre sense of humor, you know that?" he asked.

"What are you talking about?" Cooley asked.

"You have got a judge to take care of this case, I understand," D'Amico said. "This is not something you want to mess around with. You know who these people are?"

"Yes, I do," Cooley replied.

"If you mess up, you know what will happen?" D'Amico said.

"I understand, Marco," Cooley said. "If I say I can do it, I can do it."

A knock at the door interrupted the conversation. Harry walked in and shook Cooley's hand as D'Amico made the formal introduction.

"You better not be fucking around with us," Harry said. "You sure you can handle it? You sure that this judge is going to throw this case out?"

"Yes."

"Well, Maloney tells me that this guy's a straight judge," Harry said. "You're sure?"

"If I say I can do it, I can do it," Cooley said. "I talked to him and he say's he's going to do it."

"Fine," Harry said. "Now, Tom is really pissed off because he wants to try the case. He went to Pat for help and now he's being kicked off the case. You've got to convince this judge to let Tom try the case. Tom is going to be named to a judgeship real soon. He is a good friend of mine and he can be a very good friend in the future."

"It will look bad if Maloney stays on the case," Cooley explained. "He filed the SOJ and named Wilson. Now, he's gonna walk back in and ask for a bench trial in front of the guy he objected to? It will smell."

Harry just stared at him for a few tense seconds before saying, "Just see if you can do it. If you're right about this judge, you'll be on top forever. If you're not, well, that's no good," he said.

"Fine," Cooley said.

"Now," Harry said, "I've got some papers for you."

He handed Cooley the federal prison psychiatrist's report on Louie Almeida. "I got a private investigator who got this for me," he said. "Almeida is a fucking psycho. We don't have to worry about him."

"What about this guy who was walking his dog? Lowe? Bob Lowe?" Cooley asked. "He picked you out of a lineup, right? He says he identified you right after the shooting."

"We took care of that," Harry said. "We got to the cops and those reports are not going to make it to court. They're gone. This guy has some bad checks hanging out there. By the time he gets to court, it's just gonna be his word. If he says he identified me and the cops won't back it up, then what he says is bullshit. It won't hold up. The only reports left are that he identified me four years later. Who the fuck is gonna believe that?"

"OK," Cooley said.

"And I have an alibi," Harry continued. "It was Maloney's idea. Me and four or five of my friends were hitting balls at the driving range. How does that sound?"

"How are they going to remember where they were four years ago?" Cooley asked. "What if one of your buddies burns you, tells a different story?"

"Don't worry," Harry said. "That will not be a problem."

"Well, if that's the best we can do, it's the best we can do," Cooley said. "Some alibi is better than no alibi."

You talk to Wilson about Maloney?" Pat Marcy asked, two days later.

"Yes, I did," Cooley said, lying. "The judge won't do it. If you want to keep Maloney on the case, we've got to find another judge. He won't handle this if Maloney steps up and tries the case. Look, I'll find somebody else."

"No, you won't," Marcy declared. "Forget about it. I've got somebody else to try the case."

"Who?"

"An attorney that used to be here in Chicago," Marcy said. "Frank Whalen. He will come in from Florida and handle it. Check with Wilson. See if he's acceptable."

Wilson was agreeable, saying, "He's a good lawyer. I knew him when he was an assistant state's attorney and when he was a defense lawyer. But I never want to meet with him. I don't want to talk to him. If I have any questions or something I want or need or something I'm concerned about, I'll deal with you and you can relay messages back and forth."

"I'm not going to be in your chambers for a while," Cooley said. "I don't want to be seen around there for a while. You need me, you call me."

There were no calls, but within a month the case had been reassigned to Wilson. Maloney had dropped out. Whalen was in and among his first acts was to fly to Chicago and meet Cooley in a room at the Bismarck Hotel downtown.

"I've got some reports," Cooley said, handing over the case file. He included the documents that Harry had passed along.

"You sure this judge is going to throw the case out?" Whalen asked.

"Yes," Cooley replied.

"You're sure?" Whalen pressed. He sounded skeptical.

"Look, I know what I'm doing," Cooley said. "I wouldn't say he was going to if he wasn't. I know the man. It's not going to be a problem."

Whalen sat down and began leafing through the file.

"I met with the judge and he's going to do it," Cooley continued, "but he doesn't want to meet with you. If there are some things the judge wants to hear or some things he needs that will make him more comfortable, then I will be the liaison between him and you."

"Let's go through this stuff," Whalen said.

With Whalen on the case, Cooley was reduced to remaining in the background, waiting for the trial to begin. He felt like the director of a play sitting in the audience on opening night, anticipating the rise of the curtain: comfortable because he was virtually invisible, his exposure minimal, but also anxious, even nervous, because things were no longer in his control. The actors were all in place. Would they remember their lines? Would they play their parts as he had directed them? He couldn't be sure. What he didn't need were any surprises, such as the one that came four days before the trial when the phone rang at 2 A.M. Cooley picked up the receiver and listened.

"It's me."

"What's up?"

"Good news. I have to talk to you," Harry said. "You know the restaurant on Grand Avenue? The all-night place?"

"Yeah," Cooley said. "I know what you're talking about."

"It's important. Get over there right away."

Cooley roused himself, splashed his face with cold water, dressed, and drove to the restaurant, wondering if he was in some trouble he didn't know about. He parked in front and walked in. The place was empty of customers, so Cooley took a booth near the front window to watch the street and ordered a hot tea. Ten minutes passed before he noticed movement at the mouth of the alley across the street and saw two men approach—"two rats slithering across the road," he would later say—enter the restaurant, and walk toward the back without acknowledging Cooley. Harry and Butch Petrocelli ordered coffee and Cooley picked up his cup and sauntered back, sliding into the booth next to Butch.

Harry leaned toward him. "My brother, Anthony, got a hold of a girl who lives down the block from where Logan was shot," he said. "He's offered her ten grand and she will testify that it wasn't me."

"Did she see it?" Cooley asked.

"She says she saw the car pull away and she will say she knows it wasn't me in the car," Harry said. He smiled. "Let the judge know that because I'm sure that will make him happy."

"That's great," Cooley said. "That is very good."

"Now the state has no fucking case at all," Harry smirked. "Louie is a fucking schizo and that other guy is no problem. The cops are on our side with this."

That was great news and Cooley buttonholed Wilson a day later at Greco's to tell him. "Judge, they got a hold of a girl who's going to get on the stand and say that Harry was not the person," Cooley said.

"That's good," Wilson said.

"So the case is looking very good," Cooley added. "They really have no-body to identify him. The state's case is just not going to be very strong."

The trial was only two days old and Cooley had been hearing that things were going well. So he was surprised to get a phone call from Wilson, demanding a meeting at a restaurant near the courthouse.

"Is Whalen sick?" Wilson asked.

"How would I know?" Cooley said. "I never met the guy before this started. What's wrong?"

"He's screwing up," Wilson said. He drummed his fingers nervously on the table. "They're burying Aleman. The state is putting on a good case. A very good case. This guy, the driver, is a good witness and Whalen is doing a terrible job of cross-examination."

"Well," Cooley said, "I'll talk to him. But, judge, you know you have to do what you said you were going to do. Or we have a problem."

"That's not all," Wilson said. His words were clipped. His body was stiff with tension.

"They were in my chambers, the lawyers, and they talked about some girl. They offered some girl ten grand on this case," Wilson hissed. "Dammit! I'm a full circuit judge. That's what *I'm* getting!"

Cooley knew what he meant: Ella Jo DeMarco, the neighborhood woman who had reported that she had been offered $10,000 to testify that Harry was not the gunman in the Logan killing. Wilson had barred the prosecu-tors from presenting her testimony.

"Judge—" Cooley began, but Wilson cut him off.

"They are burying me," he moaned. "They are fucking burying me. I'm going to lose my job over this."

Cooley stared at Wilson, fearing that he was watching the man dissem-ble before his eyes. His mind began to leap ahead, but he did not yet want to contemplate the possibility that Wilson would back out of the deal.

"You did this to me," Wilson said angrily. "You put me in this spot. Now you've got to help me. See if you can get more money. If I'm going to lose my job over this, I need more money. I'm the judge. I deserve more."

"I'll see what I can do," Cooley said. "I will talk to my people and see if I can get you some more." He stood up and tossed a twenty-dollar bill on the table, then leaned over so his face was just inches from Wilson. "Frank, you do understand the consequences if you don't do what you are supposed to do?" Cooley didn't wait for a response. He turned and strode out of the restaurant to find Marcy.

He didn't have to look far. Cooley's first stop was Counsellors Row, and there was Marcy, hanging out in the hallway outside the restaurant.

"Pat, he's really angry," Cooley said. "He's upset because he knows that they offered this girl ten large and that's all we're giving him. Can't we give him some more?"

Marcy was unmoved. "He said he'd do it for ten and that's all he's getting," he snapped. "Not a nickel more." Marcy's face darkened. "And he better do what he said he's going to do."

Cooley knew better than to argue but, as he left the restaurant, he decided that he would boost Wilson's share with some of the money he anticipated getting from Marcy for brokering the fix. Perhaps, he thought, that would keep Wilson from splitting apart at the seams, something that was becoming a frightening, perhaps fatal, possibility.

As the trial neared its end, Cooley scoured the newspapers. Most accounts of the trial suggested that the evidence for conviction was strong. It did not ease his mind to know that the press traditionally favored prosecutors, devoting much more space to their efforts than to those of the defense. Without being in the courtroom, he couldn't gauge Whalen's effectiveness or his bumbling. And so, on the morning that the case was scheduled to end, Cooley arose and loaded a suitcase with clothes. "I was in my car and I was packed," Cooley later recalled. "I was gonna go, leave town if Wilson found him guilty. When I heard on the radio that he found Harry not guilty, I drove right back to Counsellors Row. Marcy was sitting there. He was all smiles. So was I."

"Great job," Marcy said. "Great job."

"Pat, look," Cooley said. "Can't we give the judge more money? He's going to get all kinds of heat for this. The radio's already screaming that it looks suspicious."

Marcy withdrew two sealed white envelopes from the inside breast pocket of his suitcoat. "He agreed to do it for that," he said. He handed the envelopes to Cooley and slowly walked away.

Cooley stuffed the envelopes in the pocket of his coat and left the restaurant. He didn't open them until he was alone in his law office. One contained $7,500. That was for Wilson. The other held $3,000 for him.

"Son of a bitch," Cooley said aloud. He roughly calculated his expenses, including one flight to Whalen's home in Florida to review the case just prior to the trial, and figured he'd lost money on the deal. But who was he going to complain to? Instead he went to meet Wilson at the bar of the restaurant on Western Avenue. The judge was drinking. Cooley motioned toward the bathroom and Wilson followed. Before Wilson could speak, Cooley gave the envelope containing $7,500 to Wilson, who opened it and riffled the bills.

"That's all I'm going to get?" he said, weakly.

There was such pain in his voice that Cooley felt an unfamiliar pang of regret. He had not only involved his friend in this, he had broken him.

"I would have given you more—" Cooley said before Wilson cut him off. His next words seemed to hang in the air: "You've killed me."

On a fall night in 1993, the past came roaring back at Bob, when Dave Williams telephoned for the first time in more than two years.

"Bob," Williams said. "We need to come and talk to you."

"Who's we?" Bob asked.

"Myself," he said, pausing. "And a prosecutor."

"What about?"

"When can we come by?"

"Tomorrow night? About eight?"

"Fine," Williams said. "And Bob?"

"Yeah?"

"Keep this to yourself for now."

"What the hell is this about, Dave?" Bob asked. "Be straight with me."

"I will," Dave assured him. "I will. Tomorrow."

Tomorrow was there in a flash: At eight o'clock, Williams and another man arrived at the house. They walked into the dining room and took seats at the table, empty except for an ashtray, half-filled with stubbed-out Marlboros.

"Bob," Williams said. "This is Scott Cassidy."

A baby-faced man with straight brown hair combed over to one side, a white shirt, dark blue tie, and navy blue suit stuck out his hand. Bob felt his firm handshake and a direct gaze, eye to eye.

"Anybody want coffee?" Bob asked. "I drink a lot of coffee these days, since I quit drinking. Haven't had a drop in five years. Coffee's my drug of choice now." He chuckled nervously.

"None for me," Williams said, gesturing toward Cassidy, who shook his head.

Bob sat at the head of the table. "So," he said, pressing his hands together. "What's this about?"

"It's about the Logan case," Williams began. "We—"

"What about the Logan case?" Bob interrupted. "That's a long time ago. I'm done with it. You ain't gonna bring that up again."

"Take it easy, Bob," Williams said. "Relax and listen. What you are about to hear is completely confidential. Under no circumstances can you discuss this with anyone, except Fran."

Bob shook a Marlboro out of the pack, flicked his lighter and took a long drag. He exhaled noisily. "All right," he said. "Go ahead."

"Judge Wilson is dead," Williams said.

"Good," Bob snorted. "That bastard called me a liar."

"He killed himself," Williams continued. "Shot himself in the head. He was retired out in Arizona, you know. He walked out the back door of his home in Sun City and pulled the trigger."

"Got what he deserved," said Bob.

"He did it because he was scared. He knew he was under investigation," Williams said.

"For what?" asked Bob.

"For taking a bribe to find Harry not guilty."

Bob leapt from his chair. "I knew it! I knew it was fixed! Son of a bitch! All this time—" he began to sputter. "I'm the one went to jail, dammit! He called me a liar! That bastard!"

His hand trembled slightly as he lit another cigarette. No one spoke. He exhaled and looked hard at Williams.

"Son of a bitch," Bob said. "Son of a bitch. How'd you find out? How do you know?"

"I'll let Scott here tell the rest of the story," said Williams. "Get some more coffee, Bob. Get us all some coffee. We'll be here for a while."

And they were, detailing the story as Bob chain-smoked in silence. Eventually, the ashtray was overflowing and the coffee in his cup had gone cold. He had been listening to Cassidy and Williams for more than an hour.

Their story was complicated, with too many names he had never heard, but the names he knew, most prominently Harry Aleman and Frank Wilson, held his interest like a vise.

"How do you know all this?" he asked.

"Cooley," Williams said.

"Why would he tell you?" Bob asked.

"Cooley wore a wire for the Feds for four years," Williams explained. "Now he's in witness protection. When he began cooperating, he told the Feds about the fix in Harry's case. We had to keep it quiet until now because he was still undercover."

"What happened at the trial?" Bob asked. "And what's this got to do with me now?"

"Keep listening," Williams said. "Cooley went out to see Wilson. He was wearing a body recorder and he tried to get Wilson to admit on tape that he took the bribe."

"Did he?" Bob asked.

"Not in so many words," Williams said. "It is arguable. But what's not an issue is that after the FBI contacted him about an interview, Wilson walked into his back yard and shot himself in the head."

"We are going to re-indict Harry for murder," Cassidy said bluntly.

"I didn't think you could do that, man. Isn't there some kind of law?" Bob said, an anxious feeling growing inside.

"You mean double jeopardy?" Williams said, filling in the blank.

"Yeah, that's it," Bob said. "What about double jeopardy?"

"We believe that if we can prove the first trial was fixed, then double jeopardy won't apply," Williams said. "And then, we'll want you to testify again."

Bob didn't hesitate. "No," he said, defiantly. "You saw what happened last time. I'm not going through that bullshit again. For what? So some judge can call me a damned liar and ruin my life? No way."

"Bob," Williams said, his voice calm. "It's going to be a while before the trial, maybe years. We'll talk about it. But in the meantime, we want to set up protection again for you and your family. We intend to get an indictment, I can't say when, but the word is bound to get to Harry that we are moving on this case. There are going to be federal indictments against people like Pat Marcy and John D'Arco that are going to lay out the details of the fix. Harry is going to know and he might decide that the way to take care of the case this time around is to take care of you."

"I'm not going through that bullshit again," Bob said. "I don't want protection. I don't want those guys living in my house. I won't drive from motel to motel. I don't want to lose my life, my family's life. We went through that once. We paid the price. I won't do it again."

The wheels were set in motion a few weeks later, on December 8, when a Cook County grand jury voted to indict Harry once more for Billy Logan's murder. And the grand jury also returned an additional indictment charging Harry with Anthony Reitinger's murder as well.

"Justice took a hit in 1977," declared State's Attorney Jack O'Malley as he announced the return of the indictment. "A murder case was fixed."

Standing before a crowd of reporters, O'Malley said his lawyers had determined that the indictment was not a violation of the double jeopardy clause of the U.S. Constitution. "We intend to prove Aleman was never in jeopardy of being convicted," he said. "The constitution does not protect people who fix murder cases or bribe judges. His trial was a sham and double jeopardy does not apply."

Anticipating comments from Harry's lawyers, O'Malley predicted the state would defeat a legal attack on the indictment. "This is not government oppression," he said. "Aleman brought this on himself. His bribe infected the first proceeding with fraud. The trial ended on grounds wholly unrelated to the issue of his guilt or innocence."

One of the first to weigh in was newspaper columnist Mike Royko, the man who had closely followed Harry's career for more than two decades.

Everybody in the courtroom the day Judge Frank Wilson found Harry Aleman innocent of murder knew the case was fixed. Either that, or the judge had gone nuts. That's how airtight the evidence was against the mob's star hit man. . .

The only question was, how had the mob reached Judge Wilson? Was it strictly money? Or possibly blackmail? Maybe death threats to Wilson or his family? The possibilities were talked about by lawyers, cops and reporters as matter-of-factly as if discussing a sports event. Now, 17 years later, we know. The judge was bought for $10,000. It doesn't sound like much, but in today's dollars that would be about $25,000. . .

But I'm glad O'Malley is giving it a try. Aleman will be out of prison in a few years. Unless he learned to be a barber or a librarian in prison, he has only one trade.

And if a new trial is held, we'd be able to see if Aleman still has his dapper style. During every recess in the first trial, he would cheerfully strut around the hallway, shooting his cuffs, and acting like the guest of honor at his own testimonial party. In a way, I suppose, that's what he was.

The indictment was no surprise to Harry—he had known it was coming since October, when Assistant State's Attorney Patrick Quinn came to visit him at the penitentiary in Oxford.

"We are planning on indicting you for two murders," Quinn said.

"Which ones?" Harry asked.

"Billy Logan," Quinn replied. "Harry, you remember that one? That's the one where you paid the judge for the acquittal and you got off."

"Can you do that?" Harry asked.

"Yes, we can," Quinn replied.

Harry was not impressed. After the indictment was returned, he began to read about his case and was particularly interested in an article in the American Bar Association's monthly journal that examined the double jeopardy clause. The story was illustrated with a photograph of his lawyer, Allan Ackerman. Harry was encouraged by the fact that some of those who might damage his case were dead.

Cooley had by this time testified in so many trials—he had for four years been a virtual living microphone for the government, wearing a wire in meetings with lawyers, judges, and mobsters—that he could be painted as a professional snitch, willing to testify against almost anyone. Cooley now was a protected witness in hiding.

Bob and Louie Almeida carried the heavy baggage from the first trial, in which both had been demeaned as ineffective witnesses.

And Harry's original attorney, Tom Maloney, had refused to cooperate with investigators, in large part because he had been convicted himself a few months earlier of taking bribes to fix murder cases. Harry's prediction in 1977 that Maloney would be given a judgeship in Cook County had come true. But Maloney had been unable to shake his own habits and he had been convicted in the spring of 1993, largely on the testimony of Cooley, of accepting a $10,000 bribe to fix a double murder trial of two Chicago street gang members and of receiving a share of a $100,000 bribe to acquit three New York City street gang members of murder. Maloney was facing a fifteen-year prison term.

Harry's lawyers filed a blizzard of motions, battling to bury the indictment on numerous grounds, but particularly because his acquittal in 1977 barred another prosecution. They pointed to the Fifth Amendment of the U.S. Constitution, which states: "nor shall any person be subject for the same offense to be twice put in jeopardy of life or limb . . ." Never before, they argued, had anyone in the history of American jurisprudence been retried for a murder after an acquittal.

Their arguments were rejected. Criminal Court Judge Michael Toomin, who was assigned to preside over Harry's trial, traced the roots of the double jeopardy principle back to Roman law: *Nemo debet bix vexari pro una et eadem Causa,* a phrase interpreted by modern scholars as a rule of law that a defendant "shall not be twice vexed for one and the same cause." This protection later became known as being put in jeopardy for one's freedom, and in many instances, of losing one's life upon conviction. As early as 1644, the judge declared, the provision was a keystone of early English law, the source of modern American law.

"Here, assuming the veracity of the witnesses the state offers," Toomin wrote in a forty-six-page ruling, "the former proceedings were permeated with fraud in its basest and utmost form—the bribing of a judge in the most serious of crimes to be prosecuted in this land. . . . To allow Harry Aleman to seek refuge in the fraud alleged by the state would demean the integrity of the judicial process."

Harry's lawyers appealed to the Illinois Appellate Court and lost. "Fraudulent actions by defendants have been recognized historically as exceptions to the constitutional protections afforded by double jeopardy principles," the appeals court declared.

They appealed to the Illinois Supreme Court, but the court refused to hear the case. An appeal was filed with the U.S. Supreme Court. Again, the court turned a deaf ear and declined to entertain the case at all. Finally, Toomin ordered the trial to go forward. Jury selection would begin, he declared, on Monday, September 22, 1997, just five days short of the twenty-fifth anniversary of Billy Logan's death.

Sweat burned his eyes and dripped from his chin, as Bob wrestled the last of the boxes from the loading platform into the back of his truck. He reached up and pulled the door down until it slammed shut. He jumped down to the concrete and slid the padlock through the hasp and secured it.

This was his last load for the day and he was hustling to get ahead of the late afternoon rush-hour traffic. After three years of driving his own truck as an independent delivery service, he had his routine down pat: in by 5:30 A.M. to get the best choice of loads and then hurrying back to the terminal for a second load before serious traffic kicked in. If he got in the grip of rush-hour, he risked showing up too late to deliver. A closed business takes no freight, he had learned the hard way.

As he circled around to get in the cab, he saw the loading dock dispatcher waving his arm and yelling, "Bob! Hey, Lowe!"

"Dammit, what does he want now?" Bob muttered. He raised his arm in acknowledgment and began walking quickly toward the dispatcher's office. He dodged a forklift as it glided by, then walked up the ladder to the dock.

"Some guy was here, lookin' for you," the dispatcher said.

"Who was he?" Bob asked.

"Didn't say," the dispatcher said. "Thought it might be somebody look-ing to hire your truck for a load but when I asked, he just said he was looking for you." He reached into his shirt pocket. "Left his card, though."

Bob squinted at the card. "Who the hell is this?" he asked.

"I don't know," the dispatcher repeated. "He wants for you to call him."

"All right," Bob said and turned to walk to the public phone at the end of the loading platform.

"One more thing," the dispatcher called after him.

Bob turned.

"He had a bulge in his coat. Might have been packing heat," the dis-patcher said. "You in any kind of trouble?"

Bob felt his heart leap and struggled just to say "no."

The dispatcher shrugged and returned to his office.

Digging into his pocket for change, Bob dropped several coins into the slot and dialed. A male voice answered on the third ring: "Hello?"

"I was told to call this number," Bob said.

"This Mr. Lowe?" said the voice.

"Who's this?" Bob asked, warily. It had been nearly twenty years since he had testified against Harry, but Bob still remained cautious. Particularly when a stranger asked for him by his real name. *Who is this stranger? And what does he want?*

"Is this Mr. Bob Lowe?" the man asked.

"What do you want?" Bob demanded.

"I'm looking for Bob Lowe," the man said. "The man who is a witness against Harry Aleman. I work for Mister Aleman and I want to ask you a few questions."

Instantly, his gut tightened.

"You've got the wrong guy, pal," Bob said.

"You have a wife named Fran?" the man asked. "You have a daughter named Tiffany? A son named Rob—"

"I don't know who the fuck you are," Bob snarled. "Or who you think you're talking to, but you got a wrong number." He smashed the receiver onto the hook. Hurriedly, he strode down the platform, scrambled to his truck, and slammed it into gear. "Son of a bitch!" he yelled, flooring the accelerator.

. . . And I want to know what the hell is going on!" Bob said. He clenched the telephone in a death grip. "I *told* you what he said. He starts saying, 'You got a wife named Fran and a daughter named Tiff—' No, he said he works for Harry and he wants to ask me some questions." Pacing, he exhaled dual plumes of smoke from his nostrils. Fran had been upstairs, ironing clothes and watching television, when she heard the front door bang open. By the time she had gotten downstairs, Bob was already on the phone, his voice angry.

"Dammit, Dave," he was saying. "If he knows where I work, he knows where I live. And if he knows, Harry knows too, and—" He listened, puffing furiously on his cigarette. "I don't like this shit at all. What the hell is going on? How did this guy find me?" He paused to listen again. "What? What do you mean, you've been meaning to talk to me?" He paused. "Yeah, I'll be home tonight. I'm not going nowhere until I know what's going on."

He banged the phone onto the cradle. Wide-eyed, Fran just stared, saying nothing. Bob stared back. "It's starting again," he said.

Dave Williams was at the house within the hour, and explained to Bob and Fran that Harry would be retried for the Billy Logan murder in less than a month. Williams figured the caller had been Harry's private investigator looking for Bob, reaching out, apparently in an attempt to question him about what he would say on the witness stand.

"I ain't talking to him," Bob said.

"You don't have to," Dave replied.

"Good, I don't want any part of that, ever again," Bob said. As he said it, though, suddenly the full meaning of it all hit him. "There's gonna be a trial, is that what you're saying Dave?"

"That's what I'm saying and I'm saying we expect you to testify," Dave said.

"No." His response was without hesitation. "I did it once and I got screwed. You know what happened, Dave. I ain't gonna do it."

"You need protection again," Dave said. "And we need you to testify. This time, Harry is going down for good."

"No fuckin' way I'm moving again," Bob said. "I've had enough of moving to last my whole damn life. No. No way will I move. Count me out on that."

"We could move you tonight to a motel," Dave said. He felt bad, upset that no one had contacted Bob before he got a call from one of Harry's people. It appeared that the prosecutors were concerned that the longer Bob had to prepare for (and worry about) another trip to the witness stand, the greater the possibility that he would get spooked; he might even try to disappear. They had decided to wait until the last possible minute. But they'd blown it and now Dave was doing damage control. "We can set it up right now. You said it yourself, if they can find you at work, they can probably find you at home."

These were not idle threats as far as Williams was concerned. He had a healthy respect for any convicted felon, and Harry was no exception. Williams believed that it was Harry who had ordered the hit on Petrocelli and he also believed that Harry was the unseen hand in the attempted hit on another associate in 1990.

Lucien Senese was a top-ranking Teamsters Union official who was critically burned when his car was blown to bits in the 1000 block of South May Street—just a few hundred feet from Harry's childhood home. At the time, some speculated the attack was linked to his union position. Senese was poised to succeed his father as head of Teamsters Local 703. What Williams knew, but kept to himself, was that just before he got into his car, Senese had left the home of a woman investigators believed was a close friend of Harry's. She had been, some said, Harry's girlfriend on the side, though Allan Ackerman, Harry's lawyer, told the press, "I categorically deny any connection between my client and this woman. Mr. Aleman is happily married to his wife, Ruth."

While some investigators doubted that Harry ordered the bombing from prison, Williams thought otherwise.

But what concerned him most was the report filed by prison authorities at Oxford relating to a visit from Harry's son, Jeff. Harry was heard to say,

"The two will be taken care of if this goes to trial—one after the other." He was referring to Bob and Louie, Dave suspected. Dave believed the exchange was a sign that Harry was confident that his deadly hand could reach out from behind prison bars. Of course, Williams told none of this to Bob.

"You want me to quit my job, too?" Bob said sarcastically.

"Wouldn't be a bad idea," Williams said.

Now Bob was pacing back and forth across the living room. "I gave up a hell of a lot for you a long time ago and what did it get me?" he asked. "And now you want me to do it again? Can you guarantee that he will be convicted?"

"You know I can't do that," Dave said. "But they found you. You know that Harry knows where you are. What about your family? Your kids? What about Fran?"

Bob slumped onto the couch. He lit a cigarette and propped it in an already overflowing ashtray. "You can guard my kids and Fran, but not me. I got to drive my truck," he said, exhaling. "I don't want to have to go through with that bullshit of having a shadow. Can't even take a shit without some guy in a suit standing close enough to wipe my ass."

"If we do it for them, we do it for you," Dave said. "That's the way it has to be, Bob."

"What if I run?" Bob asked.

"We'll find you," Dave said. "Or Harry will."

"It ain't that I'm scared of Harry," Bob said, "but I won't be stupid, I guess."

"Good," Williams said. "Agents will be here tonight."

Bob laughed nervously. "You had this all figured out, didn't you?"

"It's for your own good, Bob," Dave said.

"I won't move," Bob said stubbornly. "I can't move anymore."

30

arrying a briefcase in one hand and a file folder under his arm, a somber-faced Kevin McNally walked up the center aisle of Courtroom 400, angled to his right and circled behind the scarred oak table reserved for defense lawyers and their clients. He was unmistakably a lawyer: tall with salt-and-pepper hair and a neatly trimmed full beard. His suit was dark. McNally hung his overcoat over the back of a chair near the wall, sat down at the table, and began to scan through the pile of documents he pulled from the file folder, arranging the papers to catch the natural light from the windows behind him in the dimly lit courtroom.

It was early, but the room had already begun to fill with reporters, the curious, idle prosecutors, and defense lawyers, as well as Harry's family members and friends, all hoping for a good seat for the first day of an historic trial. For the first time in U.S. history, a man acquitted of murder would go on trial for the same murder a second time.

But the historical significance was secondary for many of those who filed through the swinging rear door. They whispered and pointed toward the empty chair next to McNally. Over there, they knew, Harry Aleman would soon take a seat. They had read of him and heard of him on television. Today, they would see the man that lawmen called the most feared and deadly mob hit man in Chicago, and that his family called an innocent victim of vengeful prosecutors.

McNally scanned the room briefly and returned to his reading. The prosecutors, Scott Cassidy and Neil Linehan, had not yet arrived. Judge Michael Toomin was still in chambers. But sitting at the end of the second row, shooing away those who attempted to slide in for a close view, was a swarthy, round-faced man wearing an expensive suit.

"This is saved for the family," Bobby Cruz whispered politely, holding out his left arm to anyone who looked longingly at the empty pew beside him.

Less than six months earlier, at the urging of Cruz, Harry had dismissed Allan Ackerman, the lawyer who had labored for four years on the case, and brought in McNally. The late switch in lawyers was curious. Ackerman was far more knowledgeable about the case than McNally, who wasn't even from Chicago—his office was in Frankfort, Kentucky. Although McNally had a well-deserved national reputation as a skilled defense lawyer, particularly in death-penalty cases, his late entry had prompted him to repeatedly seek a delay in the trial. But Toomin had refused to extend the case beyond this day. The indictment, after all, had been returned nearly four years earlier.

Perhaps more curious to some was that the hiring of McNally suggested that someone had found the money for such a big gun to defend Harry. After the indictment was returned, Harry had pleaded indigence and Ackerman's bills of nearly $50,000 had subsequently been paid out of court funds.

Cruz, a cousin of Harry, personally vouched for McNally's skills. In 1995, McNally had been his lawyer when Cruz was acquitted of charges, in his fifth trial, that he masterminded a contract killing in Phoenix, Arizona. After fourteen years in prison, four of it on Death Row, Cruz had been released.

In the months prior to Harry's trial, McNally bitterly fought to bar the testimony of Cooley as being so prejudicial as to taint the case unfairly against Harry. He argued that the state knew of Cooley's version of events seven years before the indictment against Harry was returned. It was, he argued, a delay in prosecution that was unfair as well.

He complained that much of the evidence from the 1977 trial was missing. Indeed, the defense trial file had disappeared; shotgun wadding and pellets recovered from Logan's body were gone, as was Logan's bloodstained clothing; diagrams and photo displays used by Iavarone and Claps in the first trial also could not be found.

And most distressing, McNally argued, was that many of those who could have provided testimony beneficial to Harry were no longer alive. These included Frank Wilson and his courtroom deputies; Harry's mother, Mary, who, McNally said, could have testified that Almeida had called her prior to the 1977 trial and claimed he was being forced to testify against Harry; Ed Whalen, Harry's defense attorney in the first trial; and Pat Marcy and John D'Arco Sr., the two men the prosecution alleged had orchestrated the bribe payment to Wilson through Cooley. Butch Petrocelli, who, McNally said, could have contradicted the bribery allegation or could have been a live suspect in the killing, was also dead.

Judge Toomin had rejected McNally's pleas, including a last-minute request that morning to move the trial out of Cook County because of newspaper articles and television reports.

"Your Honor," McNally said. "The headline in yesterday's paper referred to Mr. Aleman as a hit man. It didn't require prospective jurors to even read the article. It was on the front page in a prominently displayed manner. We feel like we have no alternative, Your Honor, but to make an oral motion for a change of venue out of Chicago."

Cassidy noted that prospective jurors would be interviewed individually in the judge's chambers to determine the extent of their pretrial knowledge and perceptions of the case and only if there were an overwhelming response suggesting prejudice against Harry would McNally's motion have merit.

"The court has already ruled that the state should not permit any of its witnesses to say that this case has anything to do with organized crime, the mob, the mafia, or the outfit," Cassidy added.

The judge agreed and, once again, a defense motion was denied. And so, the following day, after a jury was selected and sworn, Toomin gaveled the case to order.

Harry waited patiently as sheriff's deputies unlocked the shackles from his wrists and his ankles. Rubbing his wrists gently, he walked into the packed courtroom. He was grayer at the temples than many remembered, but he still carried himself proudly. He wore glasses and a black sport coat, charcoal slacks, and a maroon knit shirt. He walked confidently through the center of the courtroom and behind the defense table, where he greeted McNally and the rest of the defense team. He looked toward the spectators and smiled at Ruth, blew her a kiss, and sat down. If he was worried, it was not apparent. He turned to chat briefly with a reporter seated in the front row.

"Your story was wrong," he said.

"How so?" the reporter asked, stunned momentarily to be conversing with a man who had refused repeated requests for interviews, a man who clearly had an intense aversion to the media, for its consistent portrayal of him as a vengeful, cold-blooded mob killer.

"You said the U.S. Supreme Court upheld Judge Toomin's ruling that double jeopardy did not apply," Harry whispered. He stared directly into the reporter's eyes.

"And—?" the reporter said.

"The Supreme Court never ruled on it," Harry said. "They refused to take the case. There's a difference. You ought to know that."

McNally looked over and frowned. He touched Harry's arm, pulling him away from the reporter, who, as if awakened from a trance, began scribbling frantically.

"Everyone rise for the jury," a deputy intoned, as the eight women and four men filed into their seats. Their careers were as disparate as their hometowns. There was a musician, a stockbroker, an insurance agent, a housewife, and a marketing consultant. They came from suburbs north, south and west of Chicago. They came from the North and South sides of the city.

The courtroom was standing room only when Neil Linehan rose to make the opening statement for the prosecution. Sitting on the left side of the spectator seats, directly behind the prosecution table, were members of Logan's family, including his brother, Richard, and sister, Joanna. They would soon relive the last moments of their brother's life when their sister, Betty Romo, took the stand. They sat crammed into pews with FBI agents, many veteran defense lawyers, and numerous fellow prosecutors eager to see Linehan and Cassidy at work. Among their number was Joe Claps, still a prosecutor but soon to be named a judge. Nick Iavarone was absent. He was a prospective witness, and Toomin had ruled witnesses were not allowed into the courtroom until they testified.

Linehan's opening statement took just seventeen minutes and promised that the evidence would show that Harry was guilty beyond a reasonable doubt.

Then, McNally arose to begin Harry's defense. "Harry Aleman did not shoot Bill Logan on September twenty-seventh, nineteen seventy-two," he began. "Harry Aleman was not in the automobile from where the shots were fired that night. This is the rest of the story." He paused and looked at the jurors. "The only reason that we're here, the only reason, is because a corrupt lawyer, a corrupt former policeman, claims that he passed some money to a distinguished judge of this court in nineteen seventy-seven—alone—with no one else watching."

He predicted that the evidence would show that on the night of Logan's death, Bob was unable to identify anyone in the car containing the killer. "An important question will be whether the gunman got out of the car," he said. "This is an issue we ask you to pay a lot of attention to. Other neighbors heard this. Other neighbors looked out.

"Ladies and gentlemen. The evidence will be that no one saw Mr. Lowe, let alone the gunman standing next to the car from where the shots were fired. No one saw the gunman. Except Bobby Lowe.

"We have the police file from nineteen seventy-two. And the officers will tell you that they knew nothing about any supposed identification of Harry Aleman within a couple weeks of the killing. And Officer Griffin, who was the chief investigating officer in this case, didn't even know. The description that he was given by Mr. Lowe on that night is 'two white males.' No further identification."

McNally suggested that Bob had agreed to identify Harry as the killer for money. "You will hear of perhaps as much as fifty thousand dollars in direct money for living expenses—rent, for travel," McNally said, hammering away at Bob's credibility throughout his opening statement.

The first witness called was Betty Romo, and her testimony mirrored that of the first trial. The memory was so strong that she wept as she recalled the moment when she ran, screaming, onto the lawn and clutched her bleeding brother as his life ebbed away.

Cooley provided the most dramatic moment of the day when he described his life of corruption and, later, his career as a federal informant. He had worn a concealed tape recorder while he met with men he said killed for a living. His bravado crumbled only once—when he related the final payment to Wilson in 1977. McNally sarcastically suggested that his demeanor was an act, a performance designed to elicit sympathy from the jury and to boost his own credibility, but the testimony rang true when Cooley recalled meeting Wilson in the bathroom of the restaurant after Wilson had acquitted Harry.

"I gave him the money," Cooley said. "The seventy-five hundred dollars." He paused and silence fell over the courtroom as Cooley struggled to keep his composure. For several seconds, though it seemed longer, his face twitched and his jaw clenched tight. Harry sat quietly at the defense table, staring at Cooley. "He was a broken man," Cooley finally uttered, his voice cracking. "He said, 'That's all I'm going to get?'"

Cooley pressed his fingers to the bridge of his nose. Spectators lining the walls imperceptibly leaned forward, straining to hear the hushed words.

"I started to tell him—he turned his back on me—that I would give him more. He said, 'You destroyed me. You've killed me,' and he walked out. I knew what had happened to me and to the judge."

"What was that?" Linehan asked.

"We had been used," Cooley replied. "I destroyed him."

When Toomin recessed after Cooley's testimony, he instructed the jurors not to talk about the case among themselves or with anyone else. "If anyone should endeavor to speak to you about the matter, please bring that to the attention of the sheriffs," he said.

This was a standard warning given to jurors, but seemed more urgent in this case, and, when court convened the next day, the prosecutors and defense attorneys immediately went into Toomin's chambers for a private conference that lasted more than an hour. It was a tense meeting prompted by a juror's sudden fear for her life and her decision to telephone a friend, a prosecutor, and ask for advice.

Prior to trial, Toomin had rejected McNally's request to sequester the jury in favor of issuing his strong admonitions against reading the newspapers or watching television accounts of the case. But now, Cassidy and Linehan reported, the juror had violated her sworn promise not to discuss the case with anyone. The implications were significant. *Was this,* Cassidy wondered, *another attempt to corrupt justice?*

Toomin summoned the woman, a flight attendant and nurse, to his chambers and asked her to explain.

"Well, to be honest," she said, "I was just worried about this case and where it's going and what could happen to me as well as, you know, family members or whatever. So I just wanted to know if there was anything that I could do to take myself out of it."

Nervously, she said that after hearing Cooley's testimony and McNally's opening statement refer to numerous witnesses who were no longer alive, she became scared and could not sleep. She had once dated a journalist who had received death threats, she said, "And my mind is just racing with—the media, with everything—books, movies. Your mind plays tricks on you. I mean, when they offer that there are many witnesses who are not here to be able to testify these days, I mean, I don't know if that's all because of natural causes. Yes, it was twenty-five years ago, but—I don't know."

Toomin asked if she had discussed her feelings with any other jurors.

"I guess so," she said.

"What kind of discussions?" the judge asked.

"Just basically, you know, I hope we're around after this," she said. "We'll exchange Christmas cards and hopefully we are all around at Christmastime. Just things like that. We just kind of lightheartedly talked about it."

"In spite of my admonition not to discuss anything about the case, jurors have been discussing it?" Toomin asked, concern apparent in his tone.

"We walk in and we're not stone-faced," the woman replied. "We just kind of sigh, look at each other, 'Wow, that was interesting, can't wait for tomorrow.'"

Toomin questioned the woman at length and, finally, was convinced she had directly discussed the issue of fear for her own safety with the remaining members of the jury. His concern, as well as that of the defense team, was that the entire jury panel had been tainted.

"Our fear," McNally declared, "is that Harry the hit man is in the jury room somehow."

Ultimately, Toomin disagreed. He refused to question any of the other eleven jurors or the four alternate jurors. Instead, he dismissed the woman from the panel, replaced her with one of the alternates, and ordered the trial to continue. The lawyers, followed by Toomin, returned to the courtroom and the jury was seated.

"The court is assembled," Toomin declared. "The state has further evidence to present at this time. You may proceed, Mr. Cassidy."

Cassidy arose. "Thank you, Your Honor," he said. "May it please the court, the state would call Bobby Lowe."

31

Jim Green had been a Chicago police officer for thirty years, most of it as a detective. After retiring from the force, this solidly built native of Detroit followed a path well worn by other retired police officers. He became an investigator for the Cook County State's Attorney's Office, his work primarily involving serving subpoenas, tracking down recalcitrant witnesses, and helping prosecutors prepare cases for trial.

His duties were expanded on August 30, 1997, when he was assigned to provide security for Bob after Harry's private detective tracked him down on the loading dock.

"I am your shadow," Green told Bob when they first met. "I will be with you first thing in the morning until you get home at night."

Bob eyed Jim and pointed toward his truck parked in the driveway. "I hope you like driving," he said, "because I spend most of my day on the front seat of that truck."

Jim smiled. "My second job while I was a police officer was driving a truck," he said. "I think I can handle it."

But the routine, he soon discovered, was exhausting. Jim had to leave his home at 4 A.M. just to meet Bob by 5 A.M. After a stop for coffee, they drove to the loading dock where Bob inspected loads waiting to be delivered. On the floor, under the glove compartment, Jim kept a small leather tote bag containing a cell phone and a two-way radio to communicate with the agents who were always following them in a tail car. His nine-millimeter semiautomatic was tucked under his shirttail, which hung over his belt. The team of agents in the tail car was replaced at midday, but Jim stayed on the truck, helping Bob to load and unload. Not until Bob went home, which was usually after 7 A.M., did Jim make his way back home and to bed.

Almost from the start, they enjoyed each other's company. Bob found Jim to be a man who liked the outdoors and long rides on his motorcycle. He was a man who didn't treat him gently, but like a man. He was blunt, but honest. And in Bob, Jim found a man who seemed to want nothing more than to put in a hard day's work, get paid for it, and be able to provide for his family. "He was a down-to-earth, honest guy who was street smart and knew how to make money driving a truck," Jim later said. "He got to the dock before anyone else to look over the loads and find the most profitable ones. He bought coffee for the dispatchers and told them jokes. They liked Bob and they would do favors for him. Bob worked hard. He drove real fast because the faster he moved, the more he made. It was hard to keep up with him."

The days were long and sweaty. Bob was delivering mostly computer hardware and made several deliveries each day. As they sped from pickup to dropoff, Jim always tried to keep the conversation away from the approaching trial. But as it neared, he could see Bob get increasingly tense.

"Bob was real shook up," Jim would later say. "He was thinking that Harry's people would arrange to talk to him and nobody would ever see him again."

Just before the trial, Bob came back to Walton Street. He was brought there by Cassidy, Green, and Linehan to reenact the events on the night Billy Logan was killed. They had tried to do it with Bob in their courthouse offices, but using only pictures of the neighborhood, they had found Bob to be vague on details. He would meander, not answer their questions directly, or add details that they found superfluous. They wanted it right and so here they were, as the sun was setting, pulling their car to the curb at 5903 West Walton Street. Cassidy asked Bob to start on the top step of the stairs of his former home and it was there that he began to talk, saying, "I was just coming out of the door and Ginger ran out between my legs and down the stairs. I noticed the car sitting by the curb over there. The engine was running. I didn't take much notice of it, except for the fact that the engine was on."

He turned left through the gate in the chain-link fence and began walking west. "I seen Billy come out of his house and I started to cross the street," he said, stepping off the curb, shocked to discover that Billy's house was no longer standing. It was gone and in its place was a vacant lot. "The car came past me and stopped. Billy was walking toward his car, which was parked right there. And then I heard this voice say, 'Hey, Billy,' and then there was a shot. It was loud."

Bob stopped, as if he were visualizing the scene. "I was right behind the car. There were two shots. Billy flew back. I seen a man come out of the car. He had an object in his left hand. He was making a bending motion toward Billy. He turned and looked at me. We stared at each other. I was frozen— in shock, I guess. It was a few seconds. And then I ran."

"Where was Billy Logan?" Cassidy asked.

Bob stepped onto the curb and walked toward the sidewalk. He pointed. "Right over here," he said. "He was—"

His voice caught. For several seconds, Bob stood still, his arm extended toward the grass, as he struggled to regain his composure. He shook his head as if to dismiss the images blooming so vividly there.

"I—" he began, but choked again.

Jim stepped toward him, but Bob waved him away and turned toward the sidewalk. "I'll be OK," he said. "Give me a minute."

When they had finished, they drove to the courthouse, smuggling Bob in through a basement entrance and into Toomin's courtroom to familiarize him with the stage on which he would soon star. The attorneys had been stunned by Bob's "performance" on Walton Street. There, Bob's story was a masterful narrative, without any of the digressions that had worried them during previous debriefings. When he and Jim left the courthouse, Linehan and Cassidy exchanged confident nods.

For most of the forty-five-minute drive home, Bob and Jim rode in silence, Jim behind the wheel and Bob in the passenger seat.

"They don't need to ever ask me to do this again," Bob said abruptly.

"Huh?" Jim said.

"If they ever need me again, I'm not getting involved," Bob declared. "I'm doing fine now and then this all comes up again. Is this the way it's gonna be for my whole life?"

He cracked the window farther down and pitched out his cigarette, then promptly lit another. Jim just listened.

"I mean, I'm doing all right now, but I wasted a lot of years. And I regret that," Bob said, anger rising in his voice. "That judge called me a liar. Harry got away with murder. I got screwed. The system screwed me up so bad. You know"—he paused and then abruptly, as if a thought had just occurred to him though the questions had haunted him for more than two decades, he said, "What if I take the dog out five minutes later? What if I'm not there? None of this happens. What would my life have been like then?"

Jim shifted in his seat, but said nothing.

"This is the last time," Bob said. "I won't do this again. I've paid too high a price. We've all paid too high a price."

"Bob," said Jim, measuring his words. "Everybody pays."

I wonder what it's gonna feel like seeing him after all these years?" Bob said as he and Jim sat in the witness room behind Toomin's chambers. Bob was wearing black jeans and a blue, gray, and white shirt with broad horizontal stripes. "You think I'll recognize him?" he asked. "Will he look the same?"

"Do you look the same?" Jim asked.

Cassidy poked his head through the door.

"Bob?" he said. "You're up."

Nervously, Bob stood up, dropping his cigarette into the bottom of a half-filled coffee cup. He pushed his glasses up on the bridge of his nose, wiped his sweaty palms on his pants, and walked into the courtroom. Jim followed and stood discreetly off to the side, behind the witness stand.

As he sat down after taking the oath, Bob cast a glance toward the defense table. Harry had pushed his chair back from the table and was sitting with his legs crossed.

Cassidy wasted no time, leading Bob through a series of preliminary questions and directing him to the moment when the car pulled past him on Walton Street. Jurors craned their necks as Bob's deep voice, gravelly from his years of smoking, spilled from the witness stand.

"Where did that car come to a stop at?" Cassidy asked.

"Just in front of Billy's car."

"What happened next?"

"I heard two loud noises."

"Where from?" Cassidy asked.

"The car," Bob replied.

"What did you see Billy Logan do at this time?"

"Fly backwards."

"What happened next?"

"I seen a man get out of the car," Bob said.

Cassidy stepped to the side of the podium. "Mr. Lowe, I would ask if you can look around the courtroom and see if you see that person today that you saw twenty-five years ago."

The courtroom, with all its seats filled and spectators standing along the walls, went still. Bob's eyes darted toward the defense table.

"Yes, sir," he said.

"Can you please point to him, sir, and describe to the jury what he's wearing and where he is sitting?"

Bob raised his left arm and pointed. "The gentleman right there, wearing a gray shirt," he said.

"Why don't you get off the witness stand and walk over so we know exactly who you are pointing to?" Cassidy asked.

Bob was surprised. Cassidy had only told him he would have to point out Harry from the witness stand. But he was not afraid. Instead, he found himself immediately seized by anger, at Harry, at the justice system, at all those lost years, and at himself for losing those years.

"You want me to come down?" he asked.

"Yes, if you would," Cassidy said.

It was a confrontation twenty years in the making, a confrontation he had not dared to dream would ever occur. No one spoke. No one moved. Jurors' heads swiveled as Bob stepped off the stand and angled toward the center of the courtroom. He walked and didn't stop until he was ten feet from Harry, who sat stock still, his eyes inscrutable behind his wire-rimmed glasses.

Slowly, Bob lifted his left arm. With a finger gnarled and stained by years of work, Bob pointed to Harry's face.

"This man right here," he said, the words firm and clear and carrying just a hint of his southern accent.

Aleman didn't flinch.

For what seemed minutes, but was only a few seconds, Bob's arm remained frozen, pointing. Cassidy tried to let the moment linger, but McNally interrupted, attempting to break the spell.

"This is an identification of a man he saw in a courtroom twenty years ago, Your Honor?" he asked.

Bob dropped his arm.

"No," Toomin declared. "This is the identification in open court today by this witness of the defendant, Harry Aleman."

As Bob returned to the stand, he felt invigorated, cleansed, free. It was as if a great weight had come off his shoulders. He felt lighter, younger, and, as Cassidy continued his questions, he knew he could take whatever they tried in cross-examination.

"Now, Mr. Lowe," said Cassidy, "what, if anything happened next?"

"I guess my dog scared him," Bob said. "We faced each other and I turned and ran."

"You say your dog scared him. What did your dog do?" Cassidy asked.

"The dog sort of like leaped, jumped."

"What did you see the defendant do at that time?"

"We stared at each other," Bob said.

"You stared at him?" Cassidy repeated, hammering the point home to the jurors. There was no need. Their eyes were glued on Bob.

"Yes, sir," Bob replied.

"And he stared at you?"

"Yes, sir."

"What then did you do?"

"I ran," Bob said.

"When you ran, sir, what, if anything did you hear or see?" Cassidy asked.

Bob took a sip of water and cleared his throat. "I heard another loud noise and then I heard the car drive away," he said.

"Where did you run to?"

"Some bushes," Bob said. "I didn't see anything when I jumped behind the bushes."

Under Cassidy's careful questioning, Bob described how he had come up from behind the pile of brush on the street to see the car driving westbound on Walton Street. The car, he said, was dark. And he recounted how he had identified Harry in the police mug-shot books in the weeks after the shooting and four years later picked Harry's photo from the group shown him at the hospital by police officers Law and Mudry. And he told the jury about picking Harry out of a lineup in the weeks before Harry was indicted in 1977.

Each time, Cassidy asked Bob to point to the person he had identified, and each time Bob raised his arm and pointed to Harry at the defense table.

In all, Bob pointed to Harry seven times.

32

The cross-examination was excruciating. Repeatedly, McNally attempted to shake Bob, to confuse him, to induce a stumble. He forced Bob to retrace his testimony on direct examination in minute detail, hoping for alterations and shifts that he could use to buttress his argument that Bob was fabricating and embellishing. McNally believed—and wanted the jury to agree—that the initial police report from the night of the shooting, which gave Bob's description of the gunman as only a male white, accurately summarized all that Bob knew and that the rest of his testimony was concocted. McNally subscribed to a theory that Bob had invented the story back in 1976 to get a new start in life with a new identity and, over the years, had come to believe it as truth.

A skilled questioner, McNally had ripped into Cooley's testimony with an arsenal of Cooley's bad acts during a career of crime, and he intended to do the same when Louie Almeida hit the stand. He had wanted to attack Bob's baggage: bad checks, his convictions for the gas station heists and his alcohol and drug abuse. But that all happened more than ten years ago, some of it was more than twenty years old, and therefore legally inadmissible. Mc-

Nally's best shot was to rattle Bob, to make him appear unsure and unreliable. But he found Bob was alert, poised, and ready.

"So, the car pulls right past you?" McNally asked.

"Yes, sir."

"Within feet, right?"

"Yes, sir."

"And you did see the vehicle, right?" McNally asked.

"Yes, sir, I did," Bob replied.

"But you didn't notice the driver?"

"I wasn't anticipating anything happening," Bob said. "I heard two loud noises. I seen a gentleman come out. I seen *that* gentleman." He raised his arm again and jabbed an index finger toward Harry.

McNally grimaced and said, snappishly, "I haven't asked you if you saw any gentleman."

"You are trying to put words in my mouth, sir," Bob retorted.

"I haven't tried to put words in your mouth," McNally replied. "I'm asking you questions. OK? Do you mind?"

Irritated, Bob said, "The thing of it is, you are trying to get me to say something. I didn't notice the car. I noticed it coming by me. I assumed it was going to keep going westbound."

McNally changed the subject.

"Tell us exactly what happens when the man gets out of the car."

"I seen him walking over towards where Billy Logan was."

"You heard two loud noises," McNally summarized. "You see a long object being withdrawn through the window and Mr. Logan flies back, what, four or five feet?"

"I don't know how many feet he flew back," Bob said. "That's when I seen him get out of the car and start towards Billy."

"What was this person wearing?" McNally asked.

"I don't know, sir."

McNally paused to let the answer float in front of the jury just a little longer and to let them catch a breath. Their heads had been snapping back and forth between the defense lawyer and the witness like spectators at a tennis match.

"How far are you from this person?" McNally asked.

"Three to four feet."

Like Frank Whalen had in the first trial, McNally pounced.

"You're three to four feet from this person and you can't tell us anything that he is wearing?"

This time, Bob would not be flustered. "No, sir, I cannot," he said.

McNally fired off a rapid series of questions, Bob fired right back.

"Well, it was a male, right?

"Yes, sir, it was."

"Was it a white male?"

"Yes, sir, it was."

"And what did he have in his hand?"

"I seen an object in his hands," Bob said. "It looked like a pistol. I'm not a gun expert. I don't know."

"Where is your dog at this point?"

"She was running around," Bob replied. "I don't know where she was at. She was around me."

"How did the dog react to the first two loud noises, Mr. Lowe?" McNally asked.

"I don't remember, sir," Bob said.

"You don't remember any reaction?"

"From the dog, no," Bob replied, prompting a few snickers in the back of the courtroom from observers who apparently thought McNally wasn't making much headway.

"And what was your reaction to it?" he asked.

"It all happened so fast," Bob said. "I reacted to the whole thing by running."

McNally raised his eyebrows, feigning incredulity.

"Mr. Lowe," he said, straightening up to his full height and gripping the podium. "When you heard two loud noises and saw a long object being pulled back through the window and you saw Mr. Logan, your acquaintance, fly back a number of feet in the air, did you not turn and run at *that* point, sir?"

"No, sir, I did not," Bob replied. "Not at that point. It was like I was in shock. It wasn't like it happened: so I'll take this step, I'll take that step. The man got out of the car. That's when we faced each other, and then I realized—it hit what was happening—and then I ran."

"OK," McNally said, pursing his lips. He looked down at his notes in thought and then looked up. "So, how long did you and the man with the object in his hand face one another?"

"A couple of seconds—about four seconds," Bob said.

McNally waited.

"Four or five seconds," Bob added.

"Did you forget about lunging for your dog?"

"No, sir, I did not," Bob retorted. "You asked me what my dog was doing before then. My dog did lunge for him. I think that's why he turned around and looked at me."

Speaking as if he were addressing a small child, McNally said, "Describe exactly, Mr. Lowe, what the dog did regarding lunging."

"She like leaped up on the car," Bob said. "I grabbed at her. I grabbed at my dog's collar."

"Meanwhile, what is the man with the object in his hand doing?" McNally asked.

"That's what I said," Bob said with a note of impatience. "We faced each other."

"And then you ran?"

"Yes, sir," Bob said.

"And you'll never forget that incident, will you?" McNally asked with a tone of derision.

Bob's answer came forcefully: "It hasn't left me for twenty-five years."

McNally pulled out the police reports written up on the night of the shooting and began to pick away at Bob, asking questions designed to suggest that Bob had given certain information that he was now contradicting. A smart defense lawyer knows that police rarely report verbatim what a witness says, but instead cobble together a summary. The reports also frequently contain information that is less than accurate, but they are intended to provide a broader picture of possibilities. A witness who reports seeing a tall man might be asked to give a range of height and reply that the person was taller than six feet. If the eventual arrestee is five feet, eleven inches tall, a skillful defense lawyer can suggest that the witness is fabricating or embellishing on the stand by asking if the witness had ever told police the defendant was more than six feet tall. Such questions can confuse a witness who is not prepared, alert, or attuned to the intricacies of the inquiry.

"What you told those officers that night was that you saw two occupants in a dark, possibly black nineteen-seventy or 'seventy-one Mercury Cougar or Montego parked in front of your house?" McNally asked.

"I don't remember that," Bob replied. "No, sir, I don't."

"You told them, did you not, that you saw the car drive west on Walton and then heard three gunshots in succession?"

"I never said three," Bob said. "I said I heard two loud noises. I heard a third shot when I turned and ran."

"That night you told them you saw a man getting in the car, right?"

"I never seen a man get in the car," Bob said.

"You don't remember telling them that you saw a man get *in* the car instead of *out* of the car?" McNally asked. Again, he sounded incredulous.

Now it was Bob's turn to talk as if he were addressing a child, saying, "I seen the gentleman get *out* of the car."

In great detail, McNally revisited Bob's description of picking Harry's photograph from the police mug-shot books, suggesting again through his questions that Bob was lying.

"And so the officers thanked you for your help and said they'd be in touch, right?"

"Said they'd be in touch, yes," Bob said.

"And what happened?" McNally asked. "Nothing for four years?"

"I never heard anything else," Bob answered.

"That's your testimony?" McNally asked in disbelief.

"Right."

"And I take it you didn't call anybody up?"

"I figured I don't know anything about police business," Bob said patiently. "That was something that they had to deal with."

McNally suggested that Bob had once described the car as a two-door Cougar with bucket seats.

Exasperated, Bob retorted, "Well, I didn't see inside the car, so how can I say that it had bucket seats?"

Sensing Bob was losing his temper, McNally pushed him harder, asking a question that included at least two facts that, if Bob would agree to, could provide ammunition to attack his credibility.

"Why did you tell them that you saw the gunman get out and push the bucket seat of the Cougar forward?"

Bob flared. "Now there you go—" he said before catching himself. "Yes, I did see him get out," he said evenly. "I don't know what he was pushing forward or if he was pushing anything. I seen him get out. I don't know what he was doing."

"You did not tell them it was a two-door 1971 Cougar with bucket seats?" McNally asked again.

"I don't know if it was a Cougar," Bob said. "I don't know if it was a two-door."

McNally chipped away at Bob over the size of the barrel of the gun pulled into the car, how many feet Logan had flown back after he was hit, and whether he saw the gunman fire the third shot. As hard as McNally pushed, Bob remained firm, forcing McNally to abruptly shift gears.

"At what point, sir," he asked, "did you begin to receive benefits from the State's Attorney's Office?"

"What do you call benefits, sir?" Bob shot back.

"Rent."

Something finally snapped and, his voice rising, Bob said, "Sir, they made me quit my job. They made me move. You want to switch places with me?"

McNally tried again. "At what point did you receive—"

Bob cut him off. "I never received a *dime*, sir," he declared defiantly. "They paid my bills. They made my rent."

He glared at McNally, his brow furrowed in anger. "If you take what they gave me and you spread it over the years that I've suffered with this, it don't amount to a hill of beans. You want to switch places with me?"

McNally pushed him. "How long did the payments last, sir?"

"They took care of me until the trial was over and then they relocated me," Bob said. "And that was the last of it."

McNally asked him to estimate the total he had received.

"I'm not even going to try because I don't know what it was," Bob said. "They paid my rent. They bought my food. I'd be sitting here telling a lie if I tried to estimate it."

"You told Judge Wilson it was four thousand dollars," McNally said.

"I estimated," Bob protested. "They asked me to estimate, just like you are asking me to do, sir. I estimated four thousand because I wasn't sure what it was. They said it was seven thousand dollars. I agreed. I didn't know what it was."

"You were having a lot of financial problems around that time, weren't you?" McNally asked.

"I'm still having financial problems," Bob replied.

"You blame it all on this case, right?" McNally asked.

"The vast majority of it, yes," Bob said.

"All of the troubles that you've had are in connection with your services as a witness in this case, is that your testimony?"

"Yes, sir."

Cassidy took up immediately when McNally finished. In response, Bob explained that he had said little to the detectives on the night of the shooting because of what he had just seen and because his father's warning— "Don't say anything. You'll suffer for it later"—had given him pause.

In the questions and answers that followed, Cassidy was able to vividly paint the desolation that had come over Bob and his family in the months before and the years after the first trial.

"Isn't it true, Mr. Lowe, that in nineteen seventy-seven, the State's Attorney's Office of Cook County made you quit your job?"

"Yes, sir, they did."

"You were making two hundred forty-seven dollars a week?"

"Yes, sir."

"And they paid you two hundred fifty dollars, right?"

"Yes, sir."

"You gained three bucks, didn't you, Mr. Lowe?"

"Yes, sir."

"And they said, Mr. Lowe, take your four children and we're getting you out of town," Cassidy said. "Is that what happened, Mr. Lowe?"

"Yes, sir."

"And they pulled them out of the schools they were in?"

"Yes, sir."

"They gave up the doctors they had?"

"Yes, sir."

"You hit the road, right?"

"Yes, sir," Bob said.

"They made you change your name, didn't they, Mr. Lowe?"

"Yes, sir."

"Those kids of yours, you had to change their names," Cassidy continued. "Did you change them?"

"Yes, sir."

"And right before trial, for four or five weeks, you traveled throughout the South, isn't that right?"

"Yes, sir."

Relentlessly, Cassidy continued. It was powerful and compelling. The enormity of the impact his decision to testify had had on Bob and his family was profoundly sad to many in the courtroom.

"You were at a hotel for a week and then you moved to another hotel? You and your four kids and your wife, right?"

"Yes, sir."

"But there were other people there, weren't there?" Cassidy asked.

"Yes, sir."

"You weren't just with your family, were you?"

"No," Bob said. "I had the Illinois Bureau of Investigation living with me."

"They were part of your family for weeks, right?"

"Yes, sir."

"You made a lot of money off this, is that right, Mr. Lowe?"

For just a moment, Bob did not reply. And in that moment, the silence of the courtroom was palpable. It was a silence of awe. It was a silence of re-

spect. It was a moment when even a man such as Harry might have grudgingly conceded that the man across the room had sacrificed much. It was a
moment when even Harry might have considered, had his liberty not been
so much at stake, that Bob had been cheated so many years before.

Bob broke the silence, saying, "I made so much I lost my family and
everything."

In the second row behind the prosecution table, a single tear trickled
down the cheek of Betty Romo, overcome by the thought of what Bob had
done, had endured, for her dead brother.

"And after the trial, Mr. Lowe," Cassidy said, "with a new name, you had
to move away. You had to move up to Wisconsin, right?"

"Yes, sir."

"And *that's* where the money went, isn't that right?"

"I guess so," Bob said.

"And then, I showed up."

"Yes, sir."

"You told me to go to hell, didn't you?" Cassidy asked.

"Damn right I did," Bob said.

33

The appearance of Louie Almeida provided comic relief to the otherwise serious proceedings. Although he had been given a new identity after entry into the Federal Witness Protection Program following Harry's first trial, the aging process had provided him with the best disguise. Louie had gained perhaps twenty-five to thirty pounds and lost most of his hair, though he now sported a beard. He did not appear to have increased his level of mental ability significantly in the twenty-five years since he first hit the stand, as he described how he had become a criminal after dropping out of school at age sixteen while still in the sixth grade.

His memory, never one of his stronger assets, was of less help in 1997 than it was in 1977, and McNally's attempts to undercut his testimony with contradictions in his various statements were frequently thwarted by the same answer: "I don't remember. I forget."

One of McNally's ploys, an attempt to tie Petrocelli to Billy's murder, backfired. Armed with a copy of one of Louie's early statements to authorities, McNally pointed out that Louie had recounted how he and Butch had committed three separate bombings—a currency exchange, a tavern, and a beauty shop—on the night of October 31, 1972, a little more than a month after Billy Logan's murder. Over the objections of prosecutors, McNally had convinced Toomin to allow the testimony because, he argued, Louie and Butch were in the same car used on the night of Billy's murder. Such evidence, he argued, helped back his contention that Butch had committed the murder, not Harry.

But McNally had not bargained for Louie's penchant for remembering cars. Louie readily admitted to the bombings with Butch and said they were driving a Ford LTD.

"You remember that car because it's the same car that you used when Mr. Logan was murdered a month earlier, right?" McNally asked.

"I don't know, sir, I forgot," Louie stammered. But then he corrected himself. "It was a different car."

Cassidy exploited the mistake in his later questioning of Louie, asking, "Do you recall testifying, sir, that you drove a nineteen seventy-one Plymouth during the murder?"

"Yes, sir," Louie said.

"Is that the car that you earlier described as being a work car?"

"Yes, sir."

"The one with the souped-up engine?"

"Yes, sir."

"The one with the weights in the back?"

"Yes, sir."

"Was that the same car that you were driving with Butch Petrocelli doing the bombings or a different car?"

"I think it was a different car," Louie said.

"Thank you," Cassidy said smugly. "No further questions.

In Harry's defense, McNally presented four separate frontal attacks on the prosecution's case. None directly showed that Harry was not the killer, but all were designed to muddy the waters, to create doubt in the minds of the jury—or just one juror. That's all he would need to create a hung jury and a mistrial.

He began by calling Herbert Leon McDonald, a ballistics expert who had investigated and testified in hundreds of cases, including those of Dr. Martin Luther King Jr. and Robert F. Kennedy. McNally wanted McDonald to plant the seed that Bob was wrong about there being a third shot from a pistol. McDonald told the jury that his examination of the autopsy report and autopsy photographs of Billy Logan showed that all of his wounds were caused by shotgun pellets from a distance of six to twelve feet.

"Did you see any evidence, based on the material and the evidence you reviewed, which indicated a third wound?" McNally asked.

"No, I didn't," McDonald said. "I found nothing to substantiate another shot."

He stood in front of the jury box and held up a .45-caliber bullet to explain how a .45-caliber pistol ejects the empty shell after the slug is fired from the barrel.

"Do you know whether or not a shell casing from a forty-five was found in the crime scene search?" McNally asked.

Linehan interrupted. "We will stipulate that there was no forty-five shell casing found," he said.

"Based on the material you reviewed, Professor McDonald, is there any information or evidence that has come to your attention that William Logan received three gunshot wounds, one of which was caused by a forty-five caliber weapon?" McNally asked.

"No," McDonald said. "I found no evidence to support or substantiate that."

In an attempt to suggest that Bob's trial testimony was an exagerrated lie, detectives James Griffin and Robert Shanahan, the two police officers who interviewed Bob the night of the killing, were summoned to the stand to recount Bob's statements to them. Both men said Bob never mentioned anything about standing face to face with Harry.

"Griffin and I were the preliminary investigators assigned at the time of the homicide," Shanahan said.

"Did you interview a Bob Lowe?" McNally asked.

"Yes, we did."

"Did he give you any physical description of the gunman, other than white male?" McNally asked.

"Not that I recall," Shanahan said.

"Do you have any knowledge that Mr. Lowe identified a suspect in the murder of William Logan in nineteen seventy-two?"

"No, I do not," Shanahan replied.

Griffin told the jury, "I believe he said he was in close proximity, but he never said he came face to face with the shooter."

On cross-examination, however, Griffin said he interviewed Bob for ten minutes at most, and that he was reticent to provide information. "He really didn't want to get involved. He seemed withdrawn, fearful," Griffin said.

"At that time, did you recognize that Bob was holding something back?" Cassidy asked.

"Yes, sir, I did," Griffin said.

To further try to cast doubt on Bob's trial testimony, McNally called Detective Richard Law, who, while working for Nick Iavarone, had interviewed Bob in 1976 and showed Bob the photographs at the hospital where Bob had picked out Harry's picture. McNally confronted Law with his report of that interview that said Bob "saw the white male point the weapon towards the victim in the area of the upper body or head and fire one shot." The point was important, because Bob testified at the trial that he only heard and did not see a third shot.

"That's a summary of what Mr. Lowe told us," Law replied. "A summary of it, not his exact words."

"Would you point out where it says that he told you that he ran across the street, jumped over a bush, and heard the third shot?" McNally asked, referring to Bob's version while on the witness stand.

"Well, the shot is in there," Law said.

"Yes, the shot is in there," McNally said. "He's watching him shoot, right? Into the upper body, right? Isn't that what your report says?"

"Yes," Law said. "This is a summary of our conversation, counsel."

"Do you not see the difference in my question, sir?" McNally pressed. "Did he tell you that he saw the man shoot into the upper body or did he tell you that he ran across the street, jumped over a bush and heard it?"

"This is a summary," Law insisted. "If you'd like me to explain my conversation, I'll be more than happy to, counsel."

"No," McNally retorted. "I just want to know which version he told you. Which of those two facts did he tell you?"

"The version that he told me is that when Mr. Logan was shot by the shotgun and fell back, Mr. Aleman stepped out of the car and pointed a handgun where Mr. Logan had fallen back and as Mr. Lowe turned, he heard a shot," Law said. "I inquired, 'Did you see the fire from the gun?' He said, 'No.' I asked him if he, Mr. Lowe, had a gun. He said, 'No.' Had he seen Mr. Logan with a gun? No. Or the person who was driving the car? And those were the only persons he saw in the street. The only person that had a gun was Mr. Aleman. And when he turned, he heard the shot, right there. Not down the street or on somebody's porch—right there, as he turned. And that's my summary."

Judge "Fair Fred" Suria was called in an attempt to undermine the prosecution evidence that the first trial was fixed. Suria testified that after he excused himself from hearing Harry's case because they were distantly related by marriage, he called the clerk's office so that the case could be reassigned. He said he was aware that Wilson had previously been named in Maloney's Substitution of Judge motion.

"The state was actually antsy to get to trial and I wanted to get it down and out to whoever was going to hear it as quickly as possible," Suria declared. "As a result I made no mention. My error. I wasn't even thinking. There were no objections at that time."

Wilson, he recalled, was a hard-nosed, state-oriented judge with an impeccable reputation for honesty, a man who had no empathy or sympathy for criminals. He was asked if anyone, including Pat Marcy, had told him to get off the case.

"No one asked or suggested at any time that I should excuse myself from this case," Suria said. "I do not know Pat Marcy except by newspaper reports. I have never met him." He flatly denied anyone ever offered him money or favors to get off Harry's case.

Edward Whalen Jr. was called to rebut Cooley's testimony that he had met Frank Whalen in the Bismarck Hotel in downtown Chicago to discuss strategy prior to Harry's first trial. "There was no Robert Cooley around my uncle during this trial," he said.

"Where did your uncle stay during the trial, Mr. Whalen?" McNally asked.

"He stayed in a condominium in the John Hancock building," Whalen replied. "It was owned by a friend of my father's."

"How is it you remember he stayed at the Hancock building?"

"We had meetings there," Whalen said. "Mr. Aleman was there. My uncle was there. We met there while my uncle stayed there."

"Was there any meeting whatsoever at the Bismarck Hotel?"

"No," Whalen said.

"Was there any meeting that you were at with a Robert Cooley?" McNally asked.

"I'll say it again," Whalen said firmly. "I never met Mr. Cooley in my life. So, no."

Toomin dealt a blow to the defense when McNally asked to introduce a transcript of Wilson's findings from the bench when he acquitted Harry in 1977. McNally's purpose was apparent—he wanted to show the jury that Wilson had characterized Louie and Bob as liars in delivering his acquittal. Toomin said he would grant the request, but only if the defense agreed to allow the prosecution to introduce evidence that Wilson had committed suicide after learning he was under investigation by the FBI. McNally conferred with Harry and reluctantly backed off that line of assault.

So, McNally called criminal defense attorney William Murphy in an attempt to portray Wilson as an honest judge who was impervious to a bribe. Murphy, who had written an impassioned letter to the newspapers in defense of Wilson in the furor after the first trial, testified that he worked for several years as an assistant public defender assigned to Wilson's courtroom and that bench trials were not unusual there.

"Did you ever see any hints that he was receiving money or other benefits for determining cases?" McNally asked.

"No," Murphy replied.

"What was his reputation?"

"It was good."

Do you know Harry Aleman?"

"Yes, I do," replied Phyllis Napoles. "We are second cousins. He's a son of my cousin, Mary."

McNally stood behind the lectern, hands folded behind his back.

"Did you know William Logan in his lifetime?" he asked.

"Yes, I did."

"How did you know him?"

"I was married to him."

Phyllis was clearly sympathetic to Harry, and she told the jury how she sometimes dropped her children at Harry's home while she worked; how she had visited him in prison a few months before this trial. Her testimony was crucial to the defense—she would provide jurors with an alternative suspect: Butch Petrocelli. Further, she was eager to dirty up her husband at the same time, saying, "It was a very sad marriage. He drank a lot, was very abusive to me and the children, and my mom and dad especially."

Her marriage to Billy in 1964 was her second and she only grudgingly admitted that the child from her first marriage never saw his father after she divorced; she had likewise refused to allow Billy to see their natural son or the son from her first marriage who Billy had adopted. She admitted that she had had an affair with Petrocelli after her divorce from Billy and that even after she rejected Butch's marriage proposal and remarried a third time in 1971, Butch frequently came by to see her. Butch, she recalled, loved her children very much. "He would take them out, bring them lunch, gifts. He surprised them and bought them their first puppy."

She recounted the fistfight between Billy and Butch just prior to the killing. "Butch was there first and Mr. Logan then arrived," she said. "He asked to come in and I told Bill, 'Butch is here visiting the children.' He had been drinking heavily and was very abusive and started to kick in the door and threatened Butch and myself and the boys."

"What happened next?" McNally asked.

"Butch asked him to leave and they went to the alley," she said. "They struck each other physically and there was a lot of profanity. It was a very violent encounter." The two men, she said, had threatened to kill each other.

When police came to interview her after Billy was killed, she said she considered the possibility that Butch was responsible, but did not mention it. "I had a great deal of fear of Mr. Petrocelli," she said. "That's why I didn't marry him."

Cassidy confronted her with a copy of her statement to investigators that stated, "Phyllis referred to the homicide of her ex-husband as an accident."

"I felt it was a tragic accident," she admitted.

Eight days after the trial began, the courtroom was overflowing with a crowd eagerly awaiting the final summations from the lawyers. It was their last chance to talk directly to the jury and, for more than three hours, Linehan, McNally, and Cassidy did not disappoint.

"If you were to believe that Louie Almeida is lying, that Bobby Lowe is lying, that Bob Cooley is lying, then we have one of the unluckiest men in the world right here: Harry Aleman," declared Linehan. "That's what you would have to believe, that the poor guy is the unluckiest man in the world and that these three independent people got together and framed him."

He ridiculed the defense cross-examination of Lowe that tried to suggest his testimony was purchased. "You honestly believe that's why Bobby Lowe did that? To make money?" Linehan asked. "He came forward because it was his obligation to. He did the right thing. Bobby Lowe did it and you know that he's been paying for it."

"Who really destroyed Judge Wilson?" Linehan asked the jury. He paused and then turned to point at Harry. "Who really destroyed Judge Wilson and destroyed the system is sitting right here, with hands folded."

Harry didn't blink, staring Linehan in the eye.

Linehan turned to face the jury box and, perhaps emboldened by his own remarks, committed a blunder.

"Ladies and gentlemen, none of us would be in this courtroom if it wasn't for Harry Aleman," he declared. "That's why we are here. He's the only one in this room who didn't come on this witness stand and talk about accepting responsibility."

"*Objection to that!*" McNally yelled. He shot to his feet. "I move for a mistrial!"

Linehan had stepped over a legal boundary line. Not only is a defendant not required to testify, but it is improper to comment on a defendant's decision to remain silent. Such a comment can be an error serious enough to cause a conviction to be reversed upon appeal.

McNally wasn't going to wait for an appeal. He wanted Toomin to declare a mistrial on the spot.

"Objection sustained," Toomin said. But he would go no further and Linehan resumed, meekly.

"Again, the defendant does not have to testify," he said. "But those other witnesses told you about their accepting their responsibility."

Linehan paused. He was nearly at the end. He pressed his hands down hard onto the waist-high lectern. "Think about Bob Lowe," he said. "Think about people who want to be part of a system that isn't corrupt." He turned to and pointed once more at the defense table. "And that guys like Harry Aleman shouldn't buy their way out of it."

Turning back, Linehan took a deep breath. "Ladies and gentlemen," he said, "When you go back and deliberate in the jury room, when you look at all of the evidence from what happened in nineteen seventy-two all the way to Bob Lowe coming forward, the only fair and just thing you can do is sign a guilty verdict." The room was still as Linehan gathered his notes and sat down.

Immediately, McNally stood up and walked toward the jury box, speaking as he walked. "Something is wrong here," he exclaimed. "Something is very wrong."

He jumped on Cooley, branding him a "sick liar" and a "rat in the swamp." He suggested to the jury that if they did not believe Cooley, the case had to fall apart because, if there was no bribery, then Harry was fairly acquitted in his first trial. "Don't let Robert Cooley make fools of all of us," he said, then turned his full force on Bob.

"Bobby Lowe," he said, "was emotional that night. He was confused. He continues to be confused. And you can't check what he says."

McNally paced back and forth in front of the jury box. "Memory is not like a photograph, especially when it's a few seconds and there's a man with a gun and there's a man being shot. It's not like a photograph," he said. "And it certainly isn't like a photograph after twenty-five years."

Dripping sarcasm, he ripped Louie as a perjurer. "Is Mr. Almeida the kind of person you would want to base an important decision on? Does he inspire your confidence?" McNally asked. "We think not."

At the defense table, Harry leaned back in his chair, one leg crossed over the other. He showed not a sign of nerves. His eyes darted from the jury to McNally and back.

Methodically, McNally reviewed the prosecution evidence and compared it to the defense evidence, pointing out the conflicts and gaps. Then he came to the end.

"This is a weak case," McNally declared. "And that's why Harry Aleman was found not guilty in nineteen seventy-seven. You have worked hard this far. You have taken a lot of notes. You have a lot of information. Listen to the other jurors that harbor reasonable doubts. Remember, this is an individual decision. The reason that there are twelve of you is to make sure, absolutely sure, that an innocent man is not convicted."

McNally sat down and it was the prosecution's turn again. Cassidy's rebuttal was a tour de force. Advised by the judge that he would have only thirty minutes, he began by deriding Harry for waving to Ruth and his grandchildren in front of the jury. "Blowing kisses and I love you and all that," Cassidy said in disgust. "He is not a family man. He is not. He may walk like you do, he may talk like you do, he may look like a human being, but Harry Aleman is anything but humane. He is not. His personality is that of a hit man."

"In the last twenty-five years, since this murder occurred, we have become a society that doesn't want to take responsibility for what we do," Cassidy said. "We want to blame someone else. And that's all the defense is doing. That's why they introduced Butchie Petrocelli. So you would go back there and say Butchie Petrocelli did it."

Speaking without prepared notes, but occasionally referring to a legal pad resting on the lectern, Cassidy spoke rapidly, his words crisp and biting.

"They want to shift the blame, so you focus on someone else instead of the evidence. And I respectfully submit that if you follow the law, you cannot do that. Don't feel sorry for this guy over here," he said, jerking his thumb over his shoulder toward Harry. "Of all the people in the world, of all the people in the world, Harry Aleman should not evoke your sympathy."

Cassidy saved his sarcasm for a brief reminder on how the original murder trial was bounced from judge to judge before winding up finally in front of Wilson—just as Pat Marcy had predicted to Cooley. "Harry is in front of Fair Fred," Cassidy declared. "You have seen Fair Fred. Only person in this building with the name Fair Fred or anything about fairness. If you had to pick a judge in the whole building, you couldn't pick a better judge than Fair Fred. But they wanted him out of there. They didn't want fairness. They don't want fairness today."

Some spectators muffled snickers as Cassidy ridiculed the testimony of Billy Logan's ex-wife. "Phyllis would tell anybody what kind of rat Billy Logan was," he said. "I mean, she couldn't say enough, could she? She got up there and said he was a drunk. She couldn't stop talking. So you know her cousin knows about it. We don't have to prove alibi, but you know Harry Aleman. 'Hey, why not? My cousin's getting beat up. I'll take care of that.'

"And I respectfully submit that's what happened," Cassidy said. "Harry Aleman and Phyllis are close, and Phyllis loved to tell everybody what kind of jerk Billy is. And they were going through a custody battle. After all, ladies and gentlemen, what kind of murder is this? Certainly wasn't an armed robbery, was it? Nothing was taken. It occurred at eleven-fifteen at night. It was a personal murder and we knew when we heard, 'Hey, Billy.' This is someone he knows."

Moving to the center of the courtroom, Cassidy gripped the lectern with both hands for a moment, then took a deep breath. So did several reporters seated in the front row next to the jury box. One shook his hand to get rid of a cramp.

"I stand for Bobby Lowe," Cassidy began. "And the past, present, and future Bobby Lowes, who are scared to death of this system. Scared to death. If there's a hero in this case, it's Bobby. Heroes are not judges. They are not state senators. They are people among us who are simply doing the daily activities in their life when they are out walking the dog, shopping, driving down the street, and they see something. And they have the courage, the moral courage, to come to court and literally give up their life."

Cassidy paused to let his words sink in and then continued. "Bobby Lowe is as honest as honest could be. He's a man's man."

He flipped the pages of his legal pad back down, centered it on the lectern, and then folded his hands behind his back.

"I actually stand here for one person, whose voice you never heard and you will never hear. His name is Billy Logan. He was an ordinary Joe, so to speak—a small man in life who has become a giant in death. Great things happen through small people and Billy Logan's death stands for something. It stands for justice."

The jurors were riveted as Cassidy held up a photograph of Billy for them to see. "Billy's waited a long time for today," he said. "He does not ask for your sympathy. No, he doesn't. He's in a place much safer and peaceful than you would ever know in this world. And he stands for something. He stands for justice. Today, Billy Logan is smiling. Billy Logan looks like he does in that picture, his wide Irish smile. And he has a bunch of people around him. People similarly situated as him, who have followed him, who have been taken from this world at much too young an age through no fault of their own. And Billy has told them: 'Be patient, young people, be patient. Your time will come. Justice will be served in the unjust world you have left. Be patient.' "

Cassidy pressed his hands onto the lectern and leaned forward. "Well, you know what?" he asked. "There's a party of sorts going on right now. There is. And Billy is saying, 'Today is my day. Today is my day.' "

Cassidy looked toward the ceiling and raised up his right arm, reaching his hand upward, to address the spirit of Billy Logan.

"And I say to you, 'Hey, Billy. Justice to you today, Billy Logan. Justice to you.' "

Cassidy looked at the clock that hung on the wall above the jurors and saw that his time was nearly up. Slowly and deliberately, he turned and pointed a finger, just as Bob and Louie and Cooley had done before. He pointed at Harry, who sat at the defense table, as cool as ever.

"And I say to you, Harry Aleman," Cassidy declared, "twenty-five years later. Hey, Harry. Justice to you today, Harry Aleman. Justice to you."

And that was that. It was 3 P.M. when Cassidy sat down. Thirty minutes later the jury filed out of the courtroom to deliberate. More than six hours later, at 9:15 P.M., a phone rang in the bedroom of a white house on a quiet street of a northwest suburb. Bob Lowe picked up the receiver.

"Hello?" he said.

34

Harry Aleman is a devoted, devoted family man and a very good husband. He has been very good to his grandchildren. I know people that have come to him that didn't have anything to eat and this man has helped. I see no wrong with Harry Aleman. Everybody loves him. This man has done nothing wrong. He has family, friends, people all over that think nothing about Harry Aleman but as a good man.

MARY SIMPSON, SISTER-IN-LAW

We grew up together. We lived in the same building. In my opinion he's not the person they are talking about. He's a very caring and loving person. He was always there for me when I needed him and for people in my family. It disturbs me to hear the things they say about him on TV and the news. He's a different person than they are talking about. We love him very much in our family. We want him home.

NANCY MANCINI, COUSIN

I've known him since he was born. Very respectful. He was brought up very, very strict. Went to school. He did very good in school. He skipped grades. He went to high school and then he went to art school, the Chicago Fine Arts and graduated there and he's a beautiful artist. He married a woman with four kids and he raised those kids real, real good. They had everything that he could give them, especially love.

RAPHAELA PANTONE, AUNT

I cannot believe the lies. It's just unbelievable, unbelievable. I mean, it crushes me inside. I would lay down my life for this man; he is not a murderer, not a killer, not this or that. But all these lies—it's unbelievable.

DANIEL AMABILE, FORMER SON-IN-LAW

I know him fifty years and his character—how can I say this without sounding like I—? He's just a wonderful, wonderful dear friend for many years. As far as the monster they are creating, I have to doubt it. Believe me when I tell you, all our friends, we could have this room filled with friends from our neighborhood. Everybody knows Harry and everybody loves him. Wouldn't hurt anybody.

MARY CAVALE, FRIEND

When the jury filed out to begin deliberating Harry's fate, there was a feeling that they would reach a consensus that night, so no one strayed very far. Ruth commandeered a deputy sheriff's chair outside the courtroom doors and, surrounded by her family, sat with legs crossed, flicking a Tareyton cigarette with her salmon-colored fingernails.

For a week, she had sat quietly and patiently in court, listening to the prosecutors and their witnesses vilify her husband as a murderer. But now, the frustration came out as the tension built.

"For twenty-five years, I've lived with this," she said. "For twenty-five years I've lived under the cloud of Harry being called a hit man."

The bags under her eyes and the deepening lines on her face were the only outward signs of what likely had been a series of sleepless nights. She was particularly angry at Cassidy. "He said Harry wasn't a family man. That's wrong."

She dropped her cigarette to the floor, smashed it with her shoe and lit another. An hour passed, then two, then three, and four. A commotion in the hallway signaled that something was happening. A deputy sheriff came walking around the corner. Ruth checked her watch. It was 7:30 P.M.

"Is there a verdict?" she asked.

"There is a verdict," the deputy confirmed.

Ruth arose and walked toward the window at the end of the hall. She lit another cigarette and leaned against the wall, shooing away family members, preferring to remain alone with her thoughts. Her hand trembled.

More than thirty miles away, Bob was in his truck with his bodyguard, Jim Green, finishing up another long day of work, when Jim's pager went off. He used a portable phone to make a call.

"Verdict's been reached," Jim said, disconnecting. "They're waiting for the lawyers and then we'll know."

"Good," Bob said. "Can they give that bastard the death penalty?"

"I don't know," said Jim. "You OK?"

"Great," said Bob. "Let's go home."

Shortly before 8 P.M., the jurors filed back into the courtroom. Harry sat at the defense table, next to McNally. Across the room, Cassidy and Linehan sat at the prosecution table. Toomin warned the spectators that outbursts would not be tolerated and threatened to remove anyone who felt compelled to react emotionally.

The room was so silent that the rustle of paper was clearly audible as the jury verdict form was passed to Toomin's bailiff and then to the judge. Toomin stared at it without a trace of emotion. Directly behind the prosecutors sat Billy Logan's sister, Betty, clutching a cross pendant and seemingly holding her breath. Across the aisle, some of Harry's family held hands.

"Let the record reflect the court has examined the verdict form and finds it to be in proper order and I tender it to the clerk to read to the courtroom as assembled," Toomin declared.

The clerk stood up. "We, the jury, find the defendant, Harry Aleman, guilty of murder," he read.

At the defense table, Harry did not flinch. His eyes blinked and he stared straight ahead. Behind him, members of his family gasped and some began to weep. Across the room, Billy Logan's sister began to sob.

As the jurors were individually polled to reaffirm their verdicts, Harry's mouth flattened briefly into a tight-lipped grimace. Ruth raised a clenched fist. "This is only round one," she whispered.

In the rush to meet deadlines and to grab interviews from prosecutors and McNally, reporters overlooked Ruth as she walked slowly out of the courthouse, flanked by her daughters and grandchildren. Outside, she stepped into a car and sped off into the night.

McNally was brief in his remarks to reporters, vowing an appeal and accusing the prosecutors of committing error in delivering their final arguments. Not far away, Cassidy and Linehan had comments of their own. "This will close the books on an ugly era in Cook County," Cassidy declared into the bright lights of television cameras. "It's a great day for American justice."

"We never gave up," said Richard Logan, flanked by his sisters, Betty and Joanna. "For twenty-five years, this has been between Harry and his God. Today, the Lord spoke." Betty leaned toward reporters' microphones and said, "Thank you, Bob Lowe."

When the call to Bob brought the news of the guilty verdict, there was no celebration. No one broke out a bottle. Bob was still on the wagon. He and Fran just hugged.

"The anger is all gone. I can't get it back," Bob said. "Now Harry has to pay for what he done. It is his turn." And then they went to sleep.

On November 25, 1997, two months after the guilty verdict, the courtroom was again packed for the sentencing hearing. Many of Harry's friends and relatives took the stand to express their love for the man. His lawyer, Alex Salerno, argued that Harry had "been punished like no other person that I've ever seen. The attitude that I see in Harry shows me that he's an incredible person. Since the time of his conviction he's been on suicide watch. He's not going to commit suicide, but he's on suicide watch because it's added torture for Harry Aleman. Twenty-four hours a day, seven days a week, there's a man that sits outside his cell, watches Harry when he eats, watches him when he sleeps, watches him when he goes to the bathroom.

"And when I go to visit him he's shackled up. Every other prisoner in the prison is removed from the hallways and Harry's hands and feet are shackled and he's walked to the visiting area to talk to me.

"I've never had so many people call me about an individual defendant who's going to be sentenced. And they do that because they love Harry and they love Harry because of the kind of guy he is."

Salerno asked the court to impose the minimum sentence, concluding by saying, "He does not deserve to die in jail—he just doesn't."

But that was what Cassidy wanted and he argued vigorously, passionately, saying, "It's been a long road to justice in this case. Mr. Aleman, there are two sides to him, two sides. There is the side which is quite apparent, a side his family and friends don't know. Maybe he puts on a show. Maybe there are two different personalities. But the personality you know, Judge, shows that he is a man without a conscience.

"If Mr. Aleman ever wakes up one morning after a night's sleep and all of a sudden develops a conscience, I swear he would become a madman. He would go insane at the thought of what he has done with his life.

"I respectfully ask, Judge, that the sentence you impose upon him ensures that he will spend each day in a cage that he has built for himself, a cage he built for himself each day by the way he lived, and I ask that he just rot away in that cage and he never gets out so he can never hurt anybody again."

When everyone else had spoken, Judge Toomin was brief. He concluded that Harry had "forfeited the right to live among civilized people." He then got to the point, saying, "It will be the judgment of the court that Harry Aleman will be remanded to the custody of the Department of Corrections for a term of not less than one hundred nor more than three hundred years."

Bob did not go to the sentencing. He wasn't even tempted. And so he did not hear and never did read the final words in the murder trial of Harry Aleman.

Salerno: "Can he have five minutes with his family?"

Toomin: "Yes."

Inmate #T61648 spends his days in the dull routine of prison life. On July 29, 2000, after serving out the last of his federal sentence, Harry was unceremoniously transferred to Illinois, where he joined the population at the state prison in Joliet. Harry appealed to the Illinois Appellate Court and lost. He was rejected by the Illinois Supreme Court, but still has avenues left with the U.S. Supreme Court and the federal courts. His wife, Ruth, died in January 2000, but other family members visit him regularly and continue to maintain his innocence and fight for his freedom, their arguments based on the notion that the police reports of 1972 were accurate and that Bob never did stand face to face with Harry, and only later embellished his story for financial gain.

Among those who do not visit Harry is his cousin, Bobby Cruz, who had been instrumental in Harry's decision to change lawyers just before trial. Three days after Toomin sentenced Harry, Cruz disappeared. He was last seen hanging Christmas lights on the gutters of his suburban Chicago home.

At Joliet, Harry was put in a cell in the West Wing and was assigned the job of utility man, a rather glorified title for a job that consisted mainly of sweeping and mopping the floors and carrying out the trash. This was not much different from other prison jobs he had in the past. There is no reason to believe that he is any less diligent in these duties than he was when he was an orderly in the Oxford penitentiary and took pride in the sanitation and cleanliness of his unit. And there is no reason to believe that he is not taking college courses, adding to an academic resume that includes the study of seamanship in navigation, rational behavior therapy, and principles of success, or mentoring younger prisoners, as he once did for the kids in the Taylor Street neighborhood. He still paints.

In a broad sense, Harry still lives on Taylor Street in the memories of those who knew him. One of those people is Rico Paone. "I only saw the good side of Harry," he said. "We all have a good side and a bad side. He would only talk to me about the positive things. Go to school. Get a job."

Paone owns a popular restaurant named Rico's on Racine Avenue, a couple of blocks north of Taylor Street. On nights when there are concerts or sporting events at the nearby University of Illinois, Rico's is packed wall to wall. Still, only a few of the patrons ever take note of the paintings that hang on the wall in the back of the dining room. There are about a dozen of them, eight-by-ten oils that portray mostly bucolic scenes: a horse, an Old West gunfight, a cabin nestled against a snow-covered hill. There is something at once powerful and crude about the works that surround table twenty-eight. On the wall hangs another frame that contains the name of the artist: Harry Aleman. His paintings are pricey—$2,000 and $3,000. The proceeds go to the Harry Aleman Defense Fund. Rico first hung them in 1997. Four years later, only one had been sold.

The man who was Bob Lowe now lives in a place where winters come early. He and his wife, Fran, are alone now. Their parents are dead and the kids are grown and have moved on to other places.

The man who was Bob Lowe says he doesn't think much about Harry anymore. Nor does he dream about him. But he remains a most cautious man. More than two decades of looking over his shoulder have left him wary of the world around him. He does not talk to strangers. He changes his path at the sound of a car idling nearby and he jumps at the sound of a backfiring truck or a sudden crack of thunder.

It took nearly a year for the government to put together all the pieces for yet another identity change for Bob and Fran. "They did a better job of it this time," he says. "I got a real name change. And a Social Security number, background, the whole thing."

He has a job and he works hard. He has to. There is no IRA in the bank, no pension waiting. In the initial years after he became a protected witness, Robert Cooley received $400,000 and continuing protective custody for his efforts. The man who was Bob Lowe got his new identity, a handshake, and $10,000 for moving expenses.

"I don't like much being called a hero," he says. "From what I've learned about the system in thirty years—I don't know. This last trial really didn't have that much to do with Billy. It had to do with me. That first time around I got my ass tore up and I had a bad attitude about it for a long time. I had a lot of anger. But it's gone now. It went away when I stood there and pointed my finger at Harry. Harry ran my life for a long time, whether he knew it or not, and now he's paying his price. I wasn't no angel. But I didn't hurt nobody. Me and Fran, we're trying to take it easy now. I worked too damn hard and I went through too much."

"We both did, Bob," Fran says. "We both paid. Don't you forget it."

"I never will, babe," he says. "I never will."

If there is bitterness in his voice, and there is, it is because he believes that "they treated the criminals—Cooley and Louie—better than me. But I fight those feelings. What's it gonna get me? I've moved on."

For the man who was Bob Lowe, there is still a future to grab, a present to cherish. In the dining room of his home is a large clock that chimes loudly on the hour, a gift from him to Fran on their thirtieth wedding anniversary. On the walls of the kitchen, dining room, and living room are pictures of their children and their families. And in a handsome wooden cabinet are a few pieces of china, survivors of the agents' clumsiness on that day long ago when the Lowe family began its twenty-five-year odyssey toward justice. The china has never been used.

When the weather is pleasant, Bob and Fran will sit on the brick patio behind their ranch house. There's a playground set on the lawn where he plays with his grandchildren when they come to visit. They tell him to stop smoking, but he won't give up his Marlboros.

Fran cooks dinner every night and, on some evenings, after the dishes are put away and the neighborhood is quiet and empty, Bob takes a walk.

"Hurry back," Fran always says.